How to Start and Run a Successful Photography Business

Gerry Kopelow

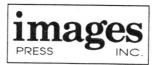

How to Start and Run a Successful Photography Business

Library of Congress Catalog Card Number: 91-078008
Gerry Kopelow
ISBN: 0-929667-13-1

Published by Images Press, 7 East 17th Street, New York, NY 10003; (212) 675-3707

Printed and bound in the United States of America

Graphic Design and Typography by Ray Noonan, ParaGraphic Artists, New York City

Cover Design by Dawn Daisley

Edited by Peter Lindsay

Photographs by Gerry Kopelow

10 9 8 7 6 5 4 3 2 1

DEDICATION

To my friend Drew Lawson at Minolta Canada who convinced me that my experience could be of value to others and to my friend Mark Simkin who convinced me I could write it all down.

ACKNOWLEDGMENTS

Many thanks to fellow photographers Barry Mallin, Art Turner and Sheila Spence for their continuing encouragement, and to Peter Lindsay, Professor of Photography at Ryerson Polytechnical Institute, Toronto, for his meticulous technical corrections.

I am grateful to Don, Bob, and Randy at Don's Photo, Walter Kaiser at Custom Images, Lindsay Bickert at Nikon Canada, Ron Berglin at Kodak Canada, Greg Emberly at Ilford Canada, Bruce Spielman at Sam the Cameraman, and to Jim Smith, Bob Wright, Ray Phillips, and Rory Landa, for their amazing patience and support.

Contents

Introduction

Commercial photographers know, or have guessed, that the money they make is not necessarily related to the cost of producing their work. That there is a significant gap between the cost of production and the selling price of commercial photos is demonstrated by the life styles of a number of high-profile shooters who support huge studios and an entourage of assistants, studio managers, accountants, stylists and groupies. You can all name several of these celebrities: you've seen them in *People* magazine. Probably you've read their glittery books or even seen their videos. You lust after their accounts and their executive jets.

I do not promise to make you into one of the photographic elite. My purpose in mentioning them is to demonstrate that there is a great deal of profit in commercial work, enough in some cases to allow an opulent style of life. Yet for every one of the celebrity photographers there are thousands of less conspicuous workers doing similar jobs in a much less ostentatious manner. Usually they work by themselves or with a part time assistant. They very likely have a black and white darkroom or even process color prints. They do not necessarily live in New York or Los Angeles. They do not want or expect to become famous. Still, they love photography. One might be billing $20,000 per year, another may be billing $150,000. If you are one of these people you can make more money in less time with less effort. This book will tell you how.

The commercial photographer who expects to make a decent living must efficiently manage three principal areas. First, all things photographic must be totally controlled. This includes buying equipment, shooting, processing, studio design, and more. Second comes everything related to the business of photography, such as selling, bookkeeping and banking. Third, to be more than just a survivor in this business a certain set of specialized intellectual and emotional skills must be acquired and maintained: they have to do with stress management because most commercial photography is produced under pressure of short deadlines acerbated by nervous clients.

I have learned how to do all this, largely by trial and error. I have learned that conventional practice is not always the best way. Some ideas look good on paper, but do not work out in real life; if you have one foot in ice water and the other foot in boiling water, statistically you are comfortable. In order to do well, one must be both clever and balanced, hardworking and harmonious, focused yet relaxed.

An example of how I solved a major problem will illustrate the approach I advocate as photographically efficient:

Clients require a professional photographer to deliver high quality results quickly. This requires the photographer to control every one of long list of variables, the last of which is processing the exposed film. In my area color prints are very popular because the only decent retoucher in town will not work on transparencies and because many clients wish to save money by gang-separating color prints which have been printed to size.

Turning exposed film into the necessary sized and color-balanced enlargements is the responsibility of the photographer but it is not usually a profitable enterprise. There are two problems here, both having to do with time.

Unless the color lab is next door, there is inevitably a lot of running around involved in deliveries and viewing proofs and test prints. Presumably this time is billed to your client through the markup on the price of the prints, but I have found that this is usually a break-even proposition rather than a major money maker. Most commercial jobs require only a few prints which must meet high standards: even if a competent printer can be found, he, rather than you, will probably make the major money from photofinishing because you are organizing and supervising the processing for him.

The 'normal' procedure of sending film out to a lab costs you in a second way by delaying the delivery of the job to your client. In most cities the business of processing film, viewing proofs, and supervising of enlargements requires three to four days. Maybe the direct costs and time lost running back and forth are not unbearable, but consider the indirect costs. For example, if the job involves a complicated setup in the studio do you leave everything set up until the final prints are made and the job has been approved by your client? Your client is also on hold while the color lab does its work. If your client is an advertising agency or designer, his or her client is on hold as well.

I found this scenario very irritating. For me it was an argument for processing color in-house but there seemed to be a lot of problems associated with this idea as well. Should I set up a film line for color negative developing? Should I process prints in tubes or buy a small processing machine? Should I hire someone to do all this? Would this person work full or part time? Could all this be expected to make a profit or would it be a break even proposition intended to increase convenience and reduce turn-around time only?

I started in photography because I love the medium. I continue in commercial work because I want to make money and spend as little time as possible doing it. The lab time and lab costs seemed fixed. To reduce either or both I would have to do it myself but the advantages would have to be substantial to make it worthwhile. The procedures would have to be simple, reliable and satisfying in

order to justify the investment. In other words, would it be efficient to undertake in-house processing of color prints?

To answer the question I made an analysis of my business. I am happy if I can shoot one or two jobs and bill seven hundred and fifty or fifteen hundred dollars per working day. I do not usually shoot every day, but even when I do, in-house lab work should not intrude. Still, a working day usually involves four hours or less of photography and four hours or more of running around, and much of that involves trips to the lab. Typically a day might produce one to ten rolls of film from which one to ten prints might be made. I had to figure out some way to handle this work at a profit while maintaining a manageable schedule for the rest of the time.

I did find a way to do what I wanted but first I had to overcome some common myths about color work. I believed that the procedures were time consuming, expensive and very complicated. But a little research revealed that this was the case only when conventional practices were followed. Processing film or prints in tubes or machines was very time consuming, at least compared to the quick and easy methods for black and white. Developing a B&W print might take five minutes while a color print, even pumped through the fastest processors, required at least fifteen minutes. This was just too long to wait, especially considering that often several tests are required to determine burning or dodging, color balance and density.

In addition to the time problem, there was the problem of low volume. The machines, even if they were faster, were too expensive to buy and too hungry for expensive chemicals when only a few films and prints were to be processed each day. Maintenance was a also consideration. Drums or tubes seemed economical for small scale work but they, as well as the machine processors, needed too much cleaning and handling.

As I thought about what exactly was required chemically for color negative film and print processing I realized that the actual steps were simple and that the problem was the conventional hardware and its attendant housekeeping. I found a better way.

In the chapter on efficiency in the darkroom I describe an unbelievably simple solution to the color processing dilemma. Processing up to nine rolls of color negative film now takes me about twenty five minutes while processing a color print takes three minutes. My costs are about fifty cents per roll or print. The system can be set up for well under a thousand dollars using easily obtained equipment. I have reduced three days of waiting and running to a couple of hours. I often make a hundred dollars an hour in the darkroom. Now I take care of my own needs faster and cheaper than an outside lab with the bonus of reduced worry and aggravation.

Even if you are not interested in darkroom work, you will find that throughout the book the same approach to problem solving and streamlining of operations yields similar results when applied to other photographic activities.

Perhaps I should limit the readership of this book to commercial photographers and their intimate friends and family. If our clients find out how cheaply and easily much of our work can be done, there will be chaos in the marketplace.

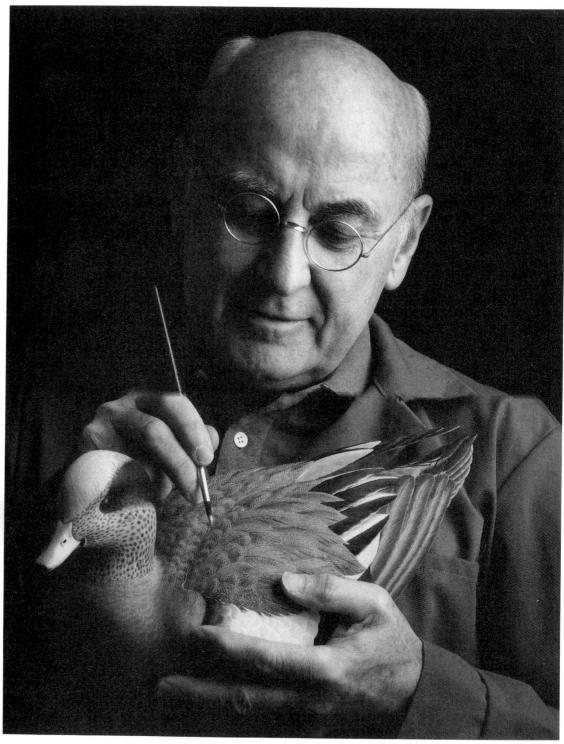

Cargil Grain is one of the largest companies in the world. The Canadian division wanted a poster image to illustrate the themes of precision and quality. The gentleman pictured here is a retired executive who has become famous making breathtakingly beautiful and life-like duck decoys. His work is not used for hunting—instead they are purchased and displayed as works of art. I made this photo in the artist's own living room using strong sidelight from a big softbox and electronic flash. The duck was complete, but I asked for a dab of light colored paint on the brush to call attention to the detail in the bird and the man's hands. You may recognize the glasses from the Great West Life cover shot. Hasselblad camera, 100mm lens, Kodak VPS film. The black and white print made on Kodak Panalure paper, a technique I use often.

1.

Who Is a Commercial Photographer?

Anyone who makes a living by producing photographs which serve the purposes of a broad range of businesses and institutions is a commercial photographer. Generally this definition excludes portrait and wedding photographers while it just barely includes photojournalists and corporate or government staff photographers.

The spectrum of commercial work is very wide, but the hard-core commercial shooter (the main beneficiary of the techniques to be described in this book) is usually found wherever there is healthy economic activity. Commercial photography is a major lubricant of the capitalist machine, and the competent commercial photographer is a respected problem solver, facilitator, and interpreter.

Photography links the objective, material world to the subjective world of impressions and ideas. A photograph is a relatively permanent two dimensional record of someone or something; it has the power to instantly induce thoughts and emotions and, to some degree, behavior. In this way, the commercial photographer, like the advertising copy writer or the television or movie script writer, is a small but surprisingly influential player in the formation of popular culture. As the servants of industry, photographers are required to present people and products in a way that conforms to the wishes of their clients. Money changes hands and persuasive images are created.

It is a demanding business. Who are these image makers? How do they learn their skills? Many are the products of technical schools and colleges. Some are self-taught. Likely they have worked as an assistant or an apprentice to some established professional. Perhaps they have crossed over from some other career or profession.

Regardless of the exact path which led them to commercial photography, the successful practitioner will exhibit three qualities: a keen aesthetic sense, an appreciation of technology, and an affinity for the intense interpersonal relationships which inevitably accompany photographic work at this level. The balance and particular manifestations of these three characteristics in an individual will determine his or her style and special strengths; unfortunately, no amount of training or self-motivation can make up for their absence. The marketplace has a way of pre-selecting its long-term participants and simply reading this book is an indicator of your desire to expand your skills. It is this desire and ability to grow that will allow the three innate qualities to really shine.

The ability to learn is particularly crucial to success as a commercial photographer who is operating a one-person studio and doing a variety of work. There are a few photographers who have developed a speciality together with a devoted clientele. Having developed a specific technique, they can enjoy the rare pleasure of refining to perfection that with which they are already familiar. Most professionals are less exalted working stiffs who cannot shoot just food, or fashion or world leaders: they must be adaptable and accommodating. It is the accomplished generalist who will do well in the shadow of the celebrity shooters.

To achieve a respectable level of skill in many areas requires stamina and an active intelligence. It is impossible to learn all that is necessary in an academic setting, and it is not sufficient to simply watch someone else work, as in an apprenticeship situation. The most effective learning is accomplished by doing, by trial and error. The successful commercial photographer will be willing to take some risks, to experiment, and to occasionally fail.

Happily, there are several motivating factors which tend to make the work of self-improvement less arduous. The more high-minded would argue that the thrill of creating fabulous images with cutting-edge photographic technology is reason enough to hang in through the rough spots: its true, of course, but do remember that a busy commercial photographer can be one of the most highly paid professionals in his or her community. Six figure incomes that compare very well with doctors, lawyers, even orthodontists, are not uncommon.

The busy professional photographer will be working in close contact with some other high-achievers: his or her client list will very likely include clever entrepreneurs, upwardly mobile corporate types, various influential politicians and civil servants, active cultural organizations and performing artists, together with designers and art directors working in the advertising industry. In short, commercial photographers associate with some of the most stimulating and intelligent individuals urban society has to offer.

Why then are there so few who achieve their full potential? I believe it is simply a lack of imagination coupled with a willingness to settle for the ordinary and the easily accessible. Oddly, such an addiction to ordinariness may be a reaction to the complex technology which is at the heart of photography. There are so many variables in photographic processes that some photographers become quite conservative in their approach: after finding a particular process or technique that works they become attached to it and fearful of change. This particular rut can be fatal. There are so many technical innovations being introduced today that the inflexible are quickly left behind.

There is no substitute for a solid grasp of the fundamentals of photography. Basic technique is a foundation for growth. Also required however, is a finely honed ability to distinguish what will help and what will hinder as high-tech materials and tools flood the photographic world. This is the thrust of the photo/efficient approach. By the application of common sense, by experimentation, and by the occasional bending of the established rules of practice, it is possible to keep ahead of the competition, make money, and still have some fun.

2.

An Overview of Commercial Work and Professional Equipment

It is unusual for a photographer to be able to specialize and do well. Everyone will find favorite disciplines within the trade but reality dictates that one has to be ready and able to do most of the work that comes through the door in order to survive. This is particularly true in the early stages of establishing a business. Such a proposition may appear intimidating to the beginner, but for a number of reasons the situation is actually a blessing in disguise to both novice and established professional.

First, a variety of work prevents boredom and stagnation, conditions that spell death in the marketplace. Second, a wide range of work compels the photographer to acquire, maintain and sharpen skills which cannot be learned any other way. Third, there is an interdisciplinary feedback effect which automatically enriches each new project. The commercial photographer works at the apex of a pyramid of creative people; it is by amplifying the creative energies of his or her clients that photographers participate in the life of the community. Finally, the willingness and ability to do a variety of work virtually guarantees that there will always be some work to

do. Variety is an insulator; a buffer which protects against downturns in particular sectors of the economy. The big corporations call it diversification.

Commercial photography embraces so many disciplines that a complete mastery of all of them is just as unlikely as the possibility of succeeding by focusing on just one. Nevertheless, it is necessary to have at least a cursory understanding of most of them if only to eliminate those which really do not appeal and to clear the way for deeper study of those that do.

The Scope of Professional Work

Advertising illustration is what most people think of as commercial photography; certainly it is its most visible and prolific incarnation. People working in this field are responsible for the images we see on billboards, bus cards, packaging and newspaper and magazine ads. These pictures are the still-life equivalents of TV commercials, and they are so big a part of the business of selling that their production attracts the biggest budgets

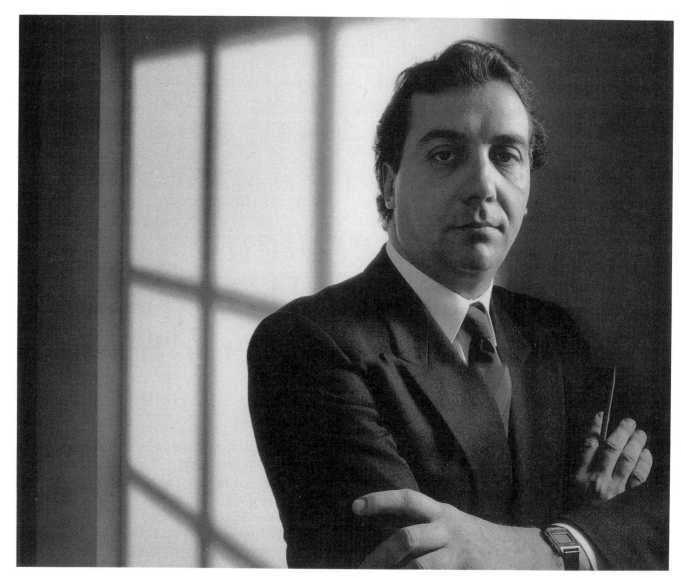

Portrait of Dennis McNight, president of the Results Group, a company that specializes in polling and public opinion surveys. The picture was part of a corporate capability brochure. The photo was made on 35mm Ilford FP4 b&w film with a Nikon F3 and a 28mm lens. I used two flash heads with 8" reflectors—one to project the shadow-image of a conveniently located grid-like glass door, and the other for strong side lighting on the subjects face. The art director of the agency accompanied me on the shoot—but the exact geometry of the image was left to me to work out. I was instructed to illustrate the qualities of competence, concentration and integrity.

and the some of the most ambitious photographers. The challenge here is to present whatever product or service is being touted in an imaginative way while maintaining both aesthetic and ethical standards. In this field one acts not only on behalf of a very visible client, usually an advertising agency, but also on behalf of a sometimes invisible client—the public. The most attractive personalities practicing the art of advertising illustration are able to tell the truth with flair.

It is a rather sobering to keep in mind that the demanding advertiser/client who pays your fees actually gets his or her money by selling something (with your assistance) to thousands, perhaps millions, of people.

Advertising illustration encompasses many subcategories, but the most significant is likely product photography, glamorized and elevated by the razzle-dazzle and big bucks of national or international advertising production. Taking pictures of objects in the studio, however, can be the most mundane of activities. Consider, for example, the black and white shot of a can of peas that appears in the newspaper ad for the local supermarket. In the middle of the spectrum is catalog photography of various levels of sophistication.

It is in this diversity we see the really outrageous potential of commercial work; some of the most ordinary product photos are shot by highly trained people using large format view cameras in well equipped studios while some of the most spectacular ad campaigns are shot with 35mm equipment and little more than available light. Who does the work is often determined only by the attitude of the photographer. This is particularly true of fashion photography, which is really a clandestine form of product photography in which people are used as props.

Style is not everything in product work, however, and special photographic skills and equipment as well as the help of outside professionals must be present to properly undertake the most ephemeral form of product work—food photography. Here the photographer relies on the technique of a food-stylist or chef whose job it is to find and prepare whatever consumables are to be photographed. Some sort of preparation area is required in the studio.

A step away from the often overheated advertising industry is the slightly more prosaic shooting which is done directly for corporations. Again, there is kind of hierarchy to this category; some would rank annual reports and portraits of CEO's (chief executive officers) at the top of both the remuneration and glamour scales followed by on-site industrial reportage of various levels of intensity which is in turn followed by public-relations and newsletter photography.

The advertising and the corporate markets will be the basic fare of most professional work in photography. But there are several other areas that can generate plenty of income for the enterprising and the adaptable photographer. Editorial photography for magazines does not pay as well as strictly commercial work, and neither does the shotgun shooting of audio-visual production. Both fields need the same talent: an ability to quickly illustrate an idea or a point of view with entertaining and cogent sequences of related images. There is a lot of this work available to those who are energetic and clear-minded enough to work at the fast pace required.

Architectural photography is engaging but fussy and specialized. Although it usually lacks the more reliable financial guarantees of regular industrial work it can be a rather elevated occupation when the architect is talented and the building is photogenic in style and situation. Working with realtors, developers and construction companies is a little less fun, but when buildings are being built or bought and sold, large sums of money will be changing hands and reasonable fees can be expected.

A little less obvious but no less demanding is the photography of the performing arts. Most urban centers support professional theater, dance, music and often TV or film production as well. Two non-photographic skills are necessary to get along in the rarefied world of entertainment: patience and tact. The main requirement in terms of technique is the ability to work unobtrusively.

A hungry commercial photographer will do the occasional wedding or private portrait, but constant contact with other professionals in the worlds of culture and business tends to erode the desire to please ordinary folks. Such work is better suited as a gift for a friend rather than to be relied upon for income.

The restoration of old photos is less trying, and it overlaps with other quite lucrative copy work such as the duplication of architectural renderings and the production of slides of graphs and charts for AV presentations. This is usually easy money for the pro who maintains his or her own processing facility. Taking in photo-finishing for other professionals or the general public can be rewarding, but a lot depends on the circumstances and the temperament of the photographer.

Equipment for Commercial Work

This book is distilled from my own experience as a professional photographer working in a mid-western city of six hundred thousand. I have, of necessity, become an "accomplished generalist" and I regularly shoot assignments from all the categories of work just listed. I am well equipped to handle whatever comes my way, yet through the years I have simplified my collection of tools into a very basic, reliable and flexible package.

Reliability of equipment is extremely important. You need to have complete confidence in your picture-making machines just as your clients need to have complete confidence in your picture-making abilities. Flexibility of equipment is also critical. Your tools must be able to keep up with what you are doing. For 35mm work I use 20mm, 28mm, 28mm PC, 35mm, 55mm Micro, 105mm, 200mm, and 300mm fixed focal length lenses. From time to time I use 28-90mm and 80-200mm zoom lenses. With my 6 X 6 camera I use 40mm, 60mm, 100mm and 150mm lenses. When shooting 4" X 5" format I use 47mm, 75mm, 90mm, 150mm, and 250mm lenses. The systems I have chosen are Nikon, Hasselblad, and TOYO. The large format lenses are Fujinons except for the 47mm, which is a Schnieder.

There are many trustworthy equipment manufacturers but no machine is totally fail-safe. For this reason I have two Nikon and two Hasselblad bodies.

For lighting equipment I have two small and two large electronic flash generators and four heads. I use five Lowel DP lights supplemented by two Photogenic mini-spots for tungsten work. I have a small collection of umbrellas, soft boxes and other light-modifying gizmos. I have two Metz 60ct-4 portable flash units as well.

Exactly why and how this particular equipment was selected will be discussed a little later, but let me say now that I believe this collection of tools to be the irreducible heart of a commercial photographer's arsenal. It is possible to own less and rent what is required for each job but eventually you will find that the extra hassle of locating and testing rental equipment is not worth the effort.

3.

Financial Considerations

Obtaining Equipment

Setting up a professional studio involves a substantial initial expenditure. Suitable premises must be found, equipment obtained, and sufficient supplies purchased to undertake the work. Some of you may be able and willing to finance these necessities out of your own pocket, but my guess is that many cannot. The catch-22 for a beginner at commercial photography is that to attract decent work one must have decent equipment but to pay for decent equipment one must have some decent work. Until the business can afford to finance the cost of equipment, the only alternatives are to borrow, rent or lease.

Borrowing professional equipment is not as outlandish as it may sound. It's amazing how much quality camera gear is in the hands of upper-middle class photo-enthusiasts. During my first couple of years as a professional I borrowed Leica and Nikon equipment from a dentist, an accountant and a doctor. Their compensation was a few custom prints or use of my studio in the evening.

Renting equipment commercially for a day or two at a time is an affordable proposition, although you must expect some delays due to the running around involved in locating, transporting and testing the gear you need. In the smaller cities it is difficult to find the more specialized professional tools. Sometimes well-equipped pros will rent out their own equipment to trustworthy individuals, but usually such things as high power studio flash gear and exotic lenses must be flown in from out of town.

Leasing is like a long term rental. It is available through most camera stores on big ticket items. In most cases the lessee is responsible for insuring and maintaining the equipment throughout the term of the lease, usually one to three years. Costs are close to the rates for bank loans, with the advantages that the payments are 100% deductible and there is no down payment required, although there will be a thorough credit check. At the end of the lease the equipment may be purchased at a depreciated price, sometimes as low as 1% of the original retail cost. The big disadvantage to leasing is that such agreements are inflexible; you are locked in for the duration and a couple of missed payments results in repossession of the equipment and the loss of your investment. The leased equipment is the property of the leasing company and as such cannot be sold or traded should it become obsolete or redundant.

Borrowing Money

If you are good at photography and even moderately successful at making a business out of it, you will soon want to own your own working tools. Likely you will turn to a bank for financing. Unfortunately, looking for money from lending institutions is not a straightforward proposition in the case of commercial photography; the size of the required loans and the nature of the risks involved make involvement relatively unattractive for banks.

An institutional lender who is not approached properly may balk at taking on a photographer as customer for a number of very understandable reasons. First, a banker sees commercial photographers primarily as professionals trading on their talents but in such a technical field, talent is difficult to evaluate, especially in the case of a relative novice. Next, the cost of equipment will likely be somewhat more than the cost of a car and somewhat less than the cost of a house but, unlike the car or house, in the event of insolvency, camera equipment is impossible to sell at anywhere near its original value. Another problem is the fact that commercial photography gives no income guarantees; billings can vary from zero up to thousands of dollars per month in the most capricious fashion. Finally, a modest commercial photography business will require several different types of bank involvement: long-term equipment loans, short-term money to cover one-time-only expenses for big jobs, as well as some kind of revolving line-of-credit supported by receivables. All these loans might total under $100,000. This is smaller than the usual house mortgage and certainly much smaller than a typical start-up loan for other types of businesses, both of which require significantly less paperwork to keep track of. In effect, smallish loans which may require unprofitable amounts of time to administer squeeze photographers into a kind of credit gap: what the bank must provide is too complex to be a personal loan but too small and fussy to be a normal business loan. Fortunately, it is possible to overcome these negative factors. The methods by which this may be done are not

in any way dishonest or even mysterious. It is essential to begin by learning how banks think.

Three conditions must exist before a bank will enter into a credit agreement. These are the three "C's": character, capacity, and collateral. Briefly, *collateral* is usually equipment or property belonging to the borrower; the bank gets title and sells the collateral should the borrower default on repayment of the loan. *Capability* is the borrower's financial ability to service the loan in an orderly way. *Character* refers to those aspects of personality which the bank considers necessary in its customers: honesty, reliability, and perseverance.

The loan approval process is simply the bank's way of determining the existence and balance of character, capacity, and collateral in each potential borrower. It is extremely important when approaching a lender to have all the information they will require assembled ahead of time and close at hand. I strongly recommend that a written proposal which takes all the bank's concerns into account be prepared as the first step in the search for financing. Even if you do not intend to borrow, making an appraisal of your financial circumstances just as a banker would do is a sensible beginning to any commercial enterprise.

Borrowing Criteria

The borrower's capacity to repay what has been borrowed is determined mathematically. A business incurs monthly expenses which are subtracted from the income generated by sales. What is left after loan payments is profit; too much debt drains a business and makes life hard. If a bank loan is to provide money to buy equipment, it is necessary to prove that the equipment will generate more than enough money to repay the loan that bought it.

It is a paradox built into the capitalist system that to borrow money when it is not required is easy; demonstrating capacity takes some ingenuity when the need for a loan is real. The saving grace for commercial photographers in search of bank money is the impressive potential for profit. What distinguishes commercial photography from other businesses is the fact that the selling price of a photograph is not determined by the cost of production, as is the case with most manufactured items; instead, its value is linked to end use. For example a photograph which costs $200 to produce might be worth $350 if it is to appear in a local newspaper, yet it could be worth five or even ten times that amount if it is to be used in a national magazine ad. In addition, because a commercial photographer is a highly skilled professional, as well as the manufacturer of a saleable product, photographic services are often billed by the day or the hour rather than by the job. Even early on in a commercial photographer's career it is not unusual for fees to exceed the rates typical of the legal or medical professions. A few tear-sheets or display prints of profitable assignments, along with a detailed accounting of expenses incurred and time spent, will go along way toward reassuring a lender. Simple, but true.

It is to your advantage to supply documentation on other long term commitments you have fulfilled. You may be seeking your very first business loan but don't be shy about listing any student loans, car loans or mortgages that you have properly discharged.

Once convinced that the capacity to service a loan exists, the lender will require security in the form of collateral. This gives the bank some recourse in case of default, but viewed in more positive light, the bank is saying that by lending money it has become a partner in your business; it wants to see that you have made a commitment as well.

If you intend to start a commercial photography business you are an accomplished student, a very advanced amateur, or a professional photographer ready to expand. You will have already acquired some cameras, lenses, and possibly a lighting system. Now you need more. A bank will generally finance up to fifty percent of the cost of new professional equipment if the equipment itself is the only collateral. That leaves the other fifty percent for you to find on your own. The bank will go farther if you can put up more security. Equipment you already own may be acceptable, as will real estate or a vehicle that is free and clear of any other encumbrances. It is the responsibility of the borrower to protect everything given as collateral by insurance.

Tying up assets might appear a bit grim, but remember that the rewards of the entrepreneurial system are offered only to creative people who extend themselves; you must take some risks in order to grow. In this regard the conservatism of banks is sometimes perceived as an impediment to growth, but forcing every credit decision through a bureaucratic review is a prudent counterbalance against debilitating overextension.

Borrowing Techniques

Proving capacity and arranging for collateral should be a pragmatic, no-nonsense procedure. While you make your pitch, however, an evaluation at a more subtle level is going on. Any long-term business relationship involves trust, so you must demonstrate that you are reliable and hard working as well as highly skilled. If you get into difficult circumstances your banker will make decisions which could have profound effects on your family and your future; the image that he or she has of your character could be the critical factor if the financial conditions are marginal or unpredictable.

In almost every case the banker will make a judgment on these subtle matters independently, that is to say without requiring letters of reference or approval by his or her superiors. As an aspiring commercial photographer you are already preselected to be intelligent, creative and sensitive. Hopefully you are honest as well. Your only concern, therefore, is to be clear about what you want, straightforward in presenting your circumstances, and candid in response to any questions.

The physical format of the loan proposal need not be overly elaborate to be effective. Obtain an attractive three-ring binder (the kind with smaller rings is best) as well as some stiff divider pages with index tabs. Make typewritten labels for each of the following topics:

education and/or work experience, credit history, business rationale, financial statements and tax records, net worth, awards and public recognition, community service activities, marketing plan, loan requirements, and examples of commercial work.

Gather together all the appropriate data and write in very plain language a short, concise, dissertation on each of the topics listed above. Be honest but not modest. If you can afford it, now is the time to obtain a few hundred sheets of quality stationery with a contemporary letter head imprinted on it. It is a conceit of many commercial photographers that they are natural designers, but my advice is to approach a real graphic artist or designer and have a suitable letterhead created. If money is a problem, an exchange of services might be suggested. Type what you have written on the stationery and perforate the left hand margin with a three-hole punch for insertion into the binder.

Under education list your academic training and if you did well mention any diplomas, degrees, awards or honors that you earned. A letter of recommendation from a favorite teacher or professor is also helpful. If you are self-taught or didn't excel academically then use this section to list your work experience and include copies of letters of reference from former employers. If you worked assisting an established photographer include samples, or a least a listing, of his or her work that you participated in producing. A few remarks relating your previous work experience to the plans for your own business could serve as a conclusion.

Your credit history is a record of what you have borrowed in the past and how you disposed of the debt. Be as detailed as possible. If you are switching banks because of a change of location and had a good relationship with your former banker, a letter of reference should be appended. If you are switching banks for some other reason, for example the loan officer with whom you had a good relationship was transferred or retired, a brief explanation of the circumstances is necessary.

A business rationale is simply a statement of the goals, intentions, and methods involved in creating and running your particular business. Describe the market you will be catering to and why your expertise is salable. A short-term projection of earnings and expenses together with medium range projection of capital spending is appropriate here. Don't be overly effusive. Remember banks want imaginative, but very pragmatic customers.

If you are already established as a commercial photographer, or have been involved in a related business such as portrait or wedding photography, insert copies of your financial statements and tax returns going back at least two years.

Your net worth is the value of your assets less the amount of your debt. On a sheet of paper make a list of everything you own such as cars, cameras, house and furniture. Indicate the fair market value of each item. Total those figures. List and add together all your debts, like car loans, mortgages, and credit cards. (Be completely frank: bankers take a very dim view of undisclosed debt.) Subtracting the debt total from the total value of your assets yields a figure for your net worth. It doesn't have to be a large number, just a positive one.

If you are good at photography, you have likely won some awards or contests. If you are in business you can list awards your clients have won for projects in which your work was included. For example, if you photographed a building for an architect, and that building later won a design award, you could add that award to your list with a footnote explaining that the architect's winning entry was illustrated with your photographs.

It is a wholesome gesture to offer some of your time and services to community institutions and groups such as the United Way. On a professional level, such work is often a central component of highly-visible campaigns so your volunteer efforts benefit yourself at the same time as they benefit others.

A marketing plan is the map of your method of entry into the commercial marketplace. You should have a clear-minded strategy for selling your services which might include direct mail of specially prepared samples, cold calls to art directors and corporate marketing people to arrange showing your portfolio, or even a contra arrangement with local magazines for advertising space.

Whatever your approach, it should be logical and specific to your skills.

You should spell out in exact detail what loans you are seeking and to what purpose they will be applied. A projection of the positive impact that the money to be borrowed will have on your income is obligatory and so is a proposal for a manageable repayment schedule and sufficient security. A description of your existing life insurance program and an indication or your willingness to buy more should it be necessary to further secure the loan (or loans) is also appropriate.

Finally, get some first-rate examples of your best work made up in 8$^1/_2$" X 11" format and have them laminated and punched for insertion into your book. Reproductions of actual magazine ads, bill-boards, or editorial layouts which feature your photographs are very effective. Be sure to include some enlargements made directly from your original negatives or transparencies; most people have never seen commercial photography close up and are very strongly impressed by carefully made first-generation prints.

After taking the trouble to put together a professional presentation, go out and do some shopping around. Remember that just like you, banks are providing a service at a price and their market is almost as competitive as yours. Look for flexibility, decent rates, and a loan officer who displays appreciation for your patronage and respect for your work; the day of the stern, paternalistic banker is long past. People overly eager to obtain much needed cash often leap at the first deal offered, forgetting they are entering a long term relationship with implications that extend far into the future. You have an obligation to yourself to ensure that any banker you deal with is empathetic and conscientious.

Maintaining Good Relations with Your Banker

Once you have entered into an satisfactory long-term arrangement with a financial institution, every effort should be made to take care of your obligations exactly as laid down. If you have established a revolving line of credit based on receivables, you will be required to provide a monthly statement of both receivables and payables; from this information the banker can gauge the health of your business. However, if things flow smoothly for some time, the monthly statements get filed without a careful look, and the relationship that you worked so hard to establish at the beginning gets a little distant. This is not a problem as long as no changes are required and times are good, but if conditions do fluctuate and you have to renegotiate, a lot of energy and time will be wasted re-establishing contact.

I recommend that from the start you consider your banker as a silent partner and keep him or her informed of what is happening in your business. If you elect to use direct mail or magazine ads as promotional tools, make sure that samples get to the bank, along with a brief note listing new clients or interesting projects that the sales efforts attract. Similarly, from time to time inform the bank of awards you win or community service work that you have undertaken. It is not inappropriate to invite your banker over to your studio when you're shooting so that he or she can develop a mental image of what you do and how you do it. Remember that commercial photography is a glamorous and mysterious business to outsiders.

The bank should be apprised of bad news as well as good. For example, if a client of yours goes bankrupt and leaves behind a bad debt or if a market sector you cater to should decline, let the bank know how your business has been affected and what counter measures you are taking. By maintaining an ongoing relationship with your bank, it will be much easier to negotiate new loans for expansion. If sudden misfortune should strike, you will receive a much more sympathetic hearing and a more generous accommodation.

If your first loan proposal does not satisfy any banks, you will have to look for money privately. This is not at all unusual for an entrepreneur just starting out. If you decide to approach a relative or friend, they deserve the same business-like attitude that you would bring to negotiations with an institutional lender.

4.

The Nuts and Bolts of Doing Business

The Basics of Establishing a Business

Before you hang out a shingle I recommend a visit to a lawyer and an accountant. These professionals will guide you through the initial red tape of licensing regulations, sales tax rules, and the basics of record-keeping. If you are about to expand an existing business, they will help you decide whether or not incorporation is necessary and can recommend banks to approach if new financing is required. It is prudent to obtain their input on the details of any loan proposals as well.

Once you have consulted with legal, accounting, and banking experts you will be ready to start normal business operations. Money will be flowing in from your clients and out, through the bank, to the various suppliers. You will have to keep track of it meticulously. I suggest that early on you establish a regular and reliable book-keeping procedure. There are two choices: pay someone to take care of the books on a monthly basis, or do it yourself. Either way, attend to it properly or your much needed concentration will be endlessly diverted by escalating paperwork.

If you elect to do the books on your own, the cheapest method is a "one-write" system.

This is a clever arrangement of specially printed forms which uses built in carbon paper strips to make journal entries automatically as you write out cheques and statements. You can find a supplier in the yellow pages of the phone book under "business forms". The sales rep will show you how to use the format that best suits your business.

Commercial Credit

Once established in business you will become both a user and a dispenser of commercial credit.

After things get rolling it will be difficult to personally run around buying all the things you need. Accounts at two or three camera shops or a photographic wholesaler will allow you to order materials by telephone which can then be delivered by the supplier or by special courier if deadlines are tight. Such accounts may be opened easily so long as you have decent references from a bank and a couple of other stores.

If you have not been in business long enough to have established a good credit rating, approach the credit manager of the store with which you want to deal and explain the nature of your business and the amount of material you expect to use each month. You might show him or her the book you prepared for the bank, deleting some of the detailed financial information which only your banker should see. In most cases, you will be expected to buy what you need with cash for ninety days or so, and then an account will be opened on a trial basis. If you pay your bills on time (typically thirty days, ninety days maximum) credit will be extended on a permanent basis. Everything depends on your reliability.

As long as you pay your bills you have a right to good service from your suppliers. Commercial photographers have to work to short deadlines and the appropriate photographic materials must be close at hand. Insist that suppliers keep your favored film, papers, replacement lamps, and chemicals in stock and that they fill your orders promptly. They should be prepared to fly in special items occasionally. If you are having problems with one of your supplier's employees, let management know and complain if the situation does not improve. It is considerate and sensible to keep your suppliers informed of what you are doing in the same way that you inform the bank. From time to time, send samples of your best work so that they can see what you do with the materials you buy from them.

Once you are using credit on a regular basis you will find that suppliers are much more flexible than banks when special circumstances arise. If you have a particularly large job coming up, they will often increase credit limits temporarily so that you can stock up with extra supplies or equipment. In tight circumstances they will allow debts to be paid off over several months, provided your previous track record has been very good.

Credit for Your Customers

The main difference between commercial photography and portrait photography is that the clients of commercial photographers are always other businesses or professionals while portrait photographers are almost always dealing with the general public. On av-

erage the business community requires at least thirty days for the processing of invoices. If you expect to be paid in cash or with an instant cheque you just won't fit in to the existing cycle. There is some pressure, therefore, to extend credit to any one who asks for it, but it is unwise to do so. Even large, seemingly well-established firms can be in financial difficulty while still maintaining an appearance of solvency.

The way in which your suppliers manage credit can serve as a model when you extend credit to your clients. Ask for references when credit is requested or expected by new clients. If you feel it might be tacky to question a new client directly, don't be shy about doing a little research and calling up their suppliers. Commercial credit-rating agencies will provide detailed information for a reasonable price. If you can find out what bank they deal with, your own bank manager can determine what the general state of their affairs might be. This approach is especially helpful with new clients calling you from out of town. A credit check is not underhanded or dishonest; it is to everybody's best interest to weed out the bad apples as quickly as possible.

Collecting Your Money

When you are uncertain about a client and they are requesting services on a very large scale, it is not unreasonable to request a partial payment in advance. Even a large corporation can understand that an independent small businessman/woman will need some guarantees when extraordinary expenses are expected to be incurred on their behalf. If they can't pay an advance they likely cannot pay at all.

In almost every case, once a healthy relationship with a reliable client has been established, you will find the extension of credit is not a problem. However it is only prudent to keep track of your receivables with an eye to early detection of trouble. You will find that each firm has a particular way of paying bills. Some pay on receipt of invoice and expect a small discount of one to three percent in exchange, which is not unreasonable. Others pay in fifteen to thirty days, and this is not unreasonable either. After sixty days things get a bit tricky.

Many advertising agencies are notoriously slow payers. Because they handle huge amounts of money intended to pay for expensive magazines space, television time, or billboards, they get into the habit of holding on to their clients' money as long as possible in order to earn the bank interest which can be a substantial part of their income. The smart ones will pay their suppliers quickly, if only to guarantee good service. However, some agencies treat their suppliers in a very arrogant fashion and don't pay for sixty, ninety, or even one hundred and twenty days. You will have to decide for yourself if this is acceptable.

The main thing is to watch for changes in the way a client pays. If cheques are too long in coming you are entitled to an explanation. Your flexibility when a client is tight for cash can earn long term loyalty and a lot of repeat business; however trust your instincts, and if a situation seems unstable or unsavory, protect yourself and insist on payment in advance or cash on delivery. Don't be intimidated by a possible loss of work; if they need you they will find the money. If they can't pay, the nicest job in the world is a waste of time.

Generally, impending insolvency is not the problem. There are firms who just habitually pay late or only after a phone inquiry. Invoices can go astray or sit forgotten on someone's desk waiting for an authorizing signature. Once in a while there will be a problem with the work you've done and the client will avoid calling; your only clue will be the delay in payment. Also, cheques do actually get lost in the mail occasionally.

The remedy for these problems is to maintain the attitude that after a job is done and the invoice sent out, that's your money out there and you have every right to receive it within a reasonable length of time. Learn the name and the telephone extension number for the comptroller or book-keeper at each of the various firms you are dealing with. If there is an unusual delay in payment get on the phone. Politely but firmly press for payment or a good explanation and some acceptable alternative, such as two or three post-dated cheques.

5.

Legal and Ethical Considerations

Copyright Law

Creativity is hard to define in any language, but the language of the law is particularly limited. Those of us who make a living inventing visual works must rely on a much amended set of regulations to protect our ability to profit from that which we create. The main instrument in our struggle is copyright, a collection of five basic rules governing the right to reproduce a work, the right to prepare derivative works, the right to distribute copies of a work, the right to perform a work publicly (important for video and broadcast technologies) and the right to display the work.

One might think that such rules could be clearly defined and simply enforced. Unfortunately, this is not always the case. In the United States the original copyright law of 1909 has been challenged many times: it was substantially revised in 1976. Under the old law all rights to an image passed to the purchaser, while under the new law rights to all images made after January 1, 1978 remain with the creator unless specified differently in a contractual agreement. Exceptions and variations are still being worked out legally.

A serious exception to the creator/copyright convention arises in the scenario called

work for hire, where the image was made by an employee—in this case the employer owns the copyright. Many clients now specify on their purchase orders that all photographs they commission are to be considered works for hire, and there is considerable tension developing over this practice. The courts have said that in the case of commercial photography such practices are valid only if the parties have signed a written agreement and if the work is specially commissioned to be part of a larger collective work to which others contribute.

Safe passage through all this demands clear, written agreements between clients and photographers.

Contracts

A contract is a promise that carries legal weight. The terms and conditions specified in a contract describe in detail the obligations which exist between two people, between a person and a business, or between two businesses.

Legal enforcement is based on proof. Memory is sufficient for some but not all circumstances—a written agreement is better. A written agreement is actually required by law in two circumstances—when the agreement will extend longer than one year, and when a the money involved exceeds $500.

A contract must include the following: a description of the product or service, the price, the date, the names of the contracting parties, and the signatures of the contracting parties. Clarity is the key. Remember that the language of contracts is not limited to legal jargon—ordinary people who are capable of stating their intentions in straightforward language can write binding contracts. For absolute peace of mind have a lawyer take a look at your final draft.

Sample contracts, model releases, and forms which are useful to photographers have been published in several different books. I recommend *The Photographers Business and Legal Handbook*, by Leonard Duboff, Images Press, New York, and *Business and Legal Forms for Photographers*, by Tad Crawford, Allworth Press, New York. Another very useful guide is *Professional Business Practices in Photography* from the American Society of Magazine Photographers.

Libel Law

Since photographs are very public documents, all photographers should have a basic understanding of the risks of publishing material that might be considered damaging or harmful to individuals or commercial entities.

To defame a person means to harm someone's reputation by subjecting them to ridicule, hatred, or contempt in some public way. If the act of defamation is verbal in nature it is called slander. If the act is written or printed it is called libel. Photographs which are defamatory fall into the latter category. Simply showing a defamatory picture to a third person is a sufficiently public event to trigger legal repercussions—i.e. a law suit.

There are variations of libel which consider whether the libelous work does the damage on its own or in conjunction with other contextual factors such as captions, text or other pictures. Advertising materials can be libelous if it impugns the quality of commercial merchandise or the practices of manufacturers.

Defenses against an accusation of libel revolve around several powerful concepts. If a defamatory photo depicts a real event then it is not libelous. If the photo clearly represents an opinion, it is not libelous. Obtaining consent for publication relieves the photographer of responsibility so long as the consent is given with a knowledge of how the image is to be used. Accurate reports of official proceedings or public meetings are exempt, as well. If a person is defamed, but allowed to reply in the same forum, then the libel is canceled. If it can be demonstrated that the defamatory material was used to clarify or amplify some debate or process of public interest without "a reckless disregard for the truth" then libel is not an issue—this defense is called *absence of malice*. Finally, public figures who launch libel actions are required to provide very substantial proof of damage or malice, since their high visibility elevates their personal lives into an arena of public concern.

There is a statute of limitations regarding defamation—libel actions must be taken within two years of publication.

Any photographer who feels that an impending job might result in some sort of libelous image should consult a lawyer. In fact, some publishers insist that the photographer assume all responsibility in case of a suit. This is a dangerous situation.

Obscenity

Free expression is a constitutional right in most enlightened democracies, but some people hold the view that there are limits to personal expression which transgress normal community standards to such a degree as to warrant legal prohibition. Since standards vary from place to place and from time to time, it is essential to maintain a working awareness of what is acceptable and what is offensive to those with whom you must live.

Common sense will tell you when your work might be considered obscene but it is impossible to be absolutely certain exactly where the boundaries are. One's best defense is to contact a lawyer familiar with the issues before getting involved in question-able projects.

Photographic Ethics

Commercial photography is deeply involved in the dissemination of basic cultural values. Many fundamental precepts of public morality were once taken for granted but are now being hotly debated. Violence against women, sex as a selling tool, the manipulation of children, materialism versus environmentalism, etc., cannot be safely left to others to consider. There is no question that photographs advocate, educate, manipulate, and stimulate. Strong images are active catalysts for both good and evil. Photographers who work without conscience or consciousness inevitably become unattractive propagandists for those who have a stake in molding specific public opinions and public desires, benign or otherwise.

The responsibility for ethical photography is of course split between the users and manipulators of photographs and photographers themselves. The viewers of photographs are not necessarily innocents either, although the exact nature of their participation varies with age, education, and life experience. Nevertheless, the photographer is the main creative instrument and the fundamental ethical filter. We are obliged, therefore, to educate ourselves and to consider the implications of our work.

6.

An Introduction to Pricing

Assuming your work is very good and that you are not wasteful of materials, how you charge for your services determines how well you live. There are no set rates in photography. There is, of course, downward pressure on prices because of competition, but if you take proper care of your clients they will become addicted to your services and what you charge them will be determined by what they can afford and how they use your photographs. Advice about producing extraordinary work will come later. For now, consider that what you offer is special and that you are hard to replace. The significance of determining the value of your work for each of your clients may be illustrated by the following story:

A young man who had worked for a time as a financial advisor with a large and respected accounting firm decided to strike out on his own. He approached two brothers who ran a big factory and offered to present a proposal for improving their operation.

The brothers had offices located side by side. Sam, brother number one, was in charge of financial matters, so he met with the young man first and was impressed. Sam asked the young man what he would charge to implement his ideas. The would-be consultant knew that his old firm would charge about

eight hundred dollars for the job, but because he was just starting out, he figured that he should ask for less. He blurted out just a single word, "Five!"

Sam hollered to his brother in the next office, "Dave, how does five thousand sound?" Immediately Dave answered, "Sounds good to me!"

"You're hired!" said Sam.

The insight of a psychic and the patience of a diplomat are required to negotiate with price conscious clients. But it pays to remember that in commercial photography setting prices is a process of negotiation, and that rates are indeed variable. Much depends on the reputation of the photographer, but to a significant degree the upper limit for a particular job is predetermined by the client's budget. If the client is an experienced buyer of photography, the budget will be reasonable. If the client is inexperienced or rapacious the budget will likely be unacceptable.

It is possible to develop an open relationship with some clients. These are the kind of people who know that they will prosper if the people they hire can also do well; such people are quickly revealed by their actions and their attitudes. Respect their egalitarian spirit by being straightforward with them. Don't hide the fact that you are working for money, but acknowledge candidly that different jobs have different values. Make it clear you always do quality work yet let them know you are willing to be flexible on rates to accommodate the range of work that might be sent your way.

For example, in your first meeting with a prospective customer you could say, "I'd like to take care of as many of your photographic needs as possible. Even if you think the budget for a certain project is too small, run it by me anyway. I can always refuse!"

In this way you will acquire a feel for what the client considers to be a small job, and by extrapolation, you will learn what is considered a large job. If you handle the small assignments gracefully, better jobs will follow naturally. Try to maintain a dialogue around the reasons for the differences between jobs in order to achieve an understanding of the economic pressures which are at work.

Information is the key to proper pricing but there is no reason to be underhanded; whatever you need to know can be discovered in an ethical manner and a little clear-headed analysis will take you the rest of the way. However, keep in mind that learning your clients' business can be a slow process. Over a period of several months you will see that each of them functions in a unique milieu. Once you've established harmonious relationships with several clients, you will have a reliable measure of the state of the marketplace and your place within it.

There are four scenarios which characterize the initiation of negotiations. The first is very rare; "I don't care what it costs, just do a fantastic job!" Much more often it will be, "Here's what I need, what will it cost?" If you have a good working relationship with a regular client, sometimes you will be told what to do and when to deliver the results, without price ever being mentioned; your previous price levels will be assumed to apply. And finally, some clients will have two or more photographers offer competitive quotes before assigning a job.

Each of these situations is handled differently but in every case the same basic information must be divined before the appropriate response can be formulated. Ask what the photos are to be used for, what size format is required and whether the client expects to keep the negatives or transparencies. Will you be required to oversee printing? Will the client find and pay for models and props if they are needed? Do you have a week to deliver the pictures or only twenty four hours? Will retouching be your responsibility or the client's? Will the client arrange access to people and places when the job must be shot on location? Keep asking until you know exactly what is required.

Because the desire for a good deal is an indelible part of both human nature and the free-enterprise system, the most difficult question is always what will a client spend on a given project? Still, it doesn't hurt to ask. You might try, "Do we have a comfortable budget to work with?", or, more directly, "What can you afford for photography on this project?". If the job is a repeat of a previous project, such as an annual report, you can ask, "Do you recall what you spent last time?" followed by, "Do you feel you got what you needed at that price?". These questions will be perceived as obnoxious if they are asked in an aggressive way. However, if your client is civilized and you are polite, a mutually beneficial exchange of information can take place.

When you're asked to produce a super product without regard to price, it is only prudent to go through the same investigative routine as if cost had been identified as an major issue. No matter what is or is not verbalized, the cost of a job is always an issue. Still, it's both flattering and inspiring when money is not a limiting factor. Enjoy the absence of financial pressure, but maintain sufficient presence of mind to pin down all the parameters of even the most deluxe assignment.

A call to quote on a job means one of four things. First, the client may be working with a tight budget and wants a bargain basement price. If the quotes are different but the photographers' skills are similar, the lowest quote gets the job. In extreme cases, price supersedes ability, and incredibly poor work results. In some markets this is the predominant mode and unavoidable. When breaking into such an environment, the instinctive response is to undercut everyone else. This kind of work inevitably involves both financial and professional sacrifices.

Second, the client might be inexperienced, ignorant or lazy and is consequently unwilling or unable to fix a proper value to the work that needs to be done. In this case the call for quotes is an easy way to get the benefit of a good photographer's advice for free. Beware of cynical people who ask you to work out the details of a complicated shoot and then give the job to somebody who will work for less.

Third, the client could be respectable but hard-nosed. Competitive quotes from competent photographers guarantee prices will be fair, all things being equal. In this case it is your professional obligation to know if the others invited to quote are in fact your equals, and if not, why not. You can ask outright who else is quoting, but do not expect an answer every time. When it doesn't seem appropriate to press for names, you might ask how many people are quoting or if the quotes are from local people only.

The final variation sometimes occurs when an advertising agency or a design house produces a project for a third party who insists on competitive quotes. If the agency or designer believes that one supplier is better suited than another to do the work, the contract may be awarded to the favorite regardless of the actual quotes tendered . Although it's unlikely that you will be told outright if you are the favored supplier, you may be given some clues such as, "be sure to mention that you specialize in (whatever) when you quote!" or "be sure to ask for enough to guarantee a quality job." In this situation a comprehensive and imaginative presentation is required if only to help your client justify a choice based on style, ability, or experience rather than price.

7.

Marketing and Promotion

A Marketing Strategy

The definition of fame is that a lot of people know your name. You will notice that this definition makes no reference to what you do or how well you do it. There is some comfort in this idea for newcomers to the photography business since it means that it is not necessary to be a Richard Avedon or a Pete Turner clone in order to attract attention—it is only necessary to spread your name around. A marketing strategy is a plan to effectively spread you name around.

Direct Mail

Your client list will build gradually if you establish a reputation for doing good work. This is psychologically satisfying but, in a small or very competitive market, business may expand too gradually if word-of-mouth is your only public relations vehicle. Self-promotion with direct mail is relatively inexpensive and highly efficient whether you intend to solicit new customers or simply keep those that have already used your services informed and interested in what you are doing.

A straightforward method of producing a memorable mailer is to photographically reproduce a striking image together with some suitable copy on 8" X 5" paper (half of a standard 8" X 10" sheet) that can be addressed and mailed like a post card. You might offer your services to a graphic artist or designer in exchange for advice on an effective layout. For one mailing you will likely need less than a hundred units. They can be made up cheaply in your own darkroom or at a commercial color lab.

Dean Collins is a successful west coast photographer. He has researched the effectiveness of the direct mail technique and has come up with some unusual insights. His informal studies have shown that most promotional material is received and almost immediately discarded by secretaries and receptionists. Collins determined that, sexist as it sounds, most secretaries are young females (18-25 years old) whose main interests are their girlfriends, men, sex, and babies. Collins tailors his direct mail items to attract the attention of these people, ensuring his stuff will not be immediately trashed. I don't endorse the perpetuation of sexual stereotypes, but the reasoning does makes sense.

If your mailer is sufficiently eye-catching it will be tacked up on walls and bulletin boards where it will quietly broadcast your skills for days, or even weeks. In highly competitive markets it helps to send out a new mailer every couple of months.

The Press Release

Personal modesty is an impediment to promoting your services. Take the example of the Hollywood flacks and abandon your reservations about self-praise and use the press release as an instrument for free advertising.

To get your material into the papers or on the air it is necessary to make a study of the local media—ask yourself the question, what constitutes an item of sufficient interest to be published or broadcast? The types of items picked up by the papers, radio, or TV depend on the size and sophistication of their markets. Very local, neighborhood media are inevitably most accessible, so start with them.

Here is a typical scenario:

Suppose you have been hired to make public relations photos of a state or federal politician in town for some special event, perhaps the announcement of some new policy initiative. You shoot the job and the photos are sent off to wherever they are supposed to go. Sometime during this particular job, however, ask someone to take a picture of you at work . . . .

Immediately after completing your assignment sit down and type up a few simply worded paragraphs under the heading "Local Photographer—Witness to History", with the subheading "For Immediate Release". The text should be double spaced and no more than a page or two in length with human-interest type details about the event gleaned from your special perspective—try to be interesting, but not gossipy. At the end of the text type -30-, which is press release language for 'end'. Send a photocopy of your press release and a copy of the picture of you at work to every local paper, etc.

You will be surprised at how often your supplied material will end up published and how quickly your reputation will be established in the community. Be alert to angles which will make your work a subject of interest to others around you—as the scope of your endeavors expands you can submit press releases to larger media outlets.

Telephone Technique

Having paved the way with a mailing or a short piece in the local paper, a personal sales call is next. In order to make a more substantial connection with a prospective customer you must make a phone call and set up an appointment.

All the businesses and institutions that commercial photographers work for are listed in the phone book. It is a simple matter to call and find out the names of art directors, communications officers, and chief designers—when you call to set up a meeting , ask for them by name. In simple language, say who you are and what you want. You will be surprised at the number of positive responses: most professional communicators want to meet new people and see new work, if only to stay abreast of current trends.

On the big day, call to confirm that your future client is available before you head out to the meeting; although you can expect civilized treatment, you are a low priority and your visit may have been forgotten or preempted. If you are forced to reschedule once or twice, be patient. If you are stonewalled three times in a row, try someone else.

The Personal Meeting

A successful meeting with potential client requires decent manners and a carefully edited portfolio of your best work.

The perfect portfolio is not necessarily a showcase for all your favorite shots—find out the kind of photography each of your potential customers usually buys and then present a few related examples of your best work. For example, a designer who specializes in corporate annual reports wants to see several first-class industrial location shots, five or six formal and 'environmental' executive portraits, plus a handful of striking product photos. Some innovative architectural shots of office towers and factories would also make sense. It would not make sense to show photographs of food, the performing arts, or women in fancy clothes, however well executed they may be.

I've found that it is most effective to show no more than twenty pieces at once. It helps if everything in your portfolio is of a uniform size. Laminated (but unbound) 11" X 14" prints with large white borders are striking to look at, satisfyingly substantial to the touch, and durable. They fit nicely into an attaché case, and they are easy to edit and assemble for specific purposes. *Tear sheets* of printed ads and magazine layouts can be carefully copied and reprinted to the same format. During your presentation remember that you are talking to an experienced professional who can judge your work quickly. Each photograph might be reviewed for only ten seconds but don't take offense. These people are busy and fifteen minutes of their time is the maximum you can reasonably expect. Have your pitch well rehearsed and do not repeat yourself. Should your work be praised, a simple thank you is sufficient. If a particular photo attracts negative attention ask why, but never, never argue. Don't overstay your welcome; when you're done, leave gracefully.

Free Radio, TV, and Print Advertising

Commercial photographers make a living largely from the advertising business. Photographers look at advertising when they want to buy or sell equipment or a vehicle. They rely on advertising to find a studio location and they advertise to sell their business or building when they retire. Why then do photographers resist advertising their own services? The personal modesty I alluded to earlier might have something to do with it, but cost is also a factor. There is a painless remedy for the latter restriction: contra—bartering between businesses—is a powerful mechanism for maintaining an effective advertising thrust with little or no cash investment.

Contra is different than the press release method of obtaining publicity because it involves a different group of people and a different reason for them to help. A press release is published when it appeals to those in the media concerned with editorial content—if a story is of interest to the reader, listeners, or viewers it is accepted. Bartering for advertising space or time requires the support of the advertising sales manager. Their help is enlisted by making a proposal which helps them do their job better. It works this way: suggest a mutually beneficial promotion where your work—an executive, family, or pet portrait, for example—is the prize. The promotion might revolve around some kind of contest or competition that would attract attention to the newspaper, radio station, or TV station. The event could be designed to go on for several days or weeks, keeping your name comfortably prominent in the community with a very minimal investment of time and materials. In the beginning this style of advertising is easier to sell to local media but the very same principals apply to sophisticated national and international promotions involving famous products and big corporations. It is only a matter of scale, with the dimensions of the project tied to the reputation of the photographer.

The Query Letter

Some photographers are not content to wait for clients to come to them with assignments. Such people are able to see profitable photographic projects all around but the problem is finding the right client to pay for the work. In this age of instant electronic communication it is comforting to note that an effective technique for making proposals to potential clients is a letter—typically a one or two page document in which a specific idea is pitched to a specific client.

The best query letters are amazingly simple and effective. The format is easy to master.

Say you are interested in producing a photo-essay on some subject of city-wide interest—the advantages of high-tech garbage incineration over old-fashioned land fills, for example. What sort of client would be as interested as you? Well, why not think big? Every city has the same garbage problems—therefore the issue is of concern everywhere. A national newsmagazine with an environmental section would be a potential client. A query letter is your method of entry.

Include the following elements: You must say why you are writing (the land-fill crisis), what you want (an assignment, film, processing, and a letter of reference for reluctant city officials), who you are and why you are the best choice for the job (lots of experi-ence, connections at city hall, you live next door to an incinerator). In closing say that a quick response would guarantee an exclusive on this particular story . . . and that is it. Clarity, and economy of expression should determine your language—competence and clear thinking should govern the tone.

Follow up your proposal with a phone call. Be prepared to take no for an answer six or seven times out of ten. Keep writing, however, and you will soon be shooting what appeals to you on a regular basis.

8.

Client Relations and Professional Standards

Following Through

A commercial photographer provides a service for a fee. Although there are some technical and aesthetic standards by which the quality of the service may be judged, it is very difficult to describe the interaction between photographer and client except to say that it is unusually intimate for a business relationship. Your interviews will inevitably lead to some assignments but what follows depends as much on your ability to deal successfully with people as on your photographic skills.

Photographers interpret and record reality on behalf of their clients. There are three steps in the process. Because each and every client has a different world view, the first task is to determine what the client wants. Next, the photographer must conjure up an appropriate mental image. Finally, a range of photographic techniques are applied to produce a tangible product.

To find out what the client wants, it is necessary to pay attention. Ask questions and listen carefully to the answers. Generally, a rendering or layout will be provided to make the exercise a little easier; study it well. Graphic artists are not constrained by the rigid optical laws that govern photography

and surprisingly often they will produce a drawing that cannot be duplicated photographically. Don't be shy about clearly calling attention to any limitations imposed by the medium. Prevent unrealistic expectations and you will save yourself a great deal of grief later on.

Having paid attention, the photographer must previsualize a creative photographic solution. Whether it is to be a variation based on past experience, or an original product of the imagination, the image must be both esthetically suitable and practical to produce. Before you start shooting, take the time to discuss your intentions with the client. Make rough sketches or use existing images to demonstrate what you propose. Bear in mind that it is not enough to just understand what you are being asked to do; the perceived need must be taken seriously. The client must feel respected.

Rules of the Game

Actually producing the work can be the easiest part of the entire process, but remember one basic principle; *your standards of quality must always exceed those of the client.* In other words, always give more than required. How much more is determined by two corollaries derived from the first principle: *'the ninety percent rule'* and *'the law of extraordinary effort'*.

Assignments fall naturally into two categories. Ninety percent of what you are asked to do may be performed to the satisfaction of all concerned provided you make good use of the skills, experience and tools you already have. The remaining ten percent of what comes your way will require a stretch of some kind. This could involve learning or inventing new techniques, acquiring new equipment, hiring an assistant, or just working extra-long hours. The prospect of extending oneself in this way can be intimidating, but demanding assignments successfully completed can offer many professional and personal rewards. A careful analysis is required. In exchange for time, money, and energy you may make a financial gain, embellish your reputation, or simply enhance your own self-esteem. However, all the costs and benefits of a complex project are impossible to anticipate in advance. Should you become involved in an undertaking that proves more difficult then anticipated, take comfort in the knowledge that any extraordinary effort made with wholesome intentions always yields a positive result.

Growth

Take proper care of your clients and they will be happy to recommend you to others in the industry. You will find that business which comes your way by referral is very good business in that the new client, having sought you out, will be predisposed to like your work. This does not mean you can lower standards, but simply that you can expect the relationship to begin on a cordial and respectful note. Bear in mind that the reputation of whoever recommended you will be affected to a degree by your performance.

Managing Professional Relationships

An astonishing variety of people will want your services but it is not always possible to predict if a new client will turn into a good client. Because a few unsavory individuals exist in every industry, you will occasionally encounter someone who is impossible to work with. Of course, you can't deal with anyone who is abusive or dishonest but (thankfully) the majority of clients are much easier to cope with. Nevertheless, even for an established professional photographer, the continuing challenge of client relations is to quickly recognize and defuse potentially troublesome situations.

Difficulties with first-time clients vary in significance according to the size of the job. The prudent buyer of photography will not usually risk offering a large project to an unknown. If you are approached to do a substantial assignment by someone you don't know, ask how they got your name and why they want to work with you. Trust your instincts as you listen to the reply. Sometimes a solid referral will connect you with a bona fide prospect who needs a job done in a hurry, but sometimes a less than legitimate outfit is simply looking for a one-shot special. All first-time clients are short-term clients until you get that second call, so don't commit valuable time and resources on unsubstantiated promises of future work. When in doubt, ask for a part-payment in advance. This will discourage triflers.

First-time clients offering modest assignments are much less of a risk. Again, ask all the proper questions, but don't be afraid to take a few chances. You will find many individuals who are worth investing in. It is exciting and satisfying to trust and be trusted. People have long memories; a small job well done could lead to substantial work six months or a year down the line. Those customers that rely on you over the long run will be your 'bread and butter', the foundation of your security. They will need special prices and preferential service from time to time, but such accommodations should be natural events within a stable, mutually beneficial relationship. Discomfort arises when a client makes too many demands and abuses your loyalty.

The secret to ensuring your regular clients don't become too cavalier with your energy is to keep them well informed about what it is you actually do for them. Tell them when you acquire new equipment or skills on their behalf. If certain jobs are particularly expensive or complicated to produce, let them know, but don't whine. When a job is particularly rewarding, either financially or professionally, tell your client in some dignified way. The idea is to demonstrate your satisfaction with the work, but not to brag about your profit margins.

Always watch for the indicators of a downhill trend in clients' attitudes. Unexpected objections to your pricing or inappropriate demands for free services are messages of dissatisfaction. Inconsiderate behaviors, such as calling at the last minute for time sensitive assignments, appearing late for shoots, or losing invoices, are all potential irritants.

As long as you are certain that your work is properly professional, the remedy for a deteriorating rapport is honesty. Set up a meeting with your client. Make it clear that you value the work that comes your way, but as diplomatically as possible point out the things that you find discouraging. A concerned, conciliatory attitude will usually be respected. In most cases your client, perhaps having been spoiled by your consistently competent service, will need only the most gentle of reminders. There is always the chance, however, that even the mildest of protests will be viewed as cheeky and misplaced, in which case you will have to decide for yourself if you can work under less than optimum conditions.

Coping with Different Types of Clients

1. *Demanding clients* come in a variety of flavors. Most of them expect miracles, even when time and money are tight. Some are congenitally insensitive and simply enjoy throwing their weight around, while others are neurotic perfectionists and assume you are as well. Experience and common sense will tell you if a client's demands are reasonable. If a demand seems unreasonable, say why, and offer an acceptable alternative. For example, there are people who create artificial

deadlines as a way of reinforcing their own importance; somehow, there's never enough time to do the job properly the first time, but there is always time to re-shoot when things screw up. Don't allow yourself to be rushed into things that you suspect will not turn out right. This requires some backbone, but believe me, an inarticulate response will mark you as incompetent, and avoiding the issue altogether will lead to ulcers.

To be fair, *competent* clients are demanding only because they are completely committed to producing excellent work; consequently, they will understand and welcome your desire for manageable working conditions. Usually, even incompetent or inexperienced clients will be grateful if you can put forward an obviously rational method of achieving their objectives. When clients ignore advice offered in good faith, however, it is better to turn down the assignment rather than participate in a fiasco.

2. *Nervous clients* buy emotional support and photography simultaneously. There are two types of nervous clients: consolable, and inconsolable.

The role of the advertising and public relations professional is very stressful so most complaints and worries are understandable and completely normal. It is an everyday part of a commercial photographer's job to reassure clients but it is important to know that the ability to reassure is a manifestation of self-confidence; there is a kind of psychic radio by which both worry and inner strength are communicated. If you are certain of your own abilities, and patiently address concerns one at a time as they arise, the *consolable* client will eventually relax.

The inconsolable client is another matter altogether. Here, the 'nervousness' is either a manipulative game that's intended to keep you on your toes or else a debilitating character defect. Conflicting feelings arise because such people transmit a double message: they want you to do the work but for some unspoken reason they want you to worry about your ability to undertake it successfully. Fortunately, the appropriate response is always the same: just do your job well and allow the emotional 'noise' to recede into the background.

3. Your clients will vary in *intelligence* and, of course, there are special considerations when dealing with people at either extreme on the scale.

Intelligent people are stimulating and frustrating at the same time. While an encounter with a powerful mind can be a delight it can also be a real challenge because intellectual power and the ability to communicate do not necessarily go hand in hand. It is sometimes difficult to understand what a really intelligent person wants, especially as their ideas may be extremely sophisticated yet poorly expressed at the same time. Complicating matters is the very human aversion to looking foolish which inhibits the asking of necessary questions. Remember that there are different kinds of intelligence and that it takes some effort to transpose concepts formed by one type of mind into concepts that another type of mind can grasp. Your clients want your special intelligence.

The word that best describes a healthy relationship between intelligent people who are working co-operatively is *engagement*. Although much of the work of commercial photography is done in solitude, there are moments of engagement with bright and inspiring people which I imagine to be similar to the harmony that musicians in a 'tight' band must experience when they are really flying.

Less intelligent clients tend to slow things down a bit. Communicating is again the key issue, but in the case of obtuse or unsophisticated customers, information moves mostly from photographer to client rather that the other way around. The problem here is that photography, particularly commercial photography, is often very complicated and time-consuming but the degree of complexity is not readily apparent just from looking at a photograph. Some clients simply cannot figure out by themselves why a photograph might be worth several hundred dollars and many hours of effort to produce. Such clients need (and will pay for) your services but you must guide them to an understanding of what it is you do, how you do it, and, most importantly, why you do it. Generally speaking, your patience and respect will be repaid with loyalty.

4. *The aggressive client* is in single-minded pursuit of business objectives, often at the expense of his or her personal life. As is the case with most strong personalities these (usually) high-achievers expect to enlist your total support by virtue of their own enthusiasm and intensity, although other kinds of emotional pressures are sometimes employed as well. Their habitual assumption that money and professional status are the only motivations of those who strive for excellence often grates on those who are in fact motivated differently.

Aggression is a major component of the sales oriented personality, and as virtually all of commercial photography is dedicated to selling, these people are everywhere. They range in disposition from 'sweetness and light' through to obnoxious; the determining factor being your usefulness to them. The truly aggressive have no loyalty; to them you are only as good as your last job. They are interested in what you do rather that what you are.

Harmonious relations with such people require you to consistently produce good work under pressure while maintaining a degree of detachment. Detachment is not disinterest or disrespect; rather it involves being able to perceive complicated situations as would a dispassionate observer. It is quite possible to maintain a very productive relationship while still keeping a little distance.

5. It is likely that you will have to treat *wealthy clients* differently than *less prosperous clients*, but that is only because they are likely to treat you differently. As a rule, clients with deep pockets pay their bills regularly, so work for them proceeds on an orderly and predictable basis, at least financially speaking. This cannot be the case for poorer clients, and greater caution is called for in pricing and collecting.

The value of your work changes according to the size of the projects of which it will be a part. As well-heeled customers are more likely to be working on a large scale, your fees to them will inevitably be higher. Both poor and rich clients might value your work equally, but tight budgets automatically put a cap on fees. The quality of your work cannot change, so your expectations must; unless you are overwhelmed with business you cannot be a snob. Be flexible in pricing when necessary, but make certain your lower paying customers are aware that they're getting reduced rates and that they can expect reasonable increases as they grow. This notion is not as unpalatable as it may at first sound; by accommodating smaller clients you will be contributing to their future success and you can reasonably expect to benefit when it arrives.

When the Client Is a Friend

The discussion so far has presupposed that the typical relationship between client and photographer is strictly business, but it is unrealistic to believe that a client cannot be, or will not become, a friend.

Although I lack the patience to deal with non-professional people on a regular basis, when a close friend asks me to photograph their wedding or family my response is always yes. However, I never take any money for the work. If they insist, I suggest they send a donation to a favorite charity.

I always refuse to shoot for acquaintances or friends of my friends. I simply tell them I'm so busy with commercial work that I cannot properly take on any other obligations. The answer is a truthful one, of course, but I have also learned over the years that friends are easy to please while those one knows less well are much pickier. It is just not worth the aggravation. I refer these jobs to a friend who does photography part time and has a more suitable disposition.

Things are easier to manage in the case of a regular client who, over time, becomes a friend, in that a basic pattern of behavior for doing business will have been already well established. My advice is try to maintain a slightly detached attitude when in the business mode; it is unfair, unprofessional, and ultimately self-defeating to expect preferential treatment.

Heal Thyself

Much of this chapter has been focused on clients' attitudes. However, a whole different range of problems arise when you yourself run out of enthusiasm. During periods of low energy, when work seems tedious and repetitious, it is easy to blame others for your own negative feelings. If you allow yourself to do this, a chain of misunderstanding and hostility develops, and your dark world view becomes a self-fulfilling prophecy.

9.

The Small Commercial Studio

The Mystique of the Studio

Good studio photography (just like a good motion picture) inspires the suspension of disbelief. The photography studio (just like the movie studio) is a place where technology and imagination work together to generate convincing illusions. Inside the studio the photographer is a minor god playing at the construction and destruction of countless little worlds.

Clients love studios. There is something whimsical and exhilarating about a place in which everything they imagine can be materialized more or less on demand. Legitimized by the ostensibly sober pretext of doing business, normally reserved adults get to play like kids in a grown-up sandbox. Both photographers and the people they work for come to regard the studio as an exotic haven comfortably isolated from the often dreary trappings of the regular corporate environment.

Finding Your Own Space

Sustaining the mystique is not impossible even if the studio is a temporary mutation of your living room or basement. At the beginning of a career, any space capable of en-compassing camera, lights, set, and photographer will do. Most assignments involving a subject smaller than a domestic appliance can be shot in a room ten feet square if necessary, although the typical eight foot ceiling places a definite limit on lighting possibilities.

Some professional photographers prefer to operate without a studio of their own. When they have to shoot in a controlled environment they rent a space and lighting equipment to go with it. My experience, however, is that such an approach is impractical for someone working in a middle-size city doing a variety of commercial work. Sooner or later the inconvenience and emotional distraction associated with a makeshift arrangement will lead to a desire for something more permanent. This means building, renting or buying.

Setting up a studio is a public act which signifies a real commitment; a marriage between you and the business community. Your bank, your suppliers, your customers, as well as your competitors, will know that you have embarked on a serious undertaking, and they will respect you for it. When others view you differently, your own self-image changes. Taking on the long-term responsibility of maintaining a commercial space increases pressure but it also encourages sober and mature behavior.

Those engaged in commercial photography tend to be stubborn perfectionists and highly involved in their work. Often they find it difficult to separate themselves emotionally from their professional obligations. This state of being puts personal peace of mind as well as harmonious family relations at risk. At first the added stress of running a studio might exacerbate this condition, but after a short while, having a separate physical space dedicated exclusively to business promotes the ability to separate oneself from worry; just walking out the door at the end of the day can be a cathartic experience.

Don't set up a studio before you can afford it. You must have enough money set aside to carry the added costs until the studio begins to pay for itself. This may take only a couple of months if you have already established a flow of studio work using your home or a studio rented on a short-term basis. However, if you are depending on the acquisition of a studio to expand your business, be prepared to cover several months' expenses with your reserves. The period of uncertainty can be reduced by careful marketing before the move.

The least expensive way to acquire a studio space is to rent and how much you pay is determined by location. Where you set up shop depends to a degree on how you intend to run your business. Commercial photography does not require a prime down-town address because there is virtually no retail component. If only couriers and the occasional client have to find you than you may quite happily locate well away from the city-center in an industrial park, a warehouse district or even in a residential subdivision.

For some photographers, a downtown location is desirable because the increased visibility and easy access for corporate clientele is an important marketing bonus, well worth the extra cost. Apart from high rent, a substantial investment in decorating and furniture will be required to maintain the appropriate upscale image. Studios of this sort usually include a small office or meeting room with a separate phone as an additional convenience for busy clients.

I recommend that you operate out of a rented space for sufficient time to acquire a thorough insight into what you really need. Then, if you find yourself totally and happily committed to one geographical area, and if the money is available, buy or build a space of your own. The cash required is significant, obviously, but the investment is returned in three ways. First, if you're the landlord you are free at any time to modify the structure to suit yourself. Second, the mortgage interest, the cost of improvements, and costs for repairs and maintenance are all deductible expenses at tax time. Third, your own building is an asset which will most likely increase in value, independent of any fluctuations in the photography business. At the end of your career, or whenever you want to make a change, you'll be able to generate cash easily by renting, selling, or refinancing the property.

Whether building, buying, or renting, you will have to determine exactly how much space your operation requires. The critical dimension is ceiling height. For any flexibility in lighting, nine feet is an absolute minimum for table-top product work, although eleven feet is infinitely more practical. Twelve feet is the minimum for photography which involves people or bulky objects like furniture. When really large sets are involved, like those required for shooting cars or fully furnished rooms, at least sixteen feet is mandatory. According to most building codes, sixteen feet is also the minimum when incorporating a mezzanine platform or balcony to facilitate shooting straight down or at an elevated angle.

The width of the studio should be about thirty-three percent greater that the width of the typical set, while the length should be twice the width to ensure enough room to maneuver with long focal length lenses. The usable dimensions may be extended by constructing a gently curved corner, called a cove, where the floor and the back wall meet. In narrow studios, the vertical corners of the back wall may be coved; in studios where height is a problem, the corner where the back wall meets the ceiling can be treated the same way. A cove may be constructed with thin plywood and plaster or else a commercial system may be obtained through one of the larger studio supply houses.

Absolute minimum studio dimensions for small product photography might be eight by sixteen feet but a more practical size for general work is fifteen by thirty feet. Shooting fashion or furniture in a space smaller than twenty five by fifty is not recommended. Extra space will be required for changing rooms for models, a washroom, as well as props, equipment storage and possibly a workshop. A darkroom will need at least one hundred square feet to be useful.

The Practical Studio

An efficiently designed studio is organized like a little ship: everything in it has a place and a purpose. The shooting area should be tidy, supplied with sufficient independently fused electrical outlets, and well isolated from extraneous daylight. Equipment should be arranged to be easy reach and replace. Heavy-duty pegboard is great for accessible storage of cables and other non-optical tools. If you are building from scratch or renovating an existing space, make hallways, doors, and stairs wide enough to ensure that moving around with bulky equipment is safe and easy. Also, consider plywood rather than plasterboard for the walls of the shooting space. Taped and sanded plywood is almost as smooth as drywall, yet much more durable.

An overhead track system for suspending lighting instruments from the ceiling is extremely handy. A fixed grid can be made cheaply from metal electrical conduit, although a more sophisticated system with movable rails and adjustable light hangers is the best way to go if you can afford it. Should you incorporate such a system in your studio, build a shelf to mount electronic flash packs a little below waist level in order to eliminate unnecessary bending and clutter. It is amazing how much bigger and more comfortable a studio seems when the floor is free of lightstands and wires.

A studio is a box in which objects and people are carefully placed and painstakingly illuminated. The main theme is control, especially control of light. Purists will argue that it is critically important to eliminate all uncontrolled reflections by painting the entire studio dead black, an idea which I find depressing. I feel that a degree of built in reflectivity is not a problem, in fact sometimes it is actually desirable. I have always painted my studio ceilings and walls white and most studio shots do not suffer from the ambient reflections induced by the white surfaces. It's easier to eliminate unwanted reflective fill with black cards and flags than it is to add additional light with more lighting instruments and reflectors. Colored walls or ceilings are an absolute no-no, however.

A white ceiling is very handy in combination with certain lighting fixtures. Some permanent source of light is necessary in any studio, if only to navigate by, but the built-in lights in my shooting area serve a double purpose. My ceiling is thirteen feet high. Three feet below the ceiling and spaced equally around the walls I have installed four permanent light fixtures, each of which use one five hundred watt quartz element. They are individually switched and directed upwards so that the light bounces evenly off the ceiling for a very pleasant effect.

Because the quartz tubes are designed to radiate at 3200K, the correct color temperature for tungsten color film, I'm able to use this broad overhead source for photographic purposes. With little or no modification, I've done large scale copy work and successfully shot a variety of outsized products. The fixtures were originally intended to be used as outdoor floodlighting and sold for forty-five dollars with lamps included. They are now five years old and the original lamps are still working fine.

Studio Accessories

There are a number of non-photographic tools and appliances that make sense in any studio. First on my list is a reliable telephone answering machine with remote message retrieval capability. The typical one-person commercial photography operation cannot, or need not, pay for someone just to answer the phone and keep track of where the photographer might be. I have found an answering machine more useful than a pager or cellular phone both of which are disruptive and on location exert distracting psychological pressure to return calls immediately. It is a case of runaway technology. There is really no need to deal with all incoming calls instantly. If you do, your life will be awfully intense; people tend to take advantage of the overly eager. When you are away from the studio, check your messages around eleven thirty in the morning and again around four o'clock in the afternoon. In this way you will be able to return important calls before lunch or before the end of the business day without having been harassed by high-tech bells and whistles. Write down your messages in your day book as the machine plays them back; you will save yourself a lot of time and aggravation in the long run.

A decent stereo system is indispensable. Good music can be inspiring when it's necessary to work late or all night long, it can soothe nervous clients, and it can motivate awkward or self-conscious models. During long hours in the darkroom, or when you're stuck with some boring assignment, music can be a life-saver.

If your work involves servicing clients from other regions, a FAX machine is a very useful tool. Many users of photography have grown impatient with the delays and expense associated with inter-city couriers and messengers, and instead they prefer to instantly FAX copy, layouts and shooting instructions directly to the photographer on the scene. If the expense of purchasing a machine outright is a problem, you might consider leasing or even sharing a machine with a business located near your studio. As with the telephone answer machine, an instant response to a FAX message is not required. If you can respond sometime during the same day most everyone will be satisfied. Those people that do expect immediate replies on a regular basis will inevitably be troublesome clients.

An electronic air cleaner is another very valuable technological gadget, particularly if a darkroom is a part of the studio. These high efficiency electro-static filters replace the conventional fiberglass filters in your furnace or air conditioner and do an amazingly thorough job of removing dust and other impurities. A one time outlay of a couple of hundred dollars plus a few minutes maintenance each month will prove to be a worthwhile investment, especially if you are a smoker. If you do maintain a darkroom, remember that your water as well as your air should be filtered with some appropriate device.

Not many photographers would consider an air compressor as a indispensable tool, but I most certainly do. I bought one in self-defense after having used up hundreds of dollars worth of 'canned' air. I installed flexible self storing coiled nylon supply lines in the shooting space, darkroom, workshop, and storage areas of my studio. A constant source of pressurized and filtered air comes in extremely handy for dusting off products, sets, cameras, lenses, equipment cases, and negatives. Once it served to make very convincing waves in a shot which required a simulation of the edge of a swimming pool.

A freezer is a relatively inexpensive appliance which makes life significantly easier for the busy photographer. Many "professional" films are intended to be stored at forty degrees Fahrenheit in order to guarantee consistent speed and color balance. To cut down on time consuming testing, it is a sensible practice to buy large quantities of favorite emulsions and store them at low temperatures for use later. This is particularly true of paper for color printing, which can often be purchased cheaply in bulk lots. Polaroid warns not to freeze their products, but I have often bought out of date instant film at a substantial discount and stored it frozen for months before using it successfully. Finally, film that has been exposed, but for some reason cannot be processed immediately, should be stored at low temperature to preserve the latent image.

To do a proper job of food photography, a fully equipped kitchen should be constructed as part of your studio. Such an expense cannot be justified in most non-specialized shops but there is a relatively economical alternative which requires only simple plumbing and wiring to install. About one thousand dollars will buy an integrated unit with a small oven, two or three adjustable elements, a stainless steel sink, a small refrigerator, and several square feet of stainless steel counter top. These clever appliances are intended for bachelor apartments, university residences, or motels. The unit I have in my studio is five feet wide by thirty two inches high by twenty eight inches deep and has a twenty-four inch oven, a five cubic foot refrigerator and a twelve by sixteen inch sink. Both smaller and larger versions are available. Mine has paid for itself many times over in lunches alone!

Sets and Props

Quite regularly you will be required to build or modify props and sets. Once I even constructed forms and poured cement for a simulated road and curb which served as the background for a shot of Puma running shoes. Hiring someone to do this kind of work is relatively expensive and usually unnecessary if the proper tools are available. Build a sturdy workbench about five feet long by thirty inches wide and attach a solid three inch vice on the right-hand corner. Put up a pegboard behind the bench and hang up a hammer, a $3/8$" capacity power drill, a staple gun, a set of screwdrivers in various sizes, a set of wrenches sized from $1/4$" to $3/4$", a set of jeweler's screw drivers, a power jig saw, wire cutters, small and medium vice-grip pliers, and a variety of files and sandpaper. If you also have handy some duct or gaffer's tape, some silicone rubber, some five-minute epoxy, a roll of eighteen gauge mechanics wire, some window putty and a spool of nylon fishing line, there will be almost nothing you can't fix, build or repair.

Locking Up Your Tools

My final non-photographic recommendations relate to security. Large free-standing safes are now out of style for banks; they can be bought used for surprisingly low prices and they're great for burglar-proof storage of cameras and lenses. I bought a second-hand sixty cubic foot safe with a four hour fire rating for three hundred dollars. A walk-in cupboard with a sturdy locking door is a good idea for expensive and fragile photographic lights. It's also wise to invest in a steel outside door, a local alarm system, and heavy wire mesh for any ground floor windows. Look in the yellow pages for suppliers. No matter how well you are insured, a robbery is an incredibly disruptive occurrence.

10.

Photographic Lighting

The Qualities of Light

Literally translated, 'photography' means drawing with light. Expert manipulation of light in all its subtle forms is the foundation of both studio and location practice; it calls for a variety of special tools, some of which are quite expensive. Nevertheless, I have worked for many years with an uncomplicated selection of relatively inexpensive lighting equipment that has served me well in many situations. The reasons for my personal choices will be more apparent after a quick review of basic principles.

Understanding photographic lighting begins with an appreciation of the technically variable qualities of light itself: color, intensity, direction, and specularity. Of these four qualities, specularity is of critical importance. In fact, most devices dedicated to the modification and control of light for photography are designed to somehow alter or enhance this trait.

Specularity is a function of the size of the light source in relation to whatever is being illuminated. For example, the sun on a cloudless day is a highly specular light source, while an overcast sky is non-specular, or highly diffused. Among photographers, specular light is referred to as *hard* and non-spec-

ular light is *soft*. An object illuminated by a 'hard' light throws a shadow with hard, precisely defined edges. A source of hard light may be altered or directed by fresnel or condenser lenses, parabolic reflectors, or mirrors. Umbrellas, diffusers, soft boxes, and hundreds of different sorts of reflectors, are used to change hard light into controlled soft light. The shadows from a 'soft' light source are fuzzy and undefined.

Synthetic Sources

Virtually all artificial light used in photography is generated by one of two sources: a tiny coil of wire made white-hot by an electrical current, or a small tube of xenon gas excited by an instantaneous electrical discharge. Because tungsten is the best material for the glowing wire, we have 'tungsten' or 'incandescent' lights. Since the xenon gas emits light for only the tiny fraction of a second during which it is energized, this source is called 'electronic flash' or 'speedlight'.

Both tungsten lamps and electronic flash tubes are relatively small so when they're used for photographic purposes without any sort of modification they are extremely 'hard' light sources. All their other attributes are markedly dissimilar.

Incandescent light is continuous; as long as electricity flows through the filament, light is produced. Electronic flash generates light much differently; electrical energy is stored in a device called a capacitor. To fully charge the capacitor with electricity takes from one to thirty seconds depending on the type of flash unit. Then the stored energy is discharged rapidly through the flash tube. The discharge begins when a small electrical signal called a trigger pulse is initiated by a switch built into the shutter mechanism of the camera. The flash must be *synchronized* with the shutter, so that the pulse of light, which may be from $1/50$ to $1/10,000$ of a second in duration, occurs when the shutter is completely open.

The brevity of the xenon flash might seem at first to be a disadvantage but it is actually a blessing in disguise. The pulse of light is so short that both subject motion and camera shake are eliminated. In order to preview the effects of the flash and to provide sufficient illumination for focusing a small tungsten lamp, called a modeling light, is mounted near the flash tube in professional studio flash units.

Due to the elaborate electronics involved, electronic flash equipment powerful enough for professional use is complicated, expensive, and heavy compared to tungsten lamps, which are simple in construction and very lightweight.

Unfortunately, tungsten lights are not very energy efficient. A lamp rated at 1000 watts might produce only 200 watts of light and as much as 800 watts of waste heat. Because incandescent lights are a fire hazard and destructive to heat sensitive subjects, they can sometimes be awkward and uncomfortable to work with.

A conventional incandescent lamp darkens and changes color with age as metal evaporating from the hot filament condenses on the inside of the glass bulb. 'Quartz-halogen' lamps are filled with inert gas and operate at extremely high temperatures so that vaporized tungsten cannot condense but instead is redeposited on the filament in a continuous

cycle. Although quartz lights last longer and behave more consistently than conventional lamps, their life expectancy is still only a few hundred hours. Both types are delicate and will burn out if they are accidentally jarred while operating. Photographers put up with all the inconveniences of 'hot lights' because the lighting effects may be easily judged and very finely controlled. In addition, some people feel that the 'warm' incandescent spectrum renders a more natural look than the 'cool' light from electronic flash.

Quantifying Color

The color of both artificial and natural light may be described more precisely with the *Kelvin Color Temperature Scale*. So called 'normal' daylight is 5500° Kelvin but this actually varies according to time of day, time of year, geographical location, and air purity. A sunset at the end of a dusty prairie day would radiate very warm light, perhaps as low as 2500° Kelvin, while high noon up in the Rocky Mountains could register a very cool 20,000° Kelvin. Incandescent lamps for photography are rated at 3200° on the Kelvin scale. Electronic flash is designed to be 5500° Kelvin.

'Daylight' color films are balanced for 5500°K and intended to be used outdoors for exposures shorter than one second, or with electronic flash. 'Tungsten' balanced films are designed for exposure under 3200°K incandescent lights. Small format tungsten transparency films, such as Kodak Ektachrome EPY, are intended for short exposure times while some large format tungsten transparency films, such as Kodak Ektachrome 6118 are intended for long exposure times. In a pinch all these films may be interchanged, provided appropriate filters are used and the corresponding exposure corrections are made.

A Simple Rule

How lighting equipment is used depends on the specific photographic problem at hand in combination with the aesthetic approach of the photographer. I generally use tungsten light when photographing inanimate objects, unless working temperature will be a problem. For lighting people and other subjects that can move, I prefer electronic flash.

A Brief History of Lighting

Over the years there have been a variety of fashions in photographic lighting. The styles have tracked changes in picture-making technology at the same time as they paralleled the broader tastes of the entire culture. Early portraiture, for example, was lit by natural daylight from large skylights built into the studios of the time; there were no artificial alternatives to sunlight. The subjects appeared rather rigid simply because they had to stay still for several minutes while the 'available light' worked its magic on the slow emulsions. Later on, with the advent of a multiplicity of marvelous incandescent fixtures, portraiture became an elaborate exercise where several types of 'hard' sources were carefully balanced to build up a highly stylized look. The glamour portraits produced in the forties by Hollywood's George Hurrell are examples of this 'heroic' style. Later still, in the sixties and seventies, electronic flash and fast films ushered in a period of unprecedented spontaneity as photographers and their subjects were freed by technical advances to catch life on the run.

The changes in portrait styles were paralleled in commercial photography. The era that's just ended in North America might be called the "decade of the soft box". We have had ten or more years of pictures of both people and products lit by very broad sources, really just counterfeit windows, filled with reflected light, and occasionally enhanced with a touch of harder rim or back-light. The look recalls the natural light work of the very first photographers, exalted by the exceptional accuracy of modern color films.

Current Trends

Today's consumers of still photography are continually inundated by a very broad spectrum of superb imagery from TV, movies and lavish magazines. Commercial photographers are expected to be able to reproduce and enhance the styles of the past as well as expertly mimic the newest visual offerings flashed by satellite from Los Angeles, New York, Paris or Berlin. Even clients with the most modest budgets are subconsciously expecting the photographs they buy to compare favorably to those produced around the world.

Although composition and perspective are important, in the calculated world of commercial photography it is mainly through the intelligent and sensitive use of light that a photograph is infused with a 'style'. Nowadays photographers need to know how to select, and tastefully apply, a multitude of lighting tools and techniques. It is absolutely essential to study the photographs which appear everywhere around you; make it a habit and you will find that it becomes fairly easy to discern the size and placement of the lights. Your own emotional responses to the images you study will teach you how lighting works to evoke an astounding range of moods.

Nuts and Bolts

After sensitizing yourself to the lighting skills of other photographers, acquiring an eclectic arsenal of both flash and tungsten hardware is an unavoidable necessity. In Chapter Two I listed my personal preferences. In Chapter Twelve I will give specific, practical details of how these tools may be used efficiently to light a range of commercial assignments, but now I'll simply outline the technical rationale for the selection of equipment.

I chose the Lowel tungsten light system because it is versatile and durable as well as light weight and compact. It was designed by a working photographer, and there are appropriate bits and pieces available to solve almost any lighting problem. The Lowel 'DP' light is the heart of the system. I am particularly fond of the DP's focusing ability; with a simple turn of knob, the beam it projects can be varied with precision from 15° to 90°. This

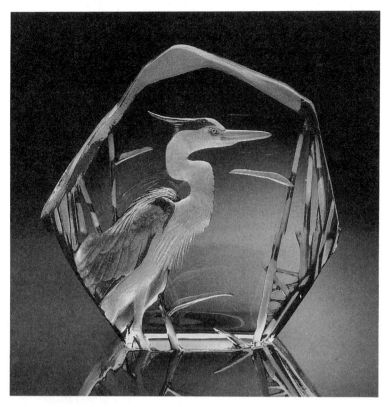

This product photo was made for a gift shop that wanted some eye-catching images sufficiently detailed to reproduce well in both newspaper and magazine ads. I like to keep things simple so I chose an 'eye-level point of view and fairly hard, edgy lighting to accentuate the graphics of the object. The crystal sculpture is sitting on a piece of black slate-surfaced formica. Hasselblad camera, 100mm lens, one 10mm extension tube, Kodak T-Max 100 film.

range may be extended with inexpensive snap-in reflectors.

The DP lights can handle up to 1000 watts each and typically use an FEL lamp. However, I prefer to the long-life 750 watt EHG bulb. Because they run a little cooler, these lamps have a slightly warmer color temperature (3000°K instead of the usual 3200°K) which I find very pleasing.

Multi-leaf barndoors and a variety of different size flags are easily attached. There is a simple but solid umbrella bracket available as well as a large, comfortably cool handle which allows the lights to be manipulated without burning fingers. A very clever system of clamps, adapters, and stands facilitates mounting the lights and accessories in all kinds of configurations. Sensibly priced fitted cases allow the entire system to pack and travel well.

Although the Lowel system can be used in a hundred different ways, my favorite approach is to bounce the DP units off strategically positioned reflector cards of various sizes, using their focusing capability in combination with the barndoors to surgically tailor the pattern and intensity of the light. By adding two little Photogenic focusing spots (sometimes called 'needle lights' or 'inkies'), and a few small mirrors, I can add highlights and accents when required.

I rely on tungsten lights and the 'system approach' when elaborate and detailed lighting is required. Really fancy lighting, however, is not called for all that often. In fact, my favorite studio light is a device I built myself for under twenty dollars out of four triangular sheets of foam-core lined with tinfoil and a tissue-paper diffuser. It never leaves the studio because it is too bulky and fragile, but for the last several years it's been my first choice for many product shots and portraits. I use it when I want a soft, but easily directed source. It is simply a home made version of the many commercially available softboxes, such as those offered by Chimera or Plume.

I use electronic flash wherever high intensities are needed and wherever subject or camera motion must be eliminated. Because the technology for generating electronic flash light is so complicated, the business end of these units, the 'flash head', must inevitably be less flexible than its incandescent counterpart. Several well developed professional flash systems, such as Balcar and Speedotron, offer a selection of reflectors and grids intended to fine tune the output of their flash heads, but the expense is unjustified if an investment has already been made for a sophisticated tungsten kit. In almost every circumstance I have encountered, flash heads bounced from umbrellas or through soft boxes were sufficient. I have, however, modified a couple of my heads to take Lowel accessories for those occasions when some fine tuning must be done.

Most situations can be handled with one big power pack and four flash heads. I think it is worth while to invest in a powerful and reliable system with a short recycle time. In the world of flash, power is measured in 'wattseconds' (ws). A small unit might generate 200ws, while a really large pack might be capable of producing 4800ws. Twenty four hundred wattseconds is typical for a heavy duty professional system, and each of the plug-in flash heads should be able to handle the unit's full output. Recycle time refers to how long the unit needs to recharge after each flash. Thirty seconds is a long time to wait between shots but two seconds is not. Big units draw heavy currents, up to thirty amperes, when recycling fast. It's wise to buy power-packs that have a switch which permits slower recycling for those locations where the electrical supply is limited. I strongly recommend you obtain a second pack as a backup against breakdown.

The heavy artillery is required outside the studio only sporadically, so save your back and obtain a bright camera-mounted flash and one or two small 'monoblocks' (self-contained flash heads and power packs) in the 200-400ws range. I have settled on the battery-powered Metz 60ct-2 for flash-on-camera, and my high-power flash heads do double duty with a couple of little 400ws generators which I clamp onto compact collapsible stands for location work. Two seventy-two inch umbrellas are my main light modifiers away from the studio, although surprisingly often, neutral colored walls or ceilings can be used for no-fuss bounce flash.

I strongly recommend that infrared or radio triggers be used in place of endlessly troublesome synch cords.

A Word About Safety

Never forget that professional electronic flash equipment operates at very high voltages and under some circumstances can be extremely dangerous. Read the manufacturer's instruction manual and religiously follow the safety recommendations! Check all connectors and cables often and replace any that look worn. Make certain that stand-mounted heads are secure and that wires are safely taped to the floor when working on location. Never allow flash equipment to be operated by people unfamiliar with it. Do not use flash equipment in a wet environment or in the presence of inflammable vapors. All extension cords for use with flash generators should have heavy duty fourteen gauge wire. Make certain that flash units are supplied by well maintained grounded receptacles of adequate size. Always switch power-packs off before connecting or disconnecting flash heads. *Always leave flash units in a discharged condition when unattended.*

11.

The Commercial Photographer's Darkroom

Why Processing Is Necessary

The heart of photographic technology is an amazing chemical event which occurs when photons of light impinge on crystals of certain silver salts (or halides), usually silver bromide. When these crystals (or *grains*) are 'exposed' to sufficient light they are subtly changed at the molecular level; if the activating light has been projected by a camera lens onto a surface coated with these crystals the changes form a pattern called a *latent image*. The latent image is not visible until chemical 'development' separates the silver from the bromine at the latent image sites. 'Fixing' the image dissolves away unexposed, and consequently 'undeveloped', crystals. What remains behind is a relatively permanent image (longevity depends on storage and handling conditions) made of metallic silver: this is what we see on b&w negatives and prints.

All color films and papers depend on this same silver-halide mechanism but in a more complex configuration. Additional chemical manipulations link special dyes to layers of light sensitive material which become the magenta, cyan and yellow components of the image. By the end of processing, all silver will have been removed. The final image in color material is composed entirely of organic dyes and is consequently much less stable than its black and white progenitor.

A Rationale for In-House Processing

Commercial photography is a technological exercise with requires an understanding of dozens of variables. To do the job right it is necessary to exercise control over all aspects of the technology, but this is obviously difficult if the last few operations are surrendered to others.

Photographic efficiency demands the streamlining of all technical procedures. I explained in the introduction how a color darkroom saves time and allows me to make more money while maintaining consistently high standards of quality. The same logic applies to black and white processing, a service which is actually unavailable in some markets.

If the technical and financial arguments are not sufficiently convincing, consider the psychological advantage; a darkroom of one's

40

own can be a much needed refuge from the frantic intensity of business deals and complex assignments. Under the amber glow of the safelights, the distractions of the outer world fade and are replaced by simpler satisfactions. Even after twenty years in the profession I am still amazed by the magical transformation of film and paper into real images.

Overview of Darkroom Procedures

In general terms, the darkroom is divided into *wet* and *dry* areas. Wet side procedures include mixing solutions, washing equipment and containers, plus all the chemical steps of processing. Dry side procedures are slide mounting, film sleeving, print trimming and mounting, as well as loading of exposed film into reels or hangars for development. The enlarger and all the operations associated with it require dry conditions. Conventional practice says that the wet and dry areas should be several feet apart or even in different rooms so that liquids or chemical powders cannot contaminate dry side materials. Kodak publishes an excellent book on conventional darkroom layout which includes several detailed floor plans. It is well worth reading.

My Darkroom

A darkroom is typically used for the following procedures:

- loading unexposed film into film-holders.
- loading exposed film onto hangars or reels.
- b&w and color film processing.
- editing/mounting/sleeving of processed film.
- b&w and color print processing.
- minor print retouching
- packaging of processed material for shipping.

Each darkroom operation involves a logical sequence which can only be performed properly if the right tools and equipment are close at hand. Ergonomics is the science of organizing the human environment so that necessary tasks may be executed precisely, efficiently and comfortably. The driver's position in a BMW is ergonomically designed: so is my darkroom. I like to work quickly and I hate cleaning up so I have incorporated a number of unusual innovations:

To begin with, nothing in my darkroom sits on the floor. All counters and sinks are mounted firmly onto the walls so that the floor is unobstructed to make mopping up simple. The floor itself is covered with a sheet of industrial grade linoleum intended for commercial kitchens, scientific laboratories and hospitals. The edges of the flooring extend six inches up the walls to form an easy-to-clean seamless baseboard.

The same people who argue for totally black studios say that darkrooms should be all black as well. My darkroom is entirely white. I've eliminated all light leaks by carefully sealing up the enlarger and the doors; the white walls are not are problem when the lights are off and they are pleasant when the lights are on. To further guarantee creature comforts the darkroom is well heated in winter and air-conditioned in the summer. The thermostat is mounted within easy reach. In addition to heating and cooling, some means of ventilation is essential; to provide economical fresh air all year round I built an *air-to-air heat exchanger* into an outside wall.

The counters and sinks are mounted at desk height (30") so that I can work while sitting in a comfortable chair. Some people might consider this an indulgence but I consider it a necessity, particularly when I have to work for an entire day or night. My chair has rollers so that I can move quickly between workstations. The layout approximates the shape of a capital 'G'. The first leg (moving counterclockwise) is a 30" X 72" sink for processing both color negative and transparency films. It is made of #618 chemical resistant stainless steel insulated with one inch of styrofoam. In the sink are several stainless tanks each of which hold $1^3/_4$ gallons, half as much as the more typical 3 gallon tanks used in larger commercial labs. The tanks are immersed in a 100°F water bath. I use inexpensive aquarium heaters to maintain the temperature.

Next (continuing counterclockwise) is a film drying cabinet with removable racks for paper. It is 18" square and 6' in height. I made it out of ¹/₂" thick *Melomine*, a high-density particle board which is laminated on both sides with a thin but very tough layer of formica. (I used the same material for the darkroom walls.) Traditional wisdom says that hot air drying is bad. I have found that modern photographic materials tolerate such treatment without any ill effects. I mounted a 'squirrel-cage' blower and a heating element near the top of my dryer. Film and paper need about five minutes to dry in the stream of 90°F filtered air.

Adjoining the dryer, and forming the north/south line of the 'G', is another stainless steel sink. It's 7" deep, 30" wide and 6' long. I use it for processing black and white prints, color prints, and black and white film. (I will describe all my processing techniques in detail later on in this chapter.)

At right angles to the printing sink is a counter which holds three paper-safes and my Super-Chromega 4" X 5" enlarger. To prevent sharpness-reducing vibration, the enlarger column is bolted directly to the counter at the bottom and to the wall at the top. It is very uncommon to have a dry counter right next to a processing sink, but you will have to wait for a little while before I tell you why I've set things up in this way.

Perpendicular to the enlarger counter is another counter with a built-in light table for editing negatives and slides. Underneath are a couple of filing cabinet drawers for current negative files. This counter is joined by another smaller one, again at right angles and separated by a double-sided pegboard wall which runs up to the ceiling. The smaller counter is used for loading color film before processing. It is oriented parallel to the film processing sink from which it is separated by three feet. The pegboard holds film hangers and reels on one side, scissors and various kinds of tape on the other.

Above the two sinks are specially designed formica covered shelf units for chemical containers, measuring graduates and other appropriate tools. Temperature controlled water (68°F for b&w, 100°F for color) is piped underneath the shelves and controlled by valves mounted on panels which drop 5" down from the bottom of the units. The water is routed to where I need it through ³/₈" flexible vinyl tubing. Two safelights and a bright white light (for previewing prints) are mounted under the printing sink shelf, as well.

Above the film editing counter is another shelf unit which holds a stereo, a telephone answering machine, film sleeves, paper cutter, slide mounts, retouch colors, shipping envelopes, labels, and several other dry-side necessities.

Black and White Film Processing

Through the years I have tried to reduce every photographic operation to its simplest possible form. Black and white processing, a fairly straightforward affair to begin with, now takes me only a few minutes and costs only pennies.

Earlier I mentioned that I develop color film in stainless steel tanks with a capacity of 1³/₄ gallons. They accommodate a rack (available from Kinderman) which holds nine rolls of 120 film or eighteen rolls of 35mm. The tanks (as well as all my stainless-steel sinks) were constructed for me at a very reasonable cost by a metal shop that specializes in stainless steel fixtures for restaurants and hospitals. I have eleven tanks for color work and another three for black and white. For b&w film runs of more than two rolls of 120 or four 35mm rolls, I mix up enough developer to fill one of the tanks sufficiently to cover however many processing reels I happen to be using.

Quite often I have only a couple of rolls of 120 film to process so a big container is not necessary. Daylight film tanks are a pain in the neck, so I use ordinary two liter plastic graduates instead. Since my darkroom is absolutely light-tight, I just 'dip and dunk' the film reels (which are stacked on a Kodak stirring rod) exactly as I do for the 1³/₄ gal tanks.

I've settled on one developer for all b&w films: Kodak DK-50. This may strike some people as a surprising choice since it is a very old formula and a little hard to find. In fact, it is the only chemical I still mix from a powder. I accept this inconvenience because DK-50 has several very useful characteristics. First, it is a wide-scale developer that yields very printable negatives. Second, it stores very well. In my lab, one gallon of stock solution gets used up in about two months, although it can sit on the shelf for much longer without any noticeable deterioration. I dilute the concentrate 1:1 with water to make a one-shot working solution which is discarded after use to ensure consistent results. The third reason DK-50 appeals to me is that it is a high-energy developer requiring short processing times (5 minutes with most films). Finally, it works well with several different b&w films in the same processing run.

After the choice of film and developer, the most important variables in b&w film developing are those factors which determine the degree of development, namely the length of time the film is immersed in the developer, the temperature of the developer, and the pattern and frequency of agitation during development. Time and temperature are the primary factors in determining *density* and *contrast*, the main technical attributes of image quality. I will be dealing with image quality in another chapter, and the range of choices for time and temperature manipulation will be discussed thoroughly at that time. Under normal conditions I use DK-50 diluted 1:1 at 68°F for five minutes for most films.

Variations in agitation, developer dilution, developer temperature, and developing time affect density and contrast. (Density is the unit of blackening employed in sensitometry and is the result of the degree of development and illumination.) Agitation is extremely important, in fact critically important, because it determines the uniformity of development, as well. Film which has been improperly agitated during development may be mottled, streaked or stained, and consequently difficult or impossible to print. As a rule, once a satisfactory agitation technique has been achieved it should not be altered.

For both tanks and graduates my method of agitation is the same. During the thirty seconds following the initial immersion, the film is gently agitated by lifting it right out of the developer and then replacing it a total of six times, i.e. five seconds for each agitation cycle. Two of these five second cycles are required every thirty seconds thereafter. In other words, agitate by raising and lowering the film six times in the first thirty seconds, then wait twenty seconds, then agitate twice during the next ten seconds, and so on. When ten seconds remain of the predetermined developing time, lift the film one last time, tilt about 15°, and allow to drain. When time is up, transfer the film to a water bath of the same temperature as the developer and agitate continuously using the same five second cycle for one minute.

Next the film is 'fixed' to dissolve away those parts of the emulsion which will not be part of the final image. I use Edwal Quick-Fix, diluted 1:5 for three minutes. Occasional agitation is satisfactory.

Fixer does not deteriorate over time, and I do so little b&w film processing that one batch lasts me about six months. The working strength of fixer, or *hypo* as it is sometimes called, may be easily checked by adding a drop of 'hypo checker' which forms a white precipitate if the fixer is exhausted. A simple method of determining fix times for black and white films is to observe how long it takes for an undeveloped piece of film to 'clear'— the proper fix time is twice the clearing time. When the clearing time finally equals the original fix time, the solution is exhausted. Small users generally discard spent chemicals, but larger users *regenerate* both b&w and color fixers by recovering the silver which has been leached from film and paper during processing. The metal is harvested by electrolysis and resold. Regeneration requires, in addition to the removal of the silver, adjustment of the pH by adding acetic acid and fresh fixing agent. Kodak has published extensive literature on this subject.

As I have described, agitation intervals vary a little in each of the three chemical steps of b&w film processing, but the technique of agitation remains the same. The key to completely uniform film development is a delicate touch. Don't yank the film out of the solutions; do it smoothly. Don't just drop the film into the solutions; lower it gently. Guarantee repeatable results by always agitating the same way.

After fixing, the film must be washed in running water (of the same temperature as the processing baths) in order to remove chemical residues which would otherwise damage the images over time. As commercial work has a life span of only a few weeks, washing thoroughly is not all that crucial. Ten minutes is adequate. If the photos are to be preserved it is important to wash for at least a half hour. *Hypo clearing agent* will shorten wash times when archival permanence is desired. After washing, film should be rinsed for thirty seconds in *Kodak Photo-Flo 600*, a 'wetting agent' which breaks down the surface tension of water to prevent drying spots. Photo-Flo itself will cause streaking if it is improperly diluted; I use a 1:1200 concentration, which is half the strength recommended by the manufacturer.

In a clean darkroom with properly filtered water supply and dryer heater, film will dry without blemishes. Negatives are very delicate when wet, so handle them by the edges only. Film should be edited for technical flaws and sleeved immediately after it comes out of the dryer. (Hands must be free of dirt and grease. Lint-free cotton gloves are available from Kodak.) I strongly recommend that all unsharp or poorly exposed negatives be discarded **before** proofs are made. This will guarantee that you are never in the position of having to explain to a client why the photo he or she has ordered is not suitable for enlargement.

A Good Print

Producing a negative is a process which begins in the camera and is finished in the darkroom. Producing a print is a process which takes place entirely within the darkroom and consequently it is very easy to con-

trol. Once the techniques are mastered printmaking becomes a profoundly enjoyable and highly profitable enterprise.

The key to making good prints is to first know what you are after. In other words, it is necessary to understand what technical elements should be present in any good enlargement. This 'understanding' is not difficult, but it is subtle. If there is any place where esthetics and technology obviously intersect, it is at the point where black and white images are evaluated.

The densitometer is a scientific device which is used to precisely measure the properties of photographic images—it is actually a special type of light meter designed to measure densities. In the case of negatives, the densitometer quantifies the amount of light transmitted through various points on the film. In scientific terms density is the common logarithm of opacity—opacity is the ratio of light incident to the negative to the light transmitted to the negative. For prints, *reflection density* is the measure. This system works because over a wide range of viewing conditions the response of the human eye is approximately logarithmic.

The 'brightness range', the range of tones from very light to very dark, may be plotted on a graph according to the densitometer readouts. These graphs, called *characteristic curves*, are different for various films and paper types, and they may be further altered by variations in exposure and development.

A scientific appreciation of image quality takes years to achieve. Some dedicated photographers are followers of an elaborate system of image control called the *Zone System*, invented by Ansel Adams. This system divides the photographic image into eleven zones, from deep black to pure white, and describes techniques which enable the photographer to 'fit' real life subjects onto the photographic tonal scale. Those proficient in the Zone System, can exactly *previsualize* how any negative and print will look before the shutter is tripped.

Although I've never owned a densitometer, and I've never practiced the Zone System, I have read two books by Ansel Adams: "The Negative" and "The Print". Together, these densely written tracts are an intense lesson in how far photographic technique can be taken in pursuit of beauty. I highly recommend them.

How does one know when a print is beautiful? Even in commercial work the design of the image is paramount, but technically speaking, a beautiful print is one that may be properly reproduced in a newspaper, magazine, or poster. Such a print must be sharp and free of mechanical defects like fingerprints, dust spots and scratches. However, a wide range of tones with significant details visible in both highlight and shadow areas is the most important factor for reproducibility. These conditions may be achieved by very straightforward means.

These days, most commercial photographs are made in color and most commercial photographers do not process their own work. To my mind this is a sad state of affairs. A working knowledge of b&w technique and a deep appreciation of a beautiful print are indispensable fundamentals.

The Technique of Printmaking in Brief

The chemistry of black and white printing is basically the same as for film, although the hardware is quite different. Developer and fixer are set out in trays rather than tanks. Unlike film, which is processed in absolute darkness and never touched while wet, prints are moved from tray to tray by hand under the surprisingly bright illumination of red or orange safelights.

Earlier I mentioned that my print processing sink is directly adjacent to the dry counter where my enlarger is located. I have things set up in this way because it is mechanically efficient. Printmaking is essentially a few simple motions which are repeated exactly the same way over and over again; to my mind, the risk of occasional contamination is insignificant compared to the convenience of having all necessary tools within easy reach.

To begin the printmaking process a negative is selected from a file, inserted in a negative carrier, dusted with compressed air, and then placed in the enlarger. A lens of appropriate focal length is selected (my enlarger has a three position turret which holds 50mm, 80mm, and 150mm lenses for 35mm, 6cm X 6cm, and 4" X 5" respectively) and the image is projected on to an easel which has been pre-adjusted to the correct size.

A piece of enlarging paper is inserted in the easel and exposed for some appropriate time, usually five to thirty seconds. Using tongs, the paper is immersed in the developer and agitated to ensure uniform development. Because the whole operation is done by safelight, it is possible to actually see the image gradually appear on the blank paper. This takes about two minutes, and then the paper is transferred to a *stopbath*, a dilute solution of acetic acid which immediately halts the process of development. The print is moved to a tray of fixer after thirty seconds of continuous agitation in the stop bath. Following a short time in the fixer, the white lights may be turned on and the print can be evaluated. If it is satisfactory, the paper is then washed and dried.

It takes hardly any more time to make a print than it does to read this short description.

B&W Printing in Detail

The Negative

I've arranged my workspace so that the printing process moves smoothly from left to right. Negatives to be printed are placed to the left of the enlarger.

Some negatives will have mechanical deficiencies which show up in enlargements. Negatives which are streaked or mottled due to improper agitation in the developer or those which have been torn or badly scratched cannot be saved in the darkroom and must be extensively retouched. Happily, most negative streaks are a result of improper washing and careful rewashing with a little judicious scrubbing by water-softened finger tips will do the trick. Exhausted fixer can stain film but this can usually be remedied by refixing in fresh fixer and rewashing.

Small scratches may be masked by the ancient 'nose-grease' method: touch the side of your nose and transfer a little of the thin natural oil from your skin to the negative. Gently rub the stuff into the scratched area. Clean the negative with film cleaner after you're finished printing.

Several negative carriers of different sizes are hung on a pegboard behind and to the left of the enlarger. Except for one, all my negative carriers are *glassless*; simply two hinged pieces of smooth metal with holes cut out of them to match the negative sizes. The exception is a glass carrier which I use for critical 35mm work where the need for edge to edge sharpness supersedes the inconvenience of cleaning and dusting the four extra surfaces of optical glass.

The Enlarger

My enlarger is a 4 X 5 Super-Chromega. Like almost all color enlargers, it uses a diffused light source rather than a condenser light source, which was the standard for black and white work many years ago. Black and white purists argued that a condenser enlarger produced a sharper image because 'hard' light, which is directed through the negative by large condenser lenses, is more organized and directional than the 'soft' light created by the *light mixing chamber* in a diffuser enlarger. This may be true to a degree, but the cost is too high. Hard sources amplify every dust particle and mechanical flaw on the negative and they require the insertion of individual color filters in the light path for color printing, both major inconveniences. Condensor enlargers are, in fact, unsuitable for printing color negatives because dye images (including Ilford XP-2 black and white film) do not scatter light (Callier effect) the same way as conventional black and white negatives.

Diffuser enlargers tend to de-emphasize negative faults and color correction may be conveniently selected with the built-in graduated filters, consequently most commercial work is done with diffusion enlargers.

As a precision optical instrument the enlarger needs proper installation and periodic maintenance to do its job well. Mine is bolted directly to the counter which eliminates the need for a baseboard. The top of the column is attached to the wall behind it with two struts in order to prevent vibration. The whole machine, including bellows, light mixing chamber, and filters, is regularly dusted with blasts of compressed air. Moving parts are lightly lubricated with machine oil or thin grease as required. I have a small level for checking the alignment of the column, the enlarger head, the negative stage, and the lens carrier. The enlarging lenses are cleaned periodically with lens-cleaning fluid and lens-cleaning tissue.

The Chromega, like many other similar enlargers, uses a low voltage quartz-halogen lamp with an integrated reflector. The lamps supplied by the manufacturer are rated at 150 watts at 21 volts and last for about seventy five hours, about a month's normal use for me. Every new lamp has an different color and they are expensive to replace. To avoid the hassle and expense, I have been using a lamp that has the same mechanical configuration, but a different electrical configuration. The EJL bulb has a filament rated at 200 watts and 24 volts. It costs fifty percent more than the recommended Omega lamp and produces about the same amount of light, but because it is considerably underrated in this application, it's lifespan is about fifteen times longer.

Many lamp failures occur because terminal pins overheat. Low voltage-lamps require high currents which can cause overheating if the electrical connections are poor. Gently clean the terminals and the socket contacts with fine emery paper whenever lamps are replaced.

Flatness and Focus

A finely tuned enlarger is useless if it's not precisely focused. Sometimes blurring caused by vibration is confused with improper focus, but if the enlarger is properly anchored, and if you allow it to 'settle down' for a few seconds before each exposure, the problem is likely optical rather than mechanical in nature.

'Blowing up' a negative is equivalent to photographing a very small object, a situation governed by the inviolable optical law which states that *depth of field* (i.e. the range of acceptable sharpness around the point of perfect focus) is inversely proportional to magnification. Since an 8" X 10" print made from a 35mm negative represents a magnification of over ten times, the margin for error when adjusting the focus of an enlarger is minute; a negative which isn't flat, or even paper which buckles in the easel, can affect sharpness.

As I mentioned earlier, glass carriers guarantee absolutely flat negatives. However, they are a real problem to keep clean and dust free. They can also cause trouble by inducing the strange optical phenomenon called *Newton's rings*, a series of irregular concentric circles of alternating light and dark which form around the point where two very smooth surfaces are separated by a distance of less than a few wavelengths of light. This condition can exist where glass contacts the glossy, non-emulsion side of photographic film. One remedy is to use glass with a slightly irregular surface, called 'anti-Newton Ring glass', but such glass degrades the image somewhat. The real cure is a 'wet' carrier which uses an optically transparent liquid between the film and the cover glass. In most circumstances all this is not worth the effort so glassless carriers are virtually standard in the industry. One precaution when using glassless carriers: negatives will 'pop', or buckle, when slightly heated by the light from the enlarger so always recheck the focus just before making an exposure.

The remedy for paper that won't stay flat is a device called a *vacuum easel* which, as the name implies, uses differential air pressure to suck enlarging paper down against a platen perforated with dozens of tiny holes. Like glassless carriers, however, these Cadillac systems are used only by perfectionists. Today, most enlarging papers are 'resin coated' which means the emulsion is coated on a paper base which has itself been coated with a thin layer of epoxy or some other plastic. Except under extremely dry conditions, in 8" X 10" size these papers may be expected to lie acceptably flat when secured at the edges by the frame of an ordinary easel. 11" X 14" paper is less predictable and sometimes needs help to flatten out by patting down with a clean, dry hand.

Accurate focusing is of the utmost importance but with the naked eye it is difficult to see exactly where the point of perfect focus occurs when the image projected by the enlarger is relatively dim. Brightness at the easel is a function of the light emitted by the enlarging lamp, the efficiency of the mixing chamber, the density of the negative, and the aperture of the enlarging lens. The lens aperture is the only readily adjustable condition. Just like all other lenses used in photography, enlarging lenses perform best when used two or three f-stops smaller than maximum.

I recommend a *grain magnifier* to make focusing as precise as possible. A grain magnifier is a special purpose microscope which is placed directly on the easel. By way of a front surface mirror, a sliver of the light beam projected by the enlarger is diverted upward through a magnifying lens and an eyepiece. With this wonderful tool, you will know that focus is incorrect if the 'grain' looks mushy and indistinct. When the crystal structure of the film is sharp and clearly visible, focus is bang on. It's quite dramatic.

Safelights and Other Conveniences

The limited sensitivity of printing papers allows the use of filtered light in the darkroom which makes it easy to navigate through the various operations of printmaking.

Typical safelights use low-wattage tungsten lamps in an enclosure which incorporates an amber filter. Very bright (but much more expensive) safelights are available which use filtered fluorescent tubes or yellow sodium-vapor lights. I prefer the incandescent variety because their light output may be adjusted with a light dimmer.

'Fogging' (an unwanted light gray tone which veils highlight and otherwise white margins) will occur if safelights are too bright. My safelights are wired through a small *variable transformer*, a type of dimmer switch which allows very fine voltage control. The standard Ilford safelight takes 15 watt bulbs and 5" X 7" type 'OC' amber filters. I have three such safelights in my darkroom and I run them at about 70% capacity for Multigrade paper. Kodak Panalure paper is supposed to be handled in total darkness, however I have found that by dimming the safelights to 20% of maximum, there is just enough light to see, but not enough to affect the paper. A simple test for safelight-induced fogging is to leave a coin on a very lightly exposed piece of paper for ten minutes. If the outline of the coin is visible after normal development, the safelights are too bright or to close. (Safelight fog is unrelated to *chemical fog*, produced by developers.)

To the right of my enlarger sits a *voltage regulator*. This clever electrical gadget ensures that regardless of fluctuations in the power lines, the electricity supply to the enlarger is always steady. This a necessary condition for consistent and repeatable results. Built into the same box as the voltage regulator is an adjustable timer which turns on the enlarger lamp for a length of time which may be preset from $1/10$ of a second to 90 seconds. The timer also operates a switched outlet which turns off the safelights whenever the enlarger is on so that the image on the easel is more visible when focusing.

Paper Choices

Once the negative is set up in the enlarger, an exposure must be made on light sensitive paper.

On top of the voltage regulator I have secured a *paper-safe* with two light-tight compartments, each of which can hold one hundred 8" X 10" sheets. Each compartment has a fold-down door. When the door is opened a single sheet of paper is automatically dispensed. This is very handy when working quickly, although care must be taken to make sure the door closes perfectly each time a piece of paper is used. I keep Ilford Multigrade or Kodak Polycontrast III glossy paper and Kodak Ektacolor Supra RA 'n' surface paper in the safebox.

Beside the voltage regulator/timer sit two other papersafes of a different type than the one I just described. They are really just light-tight boxes accessed by hinged lids

rather than pull-out drawers. I have stacked one box which holds 8" X 10" Kodak Panalure (Now available in three contrast grades) on top of another larger box which holds fifty sheets of 11" X 14" Ilford Multigrade 'pearl' surface or Kodak Polycontrast III 'n' surface and fifty sheets of 11" X 14" Kodak Ektacolor Supra RA 'n' surface. The Panalure paper is used to make b&w prints from color negatives. The two types of 11" X 14" paper are separated by a sheet of stiff cardboard and I flip over the entire hundred sheet pile to put whichever type I need on top. This sounds silly, but it is easy to do.

I've chosen Ilford Multigrade paper for black and white work because it has a number of characteristics that suit both my personal tastes and the demands of commercial work. It is mechanically durable and stands up well to tray processing and hot air drying. It's high-gloss surface reproduces fine detail accurately and is well received by my clients. It is also extremely sensitive to light and allows conveniently short exposure times. Processing times are also short. Multigrade's characteristic image is an attractive warm tone, with deep brown/black shadows and brilliant highlights.

Ilford Multigrade, like Kodak Polycontrast, is a *variable-contrast* paper. This means that the separation between light and dark tones, that is the contrast between light and dark tones, may be varied by changing the color of the light by which the paper is exposed. Yellow light lowers the contrast of the image while magenta light increases the contrast. These colors may be easily 'dialed in' using the adjustable filters in the enlarger. Exposure times remain relatively constant throughout the whole contrast range. The variable-contrast feature is convenient and economical.

Really good variable-contrast papers became available only in the last ten years; before that it was necessary to stock quantities of several papers, each with a different grade of contrast. Graded papers are still available in grades "0" (very low) through "6" (very high). Multigrade and Polycontrast both do an excellent job of matching grades "1" through "5", a range which is more than adequate to deal with most negatives. The continuous variability of the adjustable papers is a bonus when the required contrast falls between the fixed contrasts available with graded paper.

Purists say that archival or exhibition quality prints are best made on superior quality fire-based graded paper, and I agree. Single-grade papers are inevitably richer in tone than variable contrast papers. The bond between the emulsion and the paper is much stronger for fiber-based materials; when exposed to prolonged ultra-violet light, emulsions tend to separate from plastic coated stock. Also, fiber-based papers are available in beautiful and subtle surface textures. Nevertheless, the new variable-contrast resin-coated papers are so good and so convenient that they are the only practical choice for commercial printing.

I stock 8" X 10" b&w paper in glossy surface because it is what most clients expect. The glossy surface is attractive, but it is too slick for retouching. As it happens, there is a great deal of b&w work I do that does not need retouching, aside from occasional *spotting* to eliminate the small white dots caused by dust on the negative.

Retouchers prefer a rougher surface (called 'pearl' by Ilford, 'n' by Kodak) which more readily absorbs dyes and paint. Most b&w shots are reproduced to be 8" X 11" (standard page size) or smaller, but because retouchers prefer to work on prints larger that the final reproduction size, 11" X 14" paper is required quite often.

A Rationale for Tray Processing

Developing prints in trays is a technique that is as old as photography itself. To some, it may seem anachronistic at a time when small but sophisticated processors are cheap and readily available.

The fastest machines use the *stabilization* process to make a print in about three and one half minutes. This method is technically inferior to tray processing in terms of print quality and the developing image is hidden inside the machine so early evaluation is not possible. The prints have to be normally fixed and washed in order to last more than a few weeks without fading. Unwashed stabilizer prints will contaminate clean prints if they are stored together. Multiple prints must be made sequentially. Rollers, chemical troughs, and fittings must be kept scrupulously clean if processing is to be uniform. Costs are about fifty percent higher than manual methods.

Automatic machines which use conventional chemistry take up to fifteen minutes per print, dry to dry, and require meticulous cleaning and maintenance. They are, of course, expensive to buy but for mass production of very large prints or continuous processing of long rolls, operating costs are ridiculously small. Low volume work, however, is impossibly slow and inefficient.

I have chosen to use trays because this is far and away the fastest and most efficient method of producing the quantities of prints I need. The tray advantage flows mainly from the fact that an image is visible almost immediately after the print has been immersed in the developer solution. Under the light of a safelight an experienced printer can make a judgment and discard an unsatisfactory print without waiting for the rest of the processing to finish. Even taken to completion through stopbath and fixer the whole process takes only two and one half minutes with my favorite chemistry. Including time for a couple of tests, I usually have a final print in six minutes at a cost of about fifty cents. Using rubber gloves I can process fifteen or twenty prints at the same a time. Tray 'maintenance' is limited to a quick rinse in running water after discarding used chemicals plus a good scrubbing every six months or so.

Nuts and Bolts

I use 11" X 14" trays for developer, stopbath, and fixer, plus a 16" X 20" tray for the wash. As I mentioned earlier, processing prints involves moving them by 'hand' from tray to tray. It is not possible to actually use your hands; b&w chemistry is relatively mild but prolonged exposure will eventually lead to dermatitis. Encasing the hands in rubber gloves will protect them, but as I will describe a little later, this approach is impractical except for batch processing of ten or more prints at a time. For normal work the tool of choice is the lowly but indispensable print tong.

Several types of tongs are available, and like all tools one uses repeatedly, it is prudent to select the most comfortable and the most reliable to be found. Agitation is just as important for prints as for film, and agitation while printing is achieved by constantly manipulating the paper with tongs which consequently must be opened and closed continually. I have found that common bamboo tongs, one-piece plastic tongs and one-piece stainless steel tongs are unpleasant to use for more than a few minutes because they 'resist' closing. I prefer the type of stainless steel tongs which are hinged at the top and held open with a light spring.

Tongs must have soft tips so as not to scratch the delicate surface of the wet paper. I buy cheap bamboo tongs and 'harvest' their rubber tips to replace the tips on my stainless tongs when they wear out. When handling paper with tongs it is extremely important to avoid making creases in the paper's surface.

In the Trays

There is a wide range of processing chemistry available. Ilford recommends their special 'Multigrade' developer for Multigrade paper, but I prefer regular Ilfospeed developer which is actually intended for graded paper. The main reason for this choice is speed. The Multigrade developer takes two minutes to do its work but the image forms very gradually during that time. With Ilfospeed a distinct image pops up in the first fifteen seconds and then slowly darkens to completion in the next seventy-five seconds. A reliable prediction of final print quality can be made at the forty-five second mark. When required, extending development past two or three minutes adds noticeable highlight density.

Once a print has been exposed it must be quickly and completely immersed in developer so that processing begins uniformly across it's entire surface. This is facilitated by providing an ample portion of liquid in the tray (I use six liters for an 11" X 14" container) and by inserting the paper under the surface of the solution with a smooth sliding motion. Agitation begins immediately and lasts for the whole time the print is in the developer. Once the print is submerged in fluid, the tongs are used to gently stir the developer in a broad 's' shaped pattern for about ten seconds. Then the print is pulled sideways out of the developer and returned with the same smooth motion by which it was initially 'inserted'. This should take about six or seven seconds. Then the developer is stirred again, followed by another cycle of removal and reinsertion, and so on, until eighty of the ninety second development time is past. After a ten second drain period, the print is moved to the stopbath where it is agitated continually for thirty seconds. ('Stopbath' is a weak solution of acetic acid: I start with Kodak Glacial Acetic Acid which I purchase in one gallon containers. Note: glacial acetic acid requires caution in handling. Follow the safety precautions recommended by Kodak.)

From the stopbath the print is moved to the fixer (Edwal Quick-Fix diluted 1:7), and agitated continuously for 30 to 45 second, after which the room lights may be turned on and the image carefully examined. Wet prints appear about 15% lighter than dry prints. (The effect is most noticeable in the highlight areas.)

If the print is to be discarded, it goes right into the garbage at this point. If it is to be saved it must be moved directly to the wash tray. Over fixing will cause fading or staining. Resin coated papers require only a ten minute wash in running water. I use cold water for washing and usually allow twenty or so prints to accumulate before I load the dryer. On the end of the printing sink shelf nearest the dryer I have attached a Falcon squeegee; by turning a short hand-crank two rubberized rollers twelve inches wide strip off excess moisture so that prints dry quickly and evenly without spotting fro mineral residues. The addition of some diluted Photo-Flo to the wash water will guarantee a slick, high-gloss finish.

Testing

Making an acceptable black and white print takes only minutes once the basic technology is understood. Making a superb print takes a little longer. The key to perfection in printmaking is the ability to recognize an outstanding print when you see one. Some experience doing your own work will quite quickly get you to that place.

Good prints have a wide tonal range plus a wealth of detail in both highlight and shadow areas. Blacks should be rich, whites should be clean, and gray areas should look smooth. A good print appears 'natural' and 'unforced' while inducing an illusion of 'three-dimensionality'. These subtle qualities are related to the specific choice of paper and chemistry, but whatever the inherent characteristics of the materials might be, selection of the correct contrast grade and exposure time, together with proper development are absolutely necessary for first-class results.

The most easily achieved condition is proper development. Three elements are necessary: a supply of fresh chemistry diluted to the manufacturer's specifications, gentle but constant agitation to ensure a good flow of chemistry over the surface of the print, and sufficient time to let the chemistry do its work. If a print has been overexposed, it will darken too quickly in the developer. The natural response is to yank it out and slap it into the stopbath right away. What inevitably results is a mottled, streaked, and flat looking print. It is true that extended development will add some density in highlight areas, but exposure errors cannot be fixed by altering development times. Prints developed in Ilford Ilfospeed paper developer require a minimum of ninety seconds processing at 68°F. (I have a Gra-Lab timer with glow-in-the-dark numbers mounted above the developer tray.)

Photographic paper is too expensive to waste so its sensible to make a *test strip* to determine what exposure time and contrast setting best suits the negative being enlarged. I make test strips by first tearing up a sheet of enlarging paper into eight pieces and then put them in the same paper-safe as the Kodak Panalure. I then make a guess about the settings for the enlarger and the timer (say f11 at five seconds with 50 units of magenta filtration) and then place the test strip on the easel in an area which encompasses a representative tonal range. After exposure the test strip is secured in a simple clamp made out of a stainless steel print tong so that it can be handled without being lost in the trays of chemistry. Usually two or three tests are required to fine tune the settings before a full sized print is attempted.

Special Skills

Finding an appropriate contrast and exposure are not the only variables which the skilled printmaker must manage. Very often the local density of certain areas within a photograph need special attention. If a highlight is lacking in detail, it can be darkened, or *burned-in*, by giving extra exposure in that location. A tool for this purpose may be made by cutting a hole of the approximate size and shape of the area to be darkened in a piece of cardboard. After the initial exposure, an additional exposure is made with the cardboard held in place an inch or two above the surface of the easel. The cardboard must be moved about slightly in a random pattern so that the extra density at the edges of the burned-in area are *feathered* or graduated in a natural looking way. I only use cardboard tools for burning-in very tiny or irregularly shaped areas. Most often I can quickly arrange my hands into a suitable shape.

Reducing local density is called *dodging*; it will be obvious from a test print which areas need *holding back*, or lightening. For part of the time during the basic exposure one's own hands or specially formed cardboards tool are used to prevent light from striking those areas of the print that are too dense, such as deep shadows or dark clothing. Care must be taken to allow sufficient density to remain; the dark tones should stay dark. The idea is to preserve some realistic modulation in tone and detail in areas that would otherwise look unnaturally heavy and featureless.

It is impossible to know what areas need burning-in and dodging using test-strips alone. Although waste will be reduced as experience is gained, you can expect to discard several test-prints before fine-tuning density manipulations for a difficult negative.

Multiple Print Processing

Earlier I mentioned that tray processing lends itself to batch processing of ten to twenty prints at a time. This method is quite straightforward provided a consistent routine is followed so that each print is agitated and developed alike.

To make several prints at once from a single negative, first determine the correct exposure and contrast with test-strips and confirm any burning-in or dodging with test-prints. As the paper is exposed, place each sheet face down in the Panalure paper safe right on top of the test strips which were put there earlier.

With the white lights on, put a rubber glove on your right hand. Set the left-hand glove on the counter near the papersafe. Turn off the lights, and remove the exposed paper. Place it emulsion side up on top of the papersafe. (You will be able to tell where to divide the exposed Multigrade from the unexposed Panalure by locating the pile of test strips.)

Set the timer to two minutes and with the left hand start feeding the paper into the developer tray at a rate of one every three seconds. With the fingers of the gloved hand, gently submerge the prints as they arrive. When all the prints are in the tray, put on the left-hand glove by sliding your hand into the glove as far as it will go without assistance, and then pulling it on the rest of the way with your other hand. Avoid wetting the skin of your left wrist with developer. This operation may be a little ungraceful at first, but with a little practice it becomes quite automatic.

The paper, emulsion side up, will now be sitting in a pile with the first sheet at the bottom. The prints must be agitated evenly while maintaining the order in which they were inserted into the tray. This is done by curling each print up successively so as to cause a small wave of developer to flow over it's surface. When all the prints have been

curled this way, rotate the whole pile and repeat the procedure with the opposite edge. For a pile of fifteen prints, this cycle of agitation should take about thirty seconds. Be careful not to crease the paper. Try to get a feel for the fastest rate at which the paper can move the developer without deforming. I find that working with the long edge of the paper yields the most even development. Because the prints must be agitated intermittently during batch processing, an additional thirty seconds is added to the development time for a total of two minutes.

When time is up, turn the whole pile upside-down in the developer tray (the print which was placed in the tray first will now be at the top of the pile) and move the prints one at a time to the tray of stopbath. Care must be taken to keep the left hand out of the stopbath in order to prevent contamination of the developer. This is done by using the left hand to start the prints sliding into the stopbath but letting go before actually touching the chemical; use the right hand to ensure that each sheet of paper is covered with liquid before the next print arrives. If this step is carried out at a rate of one print every three seconds, then all the prints will have been developed for exactly the same length of time.

Use the same method to move the paper to the fixer after the first print has been in the stopbath for forty-five seconds. Agitate prints in the fixer for two minutes before turning on the room lights. To keep the developer free of contamination from fixer or stopbath, after each processing run rinse your hands thoroughly in running water and then dry them carefully with a clean towel before removing the gloves.

Big Dollars from 'Low-Tech'

The 'hands on' method of batch processing has been around since the turn of the century but even today I find that it is fast, convenient and economical. I can expose and process twenty prints in about fifteen minutes at a cost in materials of ten dollars. I charge five dollars each for multiple prints so twenty prints are worth one hundred dollars which means a profit of ninety dollars, or six

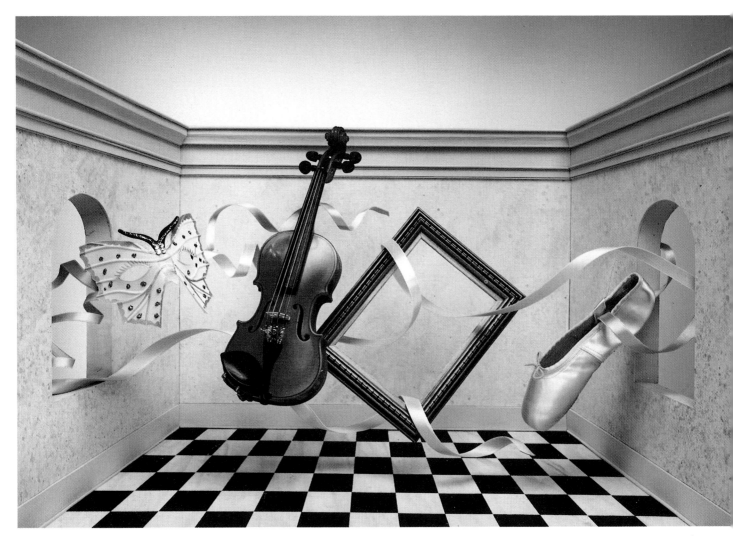

This is one of my favorite images—others must like it too, since it has won a number of prestigious awards for my client.

I was given a very detailed layout for this picture. The idea was to photographically link the performing arts with Canadian Airlines—the campaign was called The Art of Flying: the airline promised to give $5 from every ticket purchased to a performing arts institution. The image was used for magazine ads, mailers, posters, and large back-lit transparencies at airports.

Originally the art director wanted to shoot individual objects and strip them together. Instead, I suggested that a miniature room with exaggerated perspective be built to match the props—the prop-master at the local theater did the construction. The objects were glued and taped to stiff wires projecting from the back wall of the set—the wall was made of 3/4" plywood for strength. Sets of two ribbons were sewn together over thin metal strips that held the convoluted shapes aloft. Blue seamless became the 'sky'. The shot was made on 4X5" VPL film with a Toyo view camera and a 150mm lens. The main light was a broad softlight from above, supplemented by reflected fill from the front. A hidden light created the graduated density background. The single exposure required only very slight retouching to correct a couple of small imperfections in the model 'room'.

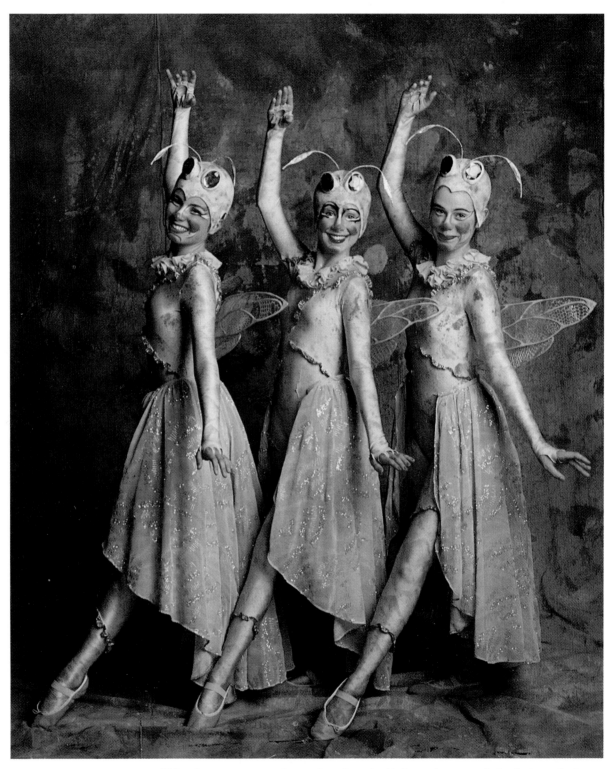

This photo was part of a series of portraits-in-costume made backstage during a production of The Wiz. *Many of the performers were amateurs—like these young girls—and sales were terrific. I don't charge for shooting the pictures but I sell 8" X 10" color prints for $10 each. This particular production had thirty or forty amateur players and I sold about $1500 worth of prints. The pictures were made on 35mm Fuji Reala film with a single large softlight and electronic flash. I provided a painted canvas backdrop.*

Brian Epperson, Principal Cellist, Winnipeg Symphony Orchestra, on stage at the Manitoba Centennial Concert Hall, Winnipeg—part of a series of ads supporting the performing arts sponsored by the large Canadian financial institution, Investor's Syndicate. The layout called for a small color image of a distinguished artist in performance that was to be inset into a larger b&w image of the same person in a rehearsal situation. There was no detailed art direction for this shot—my clients just expected some dramatic, unusual images. The image was made using Kodak VPH (ISO 400, color negative film) and a tripod-mounted Hasselblad camera equipped with a 40mm extreme wide-angle lens. Exposure was for available light—about f8 at $^1/_{15}$ sec.

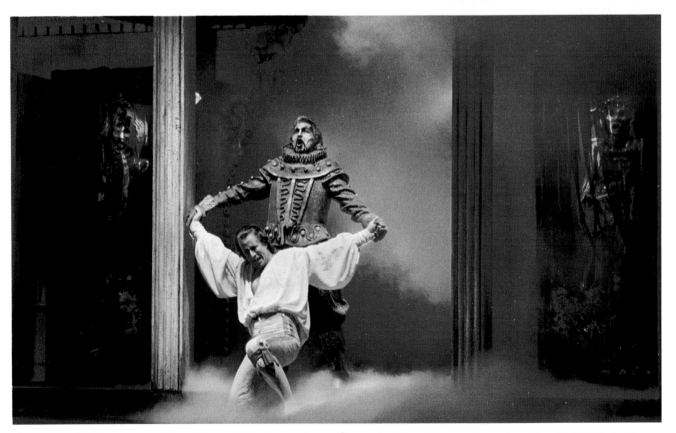

The Gates of Hell was part of a series made during a dress rehearsal of Don Giovanni, produced by the Manitoba Opera Association. The pictures were made by available light with tripod-mounted Nikons and long lenses—100mm to 300mm. I use Kodak Ektapress 1600 film for these situations. I make color prints, b&w prints (on Kodak Panalure papers), and 35mm transparencies as required from the color negatives. The Opera is traditionally lit very dimly—exposures range from f4 at $^1/_{125}$ second to f2 at $^1/_2$ second. Needless to say, the shooting ratio is quite high with the longer shutter speeds.

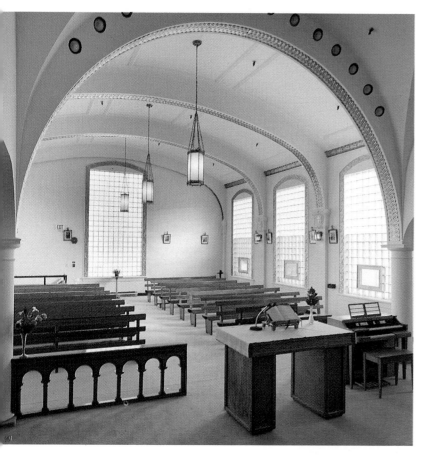

Here is an example of successful architectural photography made by available light without a view camera. I used a Hasselblad with a 40mm lens—the camera was mounted on a high tripod and carefully leveled to preserve the parallel vertical lines. I used Fuji Reala film which preserved detail even in the glass-block windows. The film also handled the mixed light sources—daylight through the windows plus tungsten artificial lights in the fixtures—in a very pleasing way. Exposure was f16 at about ¹/₂ second.

One of a series of shots used to illustrate a very highly produced 24-page color brochure for the Government of Manitoba entitled The Health Industry Development Initiative. Many location photographs were required to show the sophisticated infrastructure of health related industries. This shot was made by available light on Kodak VPS (ISO 160) color negative film in a tripod-mounted Hasselblad camera equipped with 60mm moderate wide-angle lens. Exposure was 1 sec at f11. The subject, a researcher at the University of Manitoba RH Institute was carefully positioned and asked to remain still while several exposures were made. Most people can stay fairly still from to 5 seconds, as long as the atmosphere at the location is relatively calm—I find it helpful to talk to people in very soothing tones while the shutter is open.

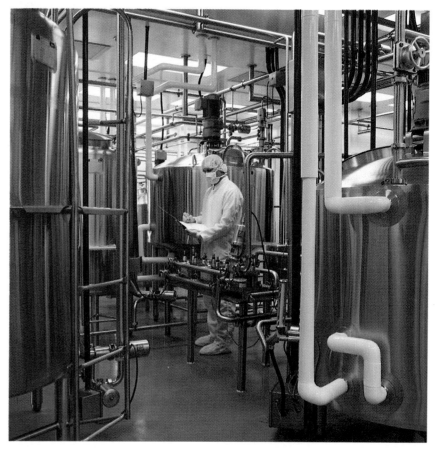

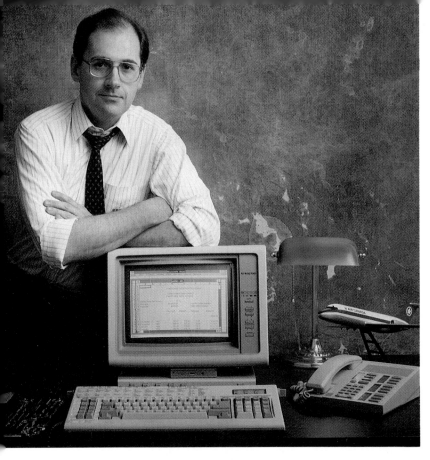

This portrait was produced as part of an expensive corporate capability brochure for a large firm of lawyers. The man pictured here was quite unusual—he was a partner in the firm, he was the author of sophisticated legal software used across the country, plus he was a jet pilot who flew for Air Canada three days a week! The photo contains hints of all this fellow's accomplishments and it was reproduced as a full page in the brochure. I tacked a painted canvas drop on his office wall and shot with available light to capture the computer screen. Kodak VPS film and a 60mm lens on my tripod-mounted Hasselblad.

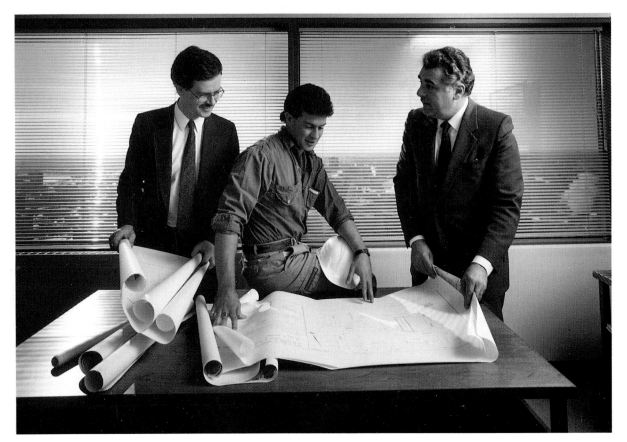

This picture was part of a lavishly produced corporate brochure for the largest firm of lawyers in my city. There was no specific art direction, but the general idea was to show lawyers interacting with their clients in an office setting. This picture includes a lawyer, a real estate developer, and a construction project manager. I used the interplay of light, shadow and reflections plus some soft bounced fill to give a feeling of naturalness—a bit of the city is visible through the slats of the blind, just enough to suggest the scope of the enterprise under discussion, but not enough to dwarf the three people. Hasselblad, 60mm lens, Kodak VPS film.

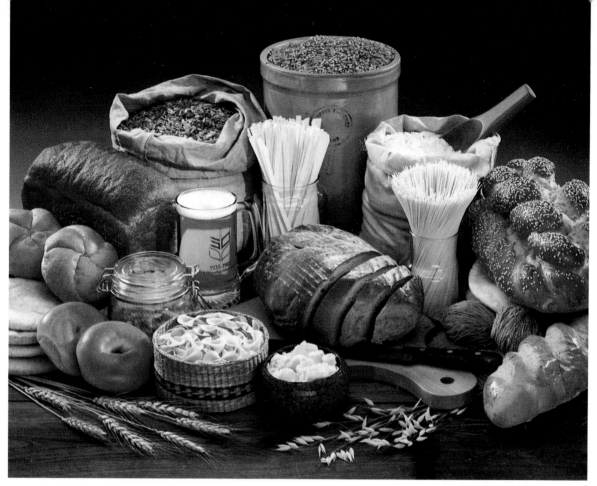

This was an illustration for a very highly produced glossy pamphlet illustrating the various corporate functions of the Canadian Wheat Board, the agency of the Federal Government of Canada responsible for marketing grains and other agricultural commodities throughout the world. I was asked to produce a photo that included as many of their products as possible so this picture shows several grains and grain products—including beer, which is made from barley. I hired someone to find or make appropriate containers. Everything was carefully arranged on a sheet of antique-looking wallboard. Illumination was based on one large softlight from above and slightly behind, plus a combination of small spots and reflectors to add appropriate highlights. There was no layout or art direction for this shot. I used Vericolor VPL film, a 4" X 5" view camera and a 250mm lens.

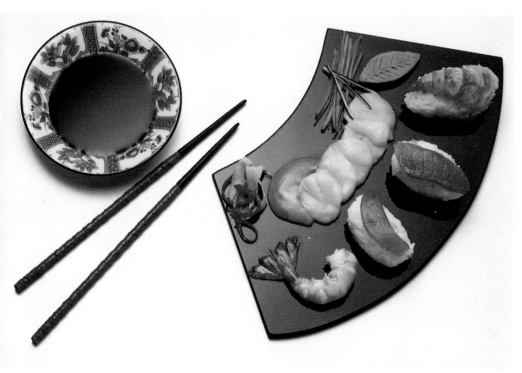

This picture was part of a series of 'food and hospitality' shots for a City of Winnipeg tourism brochure. The art director had seen another image that included an unusually shaped plate so I made this one out of black plexiglass using a power jig-saw. The food was prepared and 'accessorized' at my studio by the chef of a large local hotel. Exposed by single electronic flash on Kodak VPS and the Hasselblad, this time with a 150mm tele. The flash was projected through a large softbox.

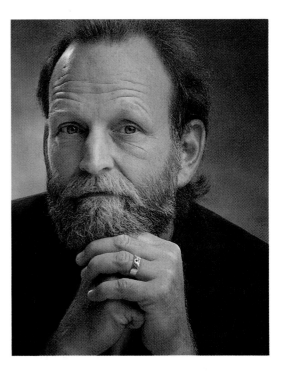

This is a studio portrait of Canadian singer/songwriter Valdy. His managers wanted a photograph that highlighted the performer's maturity and intelligence while giving a hint of the man's depth of character. The session from which this image is drawn was very productive—Valdy, myself, and the management people had a long talk before the shooting began. We were aiming to capture some subtle and elusive qualities and the shots were successful because everyone concentrated and cooperated. Fuji Reala film, Hasselblad camera, 250mm lens, electronic flash in a big softlight.

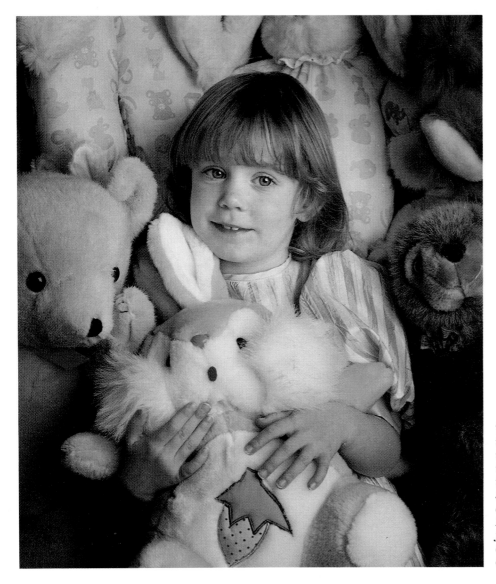

This image was part of a promotional flyer for a large mall. Each type of retailer business was illustrated with an appropriate image—this picture was for a toy store. The young model was the owner's daughter. Shot on the Hasselblad with a single bounced flash. I rearranged an existing display of stuffed toys to give a cozy grouping around the child.

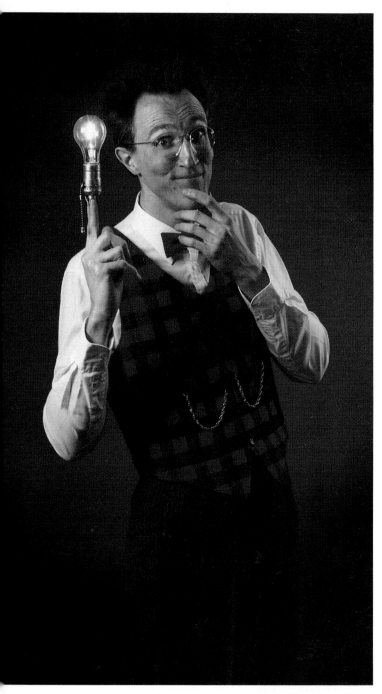

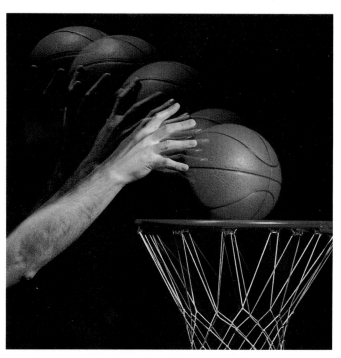

This was a cover shot of a magazine aimed at the sporting goods industry. The picture was made using a rented stroboscopic electronic flash. A microswitch was rigged to trigger a brighter conventional flash (fired through a large softlight) the instant that the ball touched the rim of the net. Everything was set up and rehearsed, then the room lights were turned off and the shutter was opened. When I started the strobe firing the model propelled the ball toward the basket. I tested the procedure on Polaroid film, and then knocked off four rolls of twelve exposures—there was only one perfect frame, but the client was ecstatic. The model is not a professional athlete, just a friend with long fingers. Camera—Hasselblad, with 150mm lens. Film—Kodak VPS.

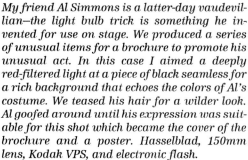

My friend Al Simmons is a latter-day vaudevillian—the light bulb trick is something he invented for use on stage. We produced a series of unusual items for a brochure to promote his unusual act. In this case I aimed a deeply red-filtered light at a piece of black seamless for a rich background that echoes the colors of Al's costume. We teased his hair for a wilder look. Al goofed around until his expression was suitable for this shot which became the cover of the brochure and a poster. Hasselblad, 150mm lens, Kodak VPS, and electronic flash.

dollars per minute! (Washing and drying add approximately fifteen minutes to the processing time, but other tasks can be done while this is going on.)

Some jobs involve a number of different negatives made under identical conditions. Such negatives may all be printed the same way after testing just one of them. Since I charge twenty dollars for the first 8" X 10" print from each individual negative, batch processing becomes even more lucrative.

Evaluating the Black and White Negative

Many of the skills in photography are interlocking. Refinement of one particular ability leads to or requires advancement in other related areas. For example, someone who regularly makes b&w prints inevitably acquires a really thorough understanding of what constitutes a good b&w negative because bad negatives are extremely difficult to print; what is not present in the negative to begin with cannot be added in the darkroom.

A scientifically minded lab manager or photographer would describe a good black and white negative qualitatively with the aid of a densitometer. Although this is certainly the ultimate in precision, other more intuitive judgments can be made as experience is accumulated.

In general terms, a negatives is too thin when shadow areas appear clear and devoid of any detail. A negative is too heavy when highlight areas are completely black, or *blocked up*; it should be possible to read newsprint viewed through the darkest part of the negative. A 'normal' negative would print easily on a #2 contrast paper.

The 'contrast' of photographic paper is a built-in characteristic determined at the time of manufacture while the 'density' of an image on photographic paper is primarily a function of exposure. This is not the case with film where both exposure and development work together to establish the density and contrast of the negative. Film can record a range of brightness of greater than 128:1.

Black and white negative film will record texture over a range of five or six f-stops, or about 64:1, and a subject brightness range of 512:1 or greater. Black and white printing papers, however, produce a reflection density or brightness range of about only 100:1. Since neither the response of the film nor the paper is linear, there will be considerable compression in both the shadows and the highlights with some subjects.

An *incident lightmeter* (the kind with a little white diffuser dome over the sensor) measures the brightness of light falling on a scene, and recommends an exposure to put an 'average' subject, such as an *18% gray card*, right in the middle of the useful density range on the negative. A *reflected lightmeter* would give the same reading under the same light provided that the reading was taken with the meter pointed directly at the 18% gray card.

The gray card is a manufactured object, a standard target which is used for testing photographic film and equipment. but objects from real-life exhibit a wide range of reflectivity. If the subject brightness range exceeds the nominal 128:1 capability of the film, it is said to be a *high-contrast* subject. If the subject brightness range is substantially less than 128:1, it is referred to as *low-contrast*.

If exposure of the film is always based on an average reading, and if development and printing are 'normal', prints made from both high-contrast and low-contrast negatives look unnatural. Within certain limits the contrast range of such negatives may be expanded or contracted by selecting a different grade of paper, but outside these limits the remedy for both excessive and insufficient contrast is based on manipulation of the relationship between exposure, development and density.

When film development is extended density continues to build up significantly, however the density of the highlight areas builds up faster than the density in the shadow areas. This allows contrast to be controlled photochemically. According to the motto of Zone System aficionados: expose for the shadows, develop for the highlights. In other words, a high-contrast subject may be compressed by over-exposure and under-development, while a low-contrast subject may be expanded by under-exposure and over-development. Again, Ansel Adams' books "The Negative" and "The Print" tell the whole story.

In general, commercial photography is carried out under controlled conditions so there is no reason why negative quality should not be consistently good. Although black and white techniques are not excessively complicated, many so-called professionals are unable to produce b&w prints for reproduction and I believe that marks a regrettable decline in standards.

12.

Darkroom Techniques for Color Processing

The Mythology

The simplicity of color processing has been obscured by many commonly held misconceptions. Most people in photography believe that color work requires a degree in chemistry and a $100,000 investment in temperamental machinery, however nothing could be farther from the truth. The complexity of color theory and the difficulty of preserving the correct *color balance* has always been greatly exaggerated.

This negatively biased situation has evolved because the technology employed by those who process color materials on a large scale is in fact complex, expensive, and quite often temperamental. Equally significant is the fact that commercial processors have a vested interest in maintaining an intimidating illusion in order to preserve their position in the market. As well, some photographers are reluctant to assume full responsibility for the work they do, and prefer instead to badmouth the technology while allowing 'the lab' to take the flak for a marginal product.

In reality, the theoretical foundation of the technology is not as impenetrable as all the elaborate machinery it has engendered, and a much simpler production approach is possible for small scale operations.

Characteristics of Color Films

Two very different families of film are available for color photography: one for color slides and one for color negatives. Each type requires different chemistry for processing and different materials and procedures for printing. I process both types of film in my own darkroom, although fully ninety-five percent of my work is shot on color negative films and I print from negative films exclusively. A brief explanation of the functional and aesthetic distinctions between negative and transparency films will clarify my choices.

Modern color materials are vastly superior to the films available even a short while ago. There is, however, a prejudice in the non-photographic printing trade that says transparencies are superior to prints from negatives. This was true ten years ago but now a color transparency has only a marginal edge.

Color negative is a tremendously flexible medium. It has a much wider *exposure latitude* than reversal films so expensive exposure bracketing may be eliminated and extensive color tests to determine filtration for exotic light sources are unnecessary. Color balance, density and cropping are easily controlled in the darkroom and multiple copies can be made quickly at a reasonable cost. Retouching a large print is easier and safer than fiddling with an original slide. Similarly, prints may be given away or lost, but the original remains secure because it never has to leave the darkroom.

There is, however, a psychological advantage to transparencies. Because they are viewed by transmitted, rather that reflected light, transparencies do appear 'richer' than an otherwise identical print. Nevertheless, the irrefutable fact is that when a transparency is reproduced on paper, whether photographically or photo/mechanically, its brightness range is reduced; it becomes a 'print' like any other.

In most circumstances a color negative and a color transparency record exactly the same degree of detail. In other words, the *resolution* (detail-recording ability) of a negative and of a transparency can be identical. A print made from either medium loses some detail by virtue of the fact that a print is one generation away from the original image. A well made original transparency, however, may be reproduced directly, which of course eliminates any losses associated with the enlarging process.

Transparencies have another significant technical advantage; they are able to reproduce delicate highlight details more accurately than prints made from negatives. This seemingly subtle superiority is important when dealing with light or pastel subjects, such as ice-cream, silverware, snow, or glass.

Finally, small format transparencies are popular because they are handy. For example, *slide files*, 8" X 11" plastic sheets with twenty 2" X 2" pockets, are the standard in the magazine business for convenient viewing, shipping and storage of 35mm transparencies.

I shoot negative whenever possible. Those clients who ask me for transparencies get a brief pitch about the alternative, but I don't push too hard if they are clear on what they want.

I always use reversal materials when shooting *high-key* subjects or editorial assignments. Eventually, when electronic manipulation of photographic images becomes com-

monplace, color negative will be universally accepted, but for now it is prudent to stay fluent in both reversal and negative techniques.

Processing Color Film

C-41 for Color Negatives

In the section on black and white processing I described my stainless tanks and the insulated sink that holds them. Altogether I use eleven tanks: three for Kodak C-41 (color negatives), seven for Kodak E-6 (transparencies). One tank is used for the final wash in both processes. This last tank has a double bottom with a stainless pipe connection. During film washing, water is directed to the bottom compartment through a vinyl hose. The water then exits through several strategically placed little holes which create small 'fountains' under the film. Chemical-laden wash-water simply flows over the top of the tank; the level in the sink is maintained by an overflow drain connected to the sewer. The wash-water is kept at the same temperature as the rest of the chemicals.

My method of processing C-41 has six steps; develop for three minutes and fifteen seconds, bleach for six minutes, wash for one minute, fix for six minutes, wash for ten minutes, then dry. White lights may be switched on after the film has been in the bleach for two minutes. Agitation is exactly the same as for b&w processing except that film is agitated twice every fifteen seconds in C-41 developer rather than twice every thirty seconds. Aside from the time required to load reels or hangars, the entire process takes only thirty-five minutes dry to dry.

Kodak calls for a pre-wet before the developer but I have found this step to be unnecessary. I don't use stabilizer either, even though Kodak says it makes color dyes more stable. I believe formaldehyde (the principal component in stabilizer) is a health hazard. Longevity, archival processing and the safe storage of color materials will be discussed later.

Color negative films consists of three separate black and white emulsions layered one on top of another. Each layer is cleverly designed to react to only one of the three primary colors: red, blue, and green. (Equal intensities of the primary colors combine to make white light. Any color can be created by adding the primary colors in some appropriate proportion.) The developer in the C-41 process develops the three black and white emulsions and causes color dyes, which are incorporated in the film at the time of manufacture, to *couple* with the silver images in proportion to the density of the silver. The dyes are complementary in color to the primary colors so the red sensitive layer accumulates cyan dye, the blue sensitive layer accumulates yellow dye, and the green sensitive layer accumulates magenta dye. (Any color can be approximated from white light by *subtracting* appropriate proportions of the complementary colors.)

The bleach removes the developed silver images and any unused dye. The fixer dissolves away all traces of the unexposed (and consequently undeveloped) parts of the black and white emulsions. What is left is a color negative made entirely of organic cyan, magenta, and yellow dyes. When printed these colored layers transmit light differently, so built into the *film base* is an overall red/orange caste which 'equalizes' the densities for easier printing.

E-6 for Color Transparencies

The E-6 process is somewhat more complicated chemically because the final image must be a positive rather than negative, hence the term '*reversal* film'.

Again, I ignore the Kodak recommendation for a pre-soak and instead put the dry film directly into the first developer for a total of six minutes with normal agitation. Next comes a two minute wash in running water followed by two minutes in the reversal bath. The film is agitated continuously for the first twenty seconds and then allowed to soak without agitation for the remaining time. After thirty seconds in the reversal bath the room lights may be turned on.

From the reversal bath the film goes to the color developer for six minutes, again

with normal agitation, followed by two minutes of constant agitation in the conditioner then six minutes in bleach, then six minutes in fixer and finally ten minutes wash in running water. As with C-41, I omit stabilizer.

The E-6 first and color developers perform the same functions in two steps as the C-41 developer does in one; the tasks of b&w development and color-coupling are divided so that in between the reversal bath can change the way the film and the dyes will interact. Thus, in reversal films the color builds up in inverse proportion to the density of the silver which yields a positive image. Because transparencies are primarily intended for direct viewing, slide film has an untinted film base.

Timing and Temperature Control

There are two very different types of reactions involved in color processing: those that continue as long as the film is in contact with the active solutions and those that proceed up to a certain point and then stop. Developers work progressively while reversal bath, conditioner, bleach and fixer all react strongly for a predictable length of time after which their activity tapers off dramatically.

The speed of the chemical reactions is dependent on temperature. Predictable results, therefore, can only be achieved if the processes take place at the same temperature every time. For this reason my film sink is well insulated, I keep thick plastic lids on the processing tanks, and the temperature of the water bath in which the tanks are sitting is precisely controlled by submerged heaters and a sensitive thermostat.

The temperature of the first developer in both the C-41 and the E-6 processes is extremely critical due to the progressive nature of the chemical activity. For this reason just before processing I always check the temperature on a digital thermometer with a stainless steel probe. A variation of only $\pm 1/2°F$ is allowed. (It is wise to check the accuracy of the process thermometer itself from time to time.) Because the developing time is just as critical as the temperature I have a Gra-Lab timer with an easy-to-read luminous dial mounted on the wall behind the film sink.

The time and temperature recommendations for the other chemicals are less critical. However, if the temperature is low or the processing time too short, the reactions may not go to completion. Film which has been incompletely bleached or fixed may be returned to the appropriate tanks until fully 'cooked'.

Color Printing the Simple Way

Overview

In the introduction I indicated that I've devised a fast, reliable and inexpensive system for making color enlargements. I have also presented a number of arguments in favor of tray processing black and white prints. Perhaps you have already put two and two together and figured out that tray processing is my secret weapon for color printing as well.

Low-tech solutions might appear tacky to those people who have succumbed to microprocessor fever, but I prefer a simple and direct approach whenever possible. The logic which justifies black and white printing in trays applies equally well to color work. Moreover, there is a powerful technical advantage to trays over machines that is unique to color processing for the low volume lab.

In b&w printing the main variables which must be attended to are contrast and density. When making enlargements in color these factors remain important but they are significant only after the correct color balance has been achieved. (Unless intentionally altered to achieve some special effect, the 'correct' color balance is a fairly specific state in which people and familiar objects appear 'natural'. There are several color markers which all of us look for more or less unconsciously such as sky blue, leaf green, or 'normal' skin tone.)

The venerable 18% gray card can be used to quantify the process of evaluating color balance. After having been photographed and reproduced, the color of the original and the color of the print can be compared using a densitometer equipped with *sharp cut-off* red, green, and blue filters. If the gray card and its copy are shown through accurate measurement of the primary colors to be identical, then the film, the paper and the processing can be said to have worked together to produce a perfect result.

Commercial labs use fancy equipment and rigorous testing to make certain that the various chemical parameters which affect color balance never change. Machines are slow but they operate continuously so large numbers of prints can be put through per hour. Professional printers expose test strips or test prints from many negatives, run them through the processor, evaluate them, and then come back to process final prints after another hour (or two or three) of work in the darkroom. The machine must be perfectly consistent so that adjustments based on the test results still apply at the time the final prints are run.

With my tray method, a test can be processed and evaluated in under three minutes and a satisfactory final print can usually be achieved after a couple of tests. With feedback this fast the exact state of the chemistry at any given time is unimportant. Changes gross enough to significantly alter the appearance of a print simply don't occur in ten or twelve minutes. In one stroke this method reduces processing time by 80% and completely eliminates the need for chemical monitoring. These economies also apply to batch processing of multiple color prints.

Special Considerations for Color Printing in Trays

Aside from the dissimilarity in chemistry and materials there are two other significant differences between color and b&w printing: the latter takes place at room temperature (68°F) under the light of bright safelights while the former is intended to be processed at high temperature (95°F) in total darkness. These technical restrictions for color work would seem to make tray processing awkward, to say the least. Nevertheless, I have been able to work out a straightforward technique which makes color printing almost as easy as black and white.

Safelight

Working in the dark can be frustrating. Processing prints in trays involves a series of mechanical manipulations which must be performed over a fairly large work area. To my delight, I have found that very dim safelight will not affect color paper if exposure to the safelights is kept short. You will recall that I equipped my b&w safelights with a variable-transformer type light-dimmer. The supply voltage must be reduced by about 75% to set the safelight levels low enough to prevent fogging yet high enough to safely navigate around the enlarger and printing sink.

Temperature Control

Some simple technology is required to keep color processing solutions at the right temperature.

I made a long shallow tray out of half inch thick plastic. At forty-eight inches long, sixteen inches wide and five inches deep, the 'sink within a sink' accommodates three ordinary plastic 11" X 14" trays placed two inches apart. The trays sit snugly on the upper edge of the larger tray with a two inch gap at the bottom. Hot tempered water is circulated through this space by a *750 Watt Calumet Temperature Regulator* connected through vinyl tubing to pipe fittings tapped into the side of the larger tray.

The first 11" X 14" tray holds six liters of Kodak RA (Rapid Access) Color Developer, the next tray holds an equal amount of the same acetic acid stopbath used for b&w processing, while the third tray is filled with Kodak RA Bleach/Fix (sometimes called 'blix').

I removed the internal temperature sensor from the Calumet heater (anyone knowledgeable in electronics can do this easily) and secured it with silicone rubber inside the smallest Pyrex test-tube I could find. The encapsulated sensor sits right in the tray of developer and is connected to the regulator with an appropriate length of wire. This way, the temperature of the water-jacket is automati-

cally adjusted to maintain the developer at the desired temperature. The actual temperature of the developer is continually monitored by a digital thermometer with a red LED (light-emitting diode) readout. The display is easily visible in the dark but harmless to paper. (LED's will fog film, however.)

The Calumet recirculating heater is a precision industrial-quality unit and costs over five hundred dollars. If this is too steep for your budget, an acceptable low-cost alternative is untempered hot water and an ordinary hand operated mixing valve; once brought up to temperature, the *thermal inertia* of the chemicals and the water-bath is sufficient to allow things to remain fairly steady with only occasional manual adjustment.

Kodak recommends that their RA paper be processed for 45 seconds at 95°F. Higher temperatures cause *edge staining* and/or cyan fog in highlight areas as well as possible emulsion separation.

Before Processing

New Variables

As discussed previously, color printing is more complicated than black and white because the 'color balance' of the image must be controlled along with density and contrast.

Unlike black and white processing which allows for a tremendous degree of control over negative contrast, the contrast of all color materials are predetermined when they are manufactured. This limitation has been imposed as a consequence of the chemical complexity of color materials in general; it is just too difficult technically to guarantee that color film will react to all colors in a linear way whenever contrast is tinkered with. The main variable affecting contrast that is actually under total the control of the photographer is the lighting, specifically the lighting ratio, at the time the photograph is taken. Just recently Kodak has introduced Ektacolor RA papers in three contrast ranges: Portra is lowest, Supra is 'normal', Ultra is highest. These papers are powerful new tools.

Density is very much a consideration in color printing, just the same as for b&w work. Beyond the actual 'lightness' or 'darkness' of the image, variations in density have a small but noticeable second order effect on color balance. With Kodak Ektacolor papers, building up density by longer exposures tends to move color balance toward yellow. (This can be problematic when burning-in a highlight, for example.)

To minimize the uncertainties some people rely on an electronic device called a *color analyzer*, a sort of highly evolved color-sensitive light meter. I don't believe such things are worth the cost. Because tray processing is so fast, my method of choice is still the test strip/test print.

The Color Enlarger

In the discussion about b&w printing, I mentioned that filtration for variable contrast papers could be selected using the built-in filters of the Super Chromega enlarger. All enlargers intended for use with color materials must have some means of changing the color of the light they project because this is the only way to adjust the color balance of the print.

Two different systems of manipulating color for photographic purposes have evolved out of the basic physical properties of light. The simplest to understand is the *additive system*, which is uses various combinations of the primary colors to generate all other colors. Enlargers which use the additive system, such as those made by Phillips or Nord, combine (in a mixing chamber) light from individually controlled red, green, and blue sources. Perfectionists say that this approach produces the purist and most saturated color, however the attendant optical and mechanical complexity adds considerable expense.

Universally accepted as the most practical solution, the *subtractive system* requires only one white light source (usually a low-voltage quartz-halogen lamp with a built-in reflector) which is modified by highly efficient yellow, cyan and magenta *dichroic* filters. (Dichroic filters work by reflecting, rather than absorbing, unwanted colors.

They are much more efficient and their characteristics are more stable over time.)

All enlargers based on the subtractive system have some precise mechanical means of controlling the degree to which the filters intersect the path of the light beam so that the projected color may be fine-tuned very carefully.

Selecting the Correct Color Balance

Some effort is required to learn what corrections to make when color printing but first it is necessary to understand how changes in the color of the light from the enlarger affect the print.

In the negative, primary colors from real life are represented by their complimentary colors: red objects result in a cyan image, blue objects appear yellow, and green object are magenta. In the print, these values are again flopped, so that things look natural once more.

To determine what needs changing in an off-color print first decide in which specific 'direction' the colors are skewed. Is the print too red, green, blue, cyan, magenta, or yellow? Even for experienced printers it helps to have on hand several prints which are properly balanced for comparison. The trick is to remember that to reduce a color cast in the print, either increase that color in the filtration, or reduce the complement. Thus:

- Magenta light from the enlarger induces green in the print.
  If a print is too magenta, increase the magenta filtration.
- Yellow light from the enlarger induces blue in the print.
  If a print is too yellow, increase the yellow filtration.
- Cyan light from the enlarger induces red in the print.
  If the print is too cyan, increase the cyan filtration.

(Note: Only two of the three subtractive filters may be used at one time. The third will only add neutral density. Also remember, there is an exposure factor associated with changes in color filtration.)

Color is just one of those things that must be studied until clearly understood. Learning how to balance color is like learning to run a personal computer: at first it seems absolutely bizarre, but after some hard work the underlying simplicity becomes apparent. Take heart in the thought that filtration varies relatively little between negatives made on the same type of film exposed under similar conditions. For example, a typical Kodak Vericolor III Type S negative exposed by electronic flash in my studio might print properly with zero cyan filtration, seventy units yellow filtration, and thirty-five units magenta or '0C 70Y 35M'. (The digits are simply the numbered intervals on the Chromega dials.) With a different emulsion batch of the same film under the same conditions the settings might change to 0C 68Y 39M. The necessary adjustment can be quickly pinned down by starting with the old settings and making a test-strip or two.

After test-strips the exposure and color balance are determined, test-prints are used to ascertain exactly where and how to burn and dodge.

Processing a Color Print

The Basic Steps of Color Printing

The technique already outlined for black and white tray processing is employed without much modification for color. One significant fact: color materials are much more sensitive to chemical contamination and mechanical stress than b&w. Always handle paper at the edges only. Keep hands clean and dry. Avoid creasing or even flexing the paper. For some reason, most kinds of abuse registers as cyan stains or marks on the finished print.

Development must be carefully timed. (I bypass the water presoak called for by Kodak.) Agitation is the same as for black and white prints. After a few minutes under the attenuated safelights it is just possible to distinguish the positions of the trays and the enlarger. Because of the low safe-light levels and because color developer turns dark green

with use so it is not possible to observe the image actually forming. (Even if it were, the print does not look right until bleaching and fixing is over.) After thirty seconds continuous agitation in the stop bath, the print is transferred to the bleach/fix. As it's name implies, this chemical does the work of the separate bleaches and fixers found in the E-6 and the C-41 processes. Prints are pulled from the bleach/fix after 45 seconds, rinsed with 95°F running water, and evaluated by white light. For the reasons I stated earlier, I omit the stabilizer recommended by Kodak. Washing and drying is the same as for b&w.

Unfortunately, there is a problem with color printing in trays that does not occur when using black and white materials; dog-eared prints. Color paper is not as physically durable as b&w paper; even gentle bumping of the paper against the walls of the trays during agitation and washing damages their corners. To rectify this situation I trim about $1/16$th of an inch off opposing edges of each print with a rotary paper cutter.

The Bottom Line

Altogether the chemical steps of tray processing require only two minutes. Costs are about fifty percent higher than black & white due to the more expensive chemistry. Batch processing of color prints is exactly the same as for b&w, and all the previously described economies of this technique remain intact. (However, I recommend reducing the processing temperature so that multiple prints can be processed for longer times: 45 seconds is too short for adequate agitation.) My clients are all hopelessly dependent on my super-fast service. Yours will be, too.

Evaluating Wet Prints and Test-Strips

I mentioned earlier that wet black and white prints appear lighter than they do when dry. This is because the silver image is suspended in a gelatin emulsion which expands when saturated with water; the particles of silver spread apart therefore their ability to absorb light is reduced. When the gelatin contracts upon drying, the image becomes denser and therefore darker. This effect is most obvious in the highlight or middle-gray areas. It takes experience to correctly second-guess the exact degree of change. The evaluation of color prints is a more complicated business. Overall, wet prints look more blue and somewhat less dense than dry prints. This effect is more prominent in dark areas. There are, in fact, no real blacks apparent at all in a wet color print so it is particularly difficult to gauge how much dodging is required to properly lighten excessively dark shadows. I recommend that at the beginning you dry prints before making a judgment; keep a 1500 watt hair dryer nearby to use on the occasional problem print.

How to Buy and Maintain Color Processing Chemicals

Stocking Up

I've already told you that there is no need to be a chemist to properly maintain a color darkroom. All the 'active ingredients' are available in convenient liquid form and they are relatively inexpensive in terms of cost-per-print or film. Most of the chemicals come divided into two or more component parts which must be mixed together before use; this promotes long shelf-life which, in turn, allows large, economically sensible quantities to be stored safely.

Mixing Chemicals

Because processing chemicals come in liquid form, preparing working solutions from the concentrates is simple. All the products are packed with mixing instructions and safety hints; follow them faithfully. Serendipitously, it is possible to split the contents of the bottles proportionately and prepare only the exact amount necessary for immediate use.

Color chemistry is extremely expensive when purchased a little at a time. I began to buy large quantities in order to benefit from the significantly lower prices. At first I was so paranoid about dividing the solutions accu-

rately that I used veterinary syringes for exact measurement. Needless to say, there was a lot of washing up to do. Eventually I realized that this degree of precision was not necessary, and now I use ordinary Peterson plastic graduates (graduated cylinders) which come in several useful sizes.

Longevity and Replenishment

All chemicals lose potency with use and some of the chemicals degenerate over time whether they are used or not. The concentrates, even in partly filled bottles, are safe on the shelf for months. However, for consistent results it is necessary to either discard or replenish working solutions as they become weakened with use or age.

The various developers are the most unstable chemicals and, as indicated earlier, the most critical. E-6 first and color developers can sit unused in tanks for about a month before they must be discarded. Because I do so little work with color transparencies, and because I usually have to process many rolls or sheets at a time when the work does appear, I generally mix fresh developers for every run. For small runs which are only a day or two apart, I will process a test roll to check the condition of used chemistry. Every second time I change developers, I change the reversal bath. Every third time I change developers, I renew the other chemicals as well.

Color negative is a forgiving process technically and Flexicolor developer is considerably more stable than the E-6 developers. I run C-41 almost daily so it is more practical to replenish than to replace partially exhausted working solutions. I use the Kodak guidelines which indicate how much fresh chemical to add in compensation for the number of square inches of film processed. (Note that developer replenisher is mixed from the same chemicals as the developer but the developer starter is omitted.) I replace all C-41 chemistry every ninety days.

If your business calls for regular processing of transparency materials it does not make good economic sense to discard used chemistry. However, the replenishment regimen must be followed exactly as laid down by

Kodak if the line is to be reliable. A test roll or sheet should be run before processing critical work. A really accurate measure of the state of your line requires densitometric analysis of *Kodak Control Strips* (Ektachrome film pre-exposed with a gray-scale and color patches). Kodak publishes a comprehensive guide to the E-6 process called the E-6 Process Control Manual which describes the proper maintenance and testing procedures in amazing detail. Also included are charts showing possible problems and their solutions.

Because there is a constant flow of visual feedback during printing, the replenishment technique can be quite relaxed. I keep a four-liter graduate of developer replenisher near the processing sink and periodically use it to 'top up' the level of solution in the tray. The developer will last virtually indefinitely with replenishment, although I usually replace it once a week due to sludge build up. (This period can be extended by decanting and filtration if desired.) Stopbath has a much greater capacity then developer and does not require replenishment. Bleach/fix may be replenished or regenerated but I prefer to discard it when cyan or magenta staining begins to occur (after about one hundred 8" X 10" prints per six liters of solution). Stopbath is

changed at the same time. (Not: please refer to the extensive Kodak and Ilford literature for advice about the safe disposal of photographic chemicals.)

The color print trays remain in the processing sink all the time. When not in use, I cover them with sheets of $1/4$" plexiglass to prevent oxidation and evaporation and to provide a surface on which to set the trays for b&w printing.

How to Charge for Processing

Clients benefit from the quick personalized service provided by an in-house lab so there is no need to compete in pricing with the commercial processors. As a rule I charge double whatever the local professional custom labs in my area charge. For special services, like same day or overnight processing, I add on an additional twenty-five to fifty percent, depending on the size of the job and the degree of inconvenience.

From time to time I will reduce my regular rates as a promotional strategy or when clients are on a tight budget. In these cases I mark the invoice "courtesy discount: —%" or "no charge for rush service (this job only)".

13.

How to Find and Use Support Services

You Don't Have to Be Alone

As your work increases in intensity and sophistication the need will arise for outside help in several areas, some of which may not seem at first to be directly related to photography. It will become necessary to find skilled, reliable and discreet people whose expertise is available on a part-time basis, often at short notice. This kind of help is not easy to locate in the phone book and your competitors are likely too self-involved or insecure to reveal their own resources. In smaller centers those few people who possess the specialized abilities commercial photographers are willing to pay for may not even exist as 'professionals' so the search becomes even more difficult.

The Photographer's Assistant

One of the first signs of overwork is a feeling of dread associated with big location assignments; the money and the job may seem fine, even exciting, but the thought of packing, transporting, then re-packing and re-transporting all that heavy-duty gear just doesn't appeal. After a certain point in the development of a photographer, it is no longer necessary or possible to take care of everything personally. It is absolutely delightful to walk into a location shoot to find that equipment and props and models have all been organized ahead of time.

An assistant can be a full time right-hand-man or woman but early on such a costly solution is superfluous. Likely a part-time assistant will be able to provide all the support needed without straining the budget assuming you can find someone with lots of spare time who is enthusiastic, intelligent, physically able, and interested in photography.

The perfect assistant might actually be an underemployed photographer. In big cities one route by which such people begin a career is to work for other more established professionals. Of course, there are some drawbacks to training your own competition, but in a part-time situation these are outweighed by the obvious conveniences of working with a helper who is already familiar with the territory. Suppliers of professional photographic equipment and materials often know who might be in a position to assist a busy pro, and if they don't they'll post a notice. (Sometimes people who work for camera stores are interested in assisting, as well.) If this doesn't work, place an ad in the 'cameras for sale' section of your local newspaper's want-ads. Wages are negotiable but for experienced assistants you can expect to pay between $75 to $150 dollars per day.

If you are prepared to invest some time teaching an enthusiastic tyro, look for a willing photography student at a technical school or in the fine arts faculty at a university. Most beginners will be satisfied with minimum wage. Although previous experience in photography is desirable, it is not a necessity. My favorite assistant is a bright, personable and strong young fellow by day and a rock musician by night.

An assistant, whether experienced or inexperienced, will expect to be taught exactly what you want him or her to do. Everything from how to answer the phone to how to sweep the floor to how to load film should be spelled out in painstaking detail at least once, and possibly twice; three times is likely a waste of time. After the equivalent of seven working days a promising assistant will start anticipating your needs and you will begin to feel a lessening of the stress which compelled you to find an assistant in the first place.

Messengers and Couriers

For some reason, many photographers automatically assume that their time is not worth anything if they're not behind a camera even though it clearly does not make any sense to charge big bucks to shoot fancy pictures and then run around doing errands for nothing. Your clients will recognize that your time is valuable and will not object to reasonable charges for pick-up of layouts, props and finished work. If they do object, the actual costs for these services are so low that they can be discretely folded into other fees. From time to time it will make 'political' sense for you to personally deliver a finished job, but most often this is not the case.

The packages that messengers move around have to reach their assigned destinations quickly. There is lots of competition in this field so don't be shy about switching around until you find an outfit that you can trust completely. Dispatchers and drivers must understand that your reputation (and their income) depends on always meeting deadlines.

Couriers that fly between urban centers are usually more professional and better organized than local messengers. Nevertheless, when you ship something to another city or when you are expecting something to arrive from another city, find out and make a note of the *way-bill number* of the package to facilitate tracing in case of a mixup.

Hair, Makeup, and Clothing Stylists

Any sophisticated photography which involves people, from high-power executive portraits to full-fledged fashion spreads, will be enhanced by the skills of *stylists*. These people know what looks appropriate according to current tastes. They work with faces and bodies they same way you do with lighting and props. Hair and makeup specialists can sometimes be located through the yellow pages or friends who frequent trendy hairstyling and 'facial' salons, however, professionals with skills more specific to commercial photography often work for television stations as well as regional theater and opera companies. A few diplomatic phone calls will put you in touch with a wealth of talent. Rates vary from $10 to $50 per hour, according to experience and ability. Book-keeping headaches can be avoided if you have these people bill your clients directly.

Fashion stylists are even more difficult to track down. If another photographer will not or cannot recommend a competent professional try looking in the yellow pages under 'fashion consultant'. Sometimes the owner or buyer at a high-profile clothing store will be interested in freelancing for cash or in exchange for your services. Local newspapers or magazines often have fashion sections; the editors or writers may be willing to work for you or suggest someone who will. In a pinch, a friend or acquaintance whom you know to have a highly developed fashion sense can be enlisted.

Hair and makeup stylists always carry a supply of exotic tools and potions. They require a more or less private workspace equipped with a shelf, (mounted at waste height, at least two feet by three feet) as well as a high, comfortable chair, one or two large wall-mounted mirrors, and ample non-fluorescent lighting. A hand-sink and a supply of soft paper towels will be appreciated. Stylists work quite intimately with the people in your pictures. Consequently, their behavior on the set is just as important as their other more specialized skills. You cannot afford to hire either a wimp or a prima donna regardless of how talented they might be. On the positive side, when the person responsible for makeup or hair is cheerful and friendly they can play a valuable role in establishing a relaxed atmosphere in the studio.

Your main responsibility in working with these people is to be very clear about what 'look' you what for your pictures. If possible, show sample photographs to illustrate precisely what you're after. Tell the stylists ahead of time what type of light (i.e. hard, soft, tungsten, electronic flash) you will be using, what the color scheme of the shot will be, as well as what kind of skin and hair the model has. If you are expecting the makeup stylist to deal with serious blemishes or to produce special effects (such as a black eye) discuss it beforehand so that any unusual supplies can be obtained in good time. For high-profile high-budget jobs, stylists should be invited to attend a planning meeting or strategy conference with your client so that all expectations can be clearly spelled out.

The Prop-Maker/Finders and Set Designers

Very often in commercial work, photographic skill is secondary to the ability to find or fabricate the artifacts and sets called for by creative-directors and designers. Many photographers have the good taste and the knowledge of both materials and techniques that are fundamental to this work but they do not always have enough time to properly follow through.

It takes a tenacious personality to rent, buy, steal or make all the unlikely items that are necessary to help create convincing illusions. Such people are often employed as freelance *prop-masters* and *scenic artists* for television stations involved in dramatic productions, in the feature-film industry, in live theater, or as window-dressers for big stores. They will take on projects for photographers between regular jobs or after hours. Charges are surprisingly reasonable since they are regularly compelled to work with very tight budgets. Again, it is desirable to have them bill your clients directly.

If large or complicated sets are involved, be prepared to allow the scenic artist access to your studio after hours or on weekends. Typical building materials such as plywood, plaster of Paris, and foam-core board should be on hand. Give the prop maker/finder a supply of your business cards (or your client's business cards) and a letter of reference to make it easier for him or her to approach potential lenders or renters of needed props. It is considerate and reasonable to provide as an advance sufficient cash to cover at least half of the expenses which are to be incurred on your behalf.

For complex jobs the props person should be involved early in the planning stages so that critical elements may acquired or assembled without having to rush.

Retouch Artists

There are definite limits to photographic technology and when those limits are reached the retouch artist takes over. It is best to involve the retoucher before the job is shot by informing your client ahead of time that what he or she is requesting cannot be achieved through photography alone. In such situations the cost of retouching will be clearly identified as being the responsibility of the client. Unfortunately, it is not always possible to recognize technically troublesome jobs ahead of time, and the retoucher is very often expected to avert or mitigate a disaster in progress; in this scenario it is not always obvious who must pay the repair bill. A photographer is certainly responsible for his or

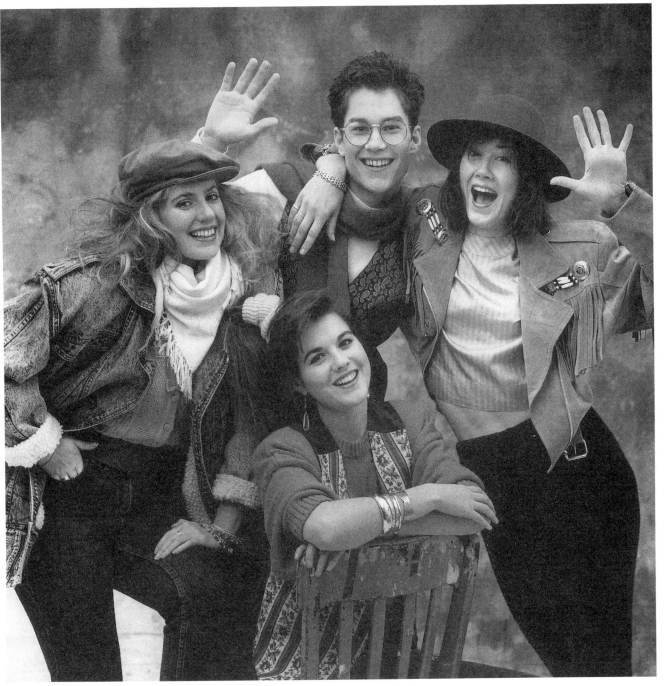

These 'youngsters', a couple of whom were almost thirty years old, were supplied by a local model agency. The shot was the center piece of a newspaper teen fashion ad for a large mall. The picture was made in the studio against a painted canvas drop illuminated with a large softlight. Hasselblad, 150mm lens, Ilford FP4 film.

her errors or lack of judgment, but clients sometimes inadvertently or deliberately misrepresent the parameters of a tricky job, in which case intense (but diplomatic) discussions are called for.

Sophisticated electronics will eventually diminish the importance of the retouch artist but for now, and for the near future, we all depend on the exotic skills of these patient and meticulous craftspeople; production managers and creative directors at advertising agencies, the people at large department stores who are responsible for flyers and catalogs, as well as high-profile portrait photographers will know where to find them.

Here are some common photographic problems that may be solved with the help of a retoucher:

1. Replacing a gray sky with blue when a tight deadline requires an exterior shoot in poor weather.
2. Eliminating unwanted elements that cannot be avoided any other way such as reflections, cluttered backgrounds, facial, or flaws which are the result of damaged negatives.
3. Restoring the lost 'edges' of light colored objects which must be photographed on white backgrounds.
4. Stripping together two or more images that were made at different times or locations.
5. Adding new elements to existing photographs.

The Food Stylist

Sooner or later all commercial photographers are called upon to shoot food. It is both prudent and efficient to hire an expert to help cope with all the hassle of finding the ingredients, preparing the dishes, and displaying the results in an attractive and original way.

Professional photographic food stylists are few and far between but independent film production companies often shoot commercials for restaurants, hotels, and food manufacturers and generally they will know of someone local who 'does food'. A really first rate job with a decent budget may warrant flying in a specialist from out of town. Head chefs at fancy restaurants and hotels are often capable of good work in the studio, as are home economists and recipe testers from agricultural marketing boards and co-ops.

In Chapter 7 I described my own 'kitchen' arrangements. Food stylists need to know well ahead of time what their working conditions will be. Many foods can be prepared elsewhere and then brought to the studio to be photographed while some dishes

must be created on the spot. Have the stylist look over your facilities and work out a practical strategy in detail; most photographs of food have to be done fairly quickly so that everything looks fresh. If the job warrants the extra effort, commercial food preparation equipment or even complete kitchens can be easily rented.

Color Labs

If you don't maintain a darkroom the professional custom lab will be your most important supplier. To be of use to a busy photographer the lab must be technically reliable and flexible enough to accommodate tight deadlines. After a reasonable period of familiarization with your preferences, the lab should consistently produce custom prints with the density and color you like.

If you are being well served by your lab, let them know; pay your bills on time and allow them the use of your best shots for self-promotion. If your lab is not performing up to par, find out why. Technical problems or poor service at the counter should be brought to the attention of the manager. If he or she cannot offer any remedy, change labs. If there is only one custom lab in town you might call up the local Kodak industrial rep (often the processor's exclusive supplier) who will likely pressure the lab to improve performance, hopefully without mentioning your name. If that doesn't work, locate an advanced amateur or a pro with his or her own color darkroom who might be willing to take care of you. If that doesn't work, re-read chapters nine and ten.

Good Relations

Everyone wants to be appreciated. It is a simple matter to make sure that samples of your work get to all the people who helped you produce it. They will have something valuable with which to sell their own skills plus the good feeling that comes with knowing someone feels they've done well.

14.

Basic Camera Technique

Much of the bread and butter work in commercial photography requires straightforward technical competence rather than incredible virtuosity. In fact, virtuosity is impossible without a good basic technique. Those of you who are attracted to commercial photography will find that it is necessary to put in at least a couple of years playing photographic 'scales' before being summoned for a 'command performance'. Regardless how mundane or exotic a particular assignment might be however, all professionally made photographs must demonstrate technical excellence.

The fundamentals for making good commercial images are:

1. Proper exposure.
2. Consistently high image resolution.
3. Appropriate choice of lens.
4. Perspective control (where required).
5. Appropriate choice of format.
6. Appropriate image composition or design.

The goal of photographic efficiency is to consistently maintain high standards in the simplest, quickest, and most economical way possible.

1. Exposure Control

Introduction

All the technical and aesthetic elements in photography are, of course, profoundly interdependent and interrelated. The design of an image depends to a large degree on the choice of optics, while the choice of optics will inevitably be limited by the choice of format, and so on. Nevertheless, everything depends on a few light-sensitive molecules receiving sufficient photo-chemical stimulation to record a permanent image. *Exposure control* is the method by which this condition may be consistently achieved.

The duration and intensity of the exposure is primarily a function of the level of light which falls on, or is reflected by the subject of the picture. In order to make an accurate determination it is necessary to keep in mind the 'quality' of the light, the f-stop required for depth-of-field, the relation between shutter speed and subject motion, and the reaction of the film to very long or very short exposure times (the *reciprocity* effect). Other indirect factors are also involved; for example, some extreme wide-angle lenses cannot project an image of even intensity across the whole frame while leaf shutters, because of their construction, are open noticeably longer at the center than at the edges for short exposure times.

Happily, most everything to do with proper exposure is both measurable and obvious. Controlled testing and careful evaluation of materials followed by accurate calibration of equipment will lead to predictable results.

Tools for Measuring Light

The initial question, "how much light?", is answered by pulling out a *light meter* of some sort. The light meter is an electronic device consisting of a sensor which changes electrically in proportion to the amount of light striking its surface and a meter scale or an array of light emitting diodes which displays those changes in numbers. A good light meter will reliably indicate the same reading whenever presented with the same intensity of light.

There are four basic categories of meters for measuring both continuous sources and electronic flash; *reflected* light meters, *incident* light meters, *spot* meters, and *behind-the-lens* light meters.

The reflected light meter measures the light coming toward the camera from an object or scene. A simple lens or baffle arrangement in front of the sensor (or *photocell*) gives an *angle of acceptance* which is usually 15° to 30°. Some units have a little optical viewfinder, but most don't so that it is necessary to guess what the meter is looking at.

The incident meter does not measure the light reflected from the subject. Instead of a lens the photocell is covered with a small diffuser, usually a white translucent plastic dome. The reading is taken from the subject position with the dome pointing at the camera. The diffuser integrates all the light falling on the subject (*illuminance*) and the resulting measurement describes the overall level of illumination independent of the reflectivity of the subject.

The spotmeter is a highly specialized reflected light meter. Here, a sophisticated lens and view-finder arrangement permit very accurate measurements of the light coming off tiny areas of the subject. Generally spot meters provide a view-finder image with a 10° angle of acceptance surrounding a 1° 'spot' of sensitivity.

Like the spotmeter, the behind-the lens (BTL) meters are specialized versions of the reflected light meter. In this case the sensing element and readout are located on board a camera. The photocell (or cells) read the light entering the camera through the taking lens. The reading is obtained off the ground-glass viewing screen, through minute perforations in the reflex mirror, or from the film surface itself. The beauty of the BTL approach is that all factors affecting the intensity of the light reaching the film, such as filters and lens transmittance, are automatically taken into account.

It's a Gray World Out There

Refinements in technology give us a wide choice of equipment, yet all light-meters, past and present, have one common characteristic; they're dumb. Some manufactures and many photographers pretend this is not the case, but they are deluding themselves, microprocessors notwithstanding. A meter can tell you how much light it sees, and that's it. No machine can interpret quantitative measurements in a way that will guarantee the appropriate exposure every time. This decision is the responsibility of the photographer and it involves some thought.

Earlier I told you that a certain film, exposed to a certain amount of light, and developed for a certain amount of time at a certain temperature will yield, when printed under controlled conditions, a tone equivalent to that of an 18% gray card. In other words, if every other step of the process is known and predetermined, exposure alone will determine the density of the final tone. If a reflected light meter of known accuracy is pointed at an 18% gray card, then the indicated exposure will end up as a print which looks exactly like the gray card. Light meters think the whole visual world is one big gray card. The underlying logic is that all the various tones in a typical scene, when randomly scrambled, will average out to the equivalent of 18% gray. Unfortunately, in the real world, such an approach is not sufficiently flexible.

Consider the photographic implications of a man—standing in direct sunlight—wearing a white shirt and a black suit. A reflected light meter pointed at this scene from the camera position might indicate f11 at $^1/_{125}$sec for ISO 100 film. If a closer reading is made from the shirt, the reading might be f22 at $^1/_{250}$sec. Another reading made from a shadow area on the dark suit might indicate f4 at $^1/_{60}$sec. A comparison of the two close-up readings indicates a span of eight f-stops: negative films cannot record detail beyond six f-stops and printing papers cannot reproduce a range of tones beyond 100:1 under the very best viewing conditions. This means the shadow side of the man's suit will drop off the dark end of the spectrum and print jet black while the sunlit white of the shirt will shoot over the top of the reproducible tonal scale and consequently print bald white. The human eye and brain working together can tolerate a brightness range of almost 100,000:1 which means what we see in real life and what we see in a photograph will not necessarily coincide. Some skill is required to reconcile the eye/brain response to the film/paper response.

The Truth About Film and Light Meters

Reflected light meters should not be considered *exposure meters*, but rather *brightness* meters.

Individual readings indicate specific intensities of light but no single reading can be trusted as an overall exposure. Instead, the meter must be used to 'poke around' the subject in order to determine the *relative brightness* of the significant tones. Once this is obtained, a decision can be made as to whether or not the tonal scale of the subject corresponds to the tonal range of the film. If the two are desperately out of alignment a decision a has to be made as to which tones in the subject are to be sacrificed to the shortcomings of the medium.

Many photographic materials are profoundly limited in ways that cannot be significantly altered by the photographer. For example, most color slide emulsions can faithfully record a brightness range of only three f-stops ($\pm1^1/_2$ stops) which means that the choice of tonal placement is drastically limited where light conditions are harsh.

The Four Levels of Exposure Control

An awareness of the relationship between subject contrast and the appearance of the final photograph is the first level of exposure control. An accurate knowledge of highlight versus shadow levels allows the exposure to be 'placed' within the film's characteristic tonal range so that the main areas of interest will be satisfactorily recorded. The relatively broad latitude of negative films allow good results in a variety of common situations however color slide materials are much more difficult to manage. The exposure for transparency film is often determined by highlight levels alone because overexposure creates terrible looking blank spaces.

The second level of exposure control is the selection and manipulation of lighting conditions. Just as one can acquire a knowledge of the properties of film, one can acquire a knowledge of the properties of light. In Chapter Eight I discussed the esthetics of light in relation to photographic 'style'; now we must consider how to deal with the technicalities.

In clear weather, in areas of low pollution, light from the sun travels directly through the atmosphere and illuminates the surface of the earth with a sometimes painful precision. This harshness may be infinitely modified by reflection, diffraction, and diffusion caused by variables such as weather, suspended particles in the air, and the angle at which the sunlight falls. Physical objects affect contrast by reflection or by creating shade. Under heavy overcast conditions the sky becomes a gigantic soft-light which dissolves all shadows completely.

Moving the subject into or out of shaded areas or placing the subject nearer to or farther from an existing reflector (such as a white building) significantly alters the brightness range. So does rotating the subject relative to the sun or even selecting a different camera angle. Subjects of moderate dimensions which have to be dealt with in harsh light can be successfully softened by the use of portable reflectors such as white cards or foam-core covered with crinkled aluminum foil. Judicious use of fill flash can reduce contrast to manageable levels without destroying the ambience of the available light.

In the studio the task of correcting, modifying or compensating for existing conditions is superseded by the necessity to invent a lighting arrangement which will optimize the power of the image while remaining within the technical limitations of the film.

The third level of exposure control must be invoked whenever careful measurement of brightness levels and all possible modifications of the lighting are not enough; the power of the Zone System was introduced in the chapter dealing with black and white processing. Color materials cannot be manipulated chemically as easily as black & white materials. However, there are a few modifications which do in fact alter the characteristics of certain color films. (I will describe them in the next chapter.)

NOTE: Before trusting any exposure technique it is necessary to know the actual sensitivity of any film you intend to rely upon. The manufactures rate their products according to certain standards prescribed by the American Standards Association and other similar organizations. This is what gives rise to ISO/DIN film speed numbers. In real life film sensitivity is not a constant and different emulsions have to be tested and evaluated under actual working conditions before a reliable *exposure index* (EI) can be determined.

The last option in exposure control is actually a group of several photo-mechanical interventions which can 'save' some poorly exposed negatives or slides; none are particularly convenient but from time to time in professional work situations arise where heroic efforts are required to salvage substandard work.

One remedy is a method of post-exposure contrast control for color materials called *silver masking* or *contrast masking*. When printing a color negative which is too hard the tonal scale may be compressed by masking with a thin black and white positive made by contact printing the original. The areas of maximum density in the mask coincide with the areas of least density in the color negative, thus reducing the exposure in those areas when the two are printed in register; the reverse is true for soft color negatives printed together with a negative black and white mask. The same techniques work when printing excessively high or low contrast transparencies except that the masking values are inverted. Well done color masking can produce prints of exceptional quality although it is a job best done by a custom lab.

Really bad b&w negatives can sometimes be enhanced by chemical agents called *reducers* and *intensifiers* which dissolve away or build up density. The action of these chemicals is rather crude; don't expect miracles. A severely overexposed color transparencies is inevitably a write-off but mildly over or under-exposed slides can be saved by re-photographing them; sophisticated duplicating techniques can modify color balance and contrast as well. There are chemical reducers for transparencies that will lighten either specific colors or overall density. As a last resort, a botched negative or slide can be printed, then retouched and carefully copied.

Regardless of even the most heroic of remedial efforts, imperfectly exposed negatives and slides will never look as good as perfectly exposed negatives and slides, regardless of the degree of effort that goes into making corrections.

Useful Definitions

EXPOSURE LATITUDE is the factor by which the minimum camera exposure required to give a negative with adequate shadow detail may be multiplied without loss of highlight detail.

USEFUL EXPOSURE RANGE depends upon the film and the degree of development and is measured from the least to the most exposure a film can receive and produce a printable tone.

SUBJECT LUMINANCE RANGE is a useful expression of subject contrast as it is a product of both the illuminance and the reflection range of the subject.

DENSITY RANGE is the difference between the minimum and the maximum density in the negative. The major effect in the variation of density range is degree of development.

TONE REPRODUCTION is the relation of the reflectances in the print to the corresponding luminances in the subject. The usual goal is to obtain an acceptable reproduction of the various luminances in the original scene.

TONE SEPARATION refers to our attempt to keep each tone in the original subject in approximately the same position in the tonal scale of the print. Because the luminance range possible in the print is less than the average luminance range in the subject, the optimum to be aimed at is proportionality as opposed to equality.

2. Resolution

The Grand Illusion

The world is actually composed of dots. Photographic film reflects reality with dots of silver and colored dyes, while the human eye registers dots as produced by a finite number of rods and cones on the retina. The brain, seeking as it does to harmonize the various elements of perception, automatically renders our microscopically fragmented vision into a smooth, continuous image. Our perception of reality as a highly detailed visual field is, in fact, an illusion. While looking at photographs, we continually make judgments as to image quality. The brain's analytical power, though focused upon what is really only a collection of speckles on a piece of paper, allows us to make an excellent approximation of reality. At some point on the visual spectrum from barely perceivable to infinitely perceivable, the brain sends a message; "Enough! No more information is required.

This photograph looks the same as the real objects it represents"—in other words, a high-resolution photograph. This point does not occur at the same place on the perceivability spectrum for every image. There are many factors which affect the exact go/no-go threshold of acceptable resolution and a solid notion of high resolution can be induced by a range of surprisingly varied technical conditions. It is the business of the commercial photographer to always know where the outside limits of acceptable resolution are to be found in order to select the right equipment and materials. To get sufficient detail recorded on film and then reproduced on paper, everything must be right: the nature of the subject, optics, film, exposure, processing, degree of enlargement, paper surface and contrast, as well as correct conditions for viewing the final product.

Of all the characteristics that distinguish an amateur effort from a professional image high resolution is the one most quickly recognized by people in general. "It's so clear! How did you do it?" How, indeed?

Resolution and Image Content

The nature of the subject is the first consideration because its physical characteristics determine to a large degree the permissible bottom line, technically speaking. For example, a very high degree of image integrity is required to make a close-up true-to-life portrait of a young person with flawless skin. Even the finest of fine-grain films will be hard put to record an unblemished cheek or forehead as a perfect, even tone. The best optics on both camera and enlarger will be hard put to project a perfect image of the iris, lip texture, or eyelashes.

On the other hand, a photographic view of a craggy cliff at the seaside on a stormy day will be much more forgiving of technical faults. Such a scene may be recorded with equipment and materials unsuitable for the perfect portrait, yet when finally reproduced on paper, will be more than acceptable to the naked eye. The ocean scene appears very rich in detail, because a little grain, a little unsteadiness, and some extra contrast all contribute data that the brain *expects* to see. The roughness of the rock and the coarse tonality of the water may be adequately communicated with less technical trouble than the subtleties of the face.

Equipment Choices for Optimum Resolution

In photography, as in music reproduction, one is always better off with the best equipment available. A top quality stereo will reproduce all the power and nuance of a symphony undistorted, yet the manipulation of a few controls will allow the broadcasting of the roughest, toughest heavy-metal.

These days we are blessed with a plethora of fine optics. Provided lenses are kept scrupulously clean, free of scratches, and in perfect alignment with the camera body and film plane, virtually all modern name-brand equipment should perform satisfactorily. Focussing helixes should be smooth and snug with no side-to-side play. Lens mounts should be secure and positive in their action. Be certain that interchangeable viewing screens, viewfinder prisms, and reflex mirrors all seat in their proper positions.

Mechanical changes which affect resolution are to be expected with heavy use, so have your equipment looked over at least once every year. A competent repair-person will make necessary adjustments to both rangefinder and reflex focusing systems at modest cost.

Film and Format

The most photo/efficient response to any assignment is to chose the smallest format and the fastest film that will provide the degree of resolution appropriate for the job at hand. As film improves, choosing a format according to its capability to hold detail becomes more and more difficult. The impressive 8" X 10" view camera has all but disappeared and the 4" X 5" view camera is typically chosen because of its focus and perspective controls rather than for its resolution. When it does arise, the need for 4" X 5" will be fairly obvious but the distinctions

between 35mm and medium format are shrinking with each new breakthrough in film technology. Most commercial jobs will be easily handled in medium format, and many can be well done on 35mm. Often medium format equipment will be used simply because art directors insist on contact sheets that are easy to read.

In the next chapter I will deal with specific types of work and give my preferences for particular films and formats for each of them. You will see that in almost every circumstance the best technical solution is a compromise between resolution and practicality. However, by way of introduction to the thinking involved in such a compromise, consider the following general comparison between miniature and medium formats:

By virtue of the inherent optical and mechanical characteristics of 35mm equipment, pictures can be made in astounding conditions. For a steady hand and a sharp eye f1.4 at $^1/_{30}$sec. might be the bottom end of the f-stop/shutter speed spectrum. With a moderate wide-angle lens and one of the new super-speed films, almost anything that is visible can be successfully photographed. A well balanced 35mm camera, combined with the forgiving depth of field of short focal length optics will offer the best chance at accurate focus and an acceptable degree of 'hand-holdability'. Similarly, short teles, say up to 135mm, may be usefully employed with only an increase in shutter speed. For example, I wouldn't hesitate to make a head and shoulders portrait with a wide open f2.8 90mm lens at $^1/_{125}$sec. Apart from the expanding grain pattern upon enlargement, the technical performance of small format equipment for available light work is superb. Computer designed lenses and lovely new films like Kodak Ektar 25 or Technical Pan allow very fine 35mm work to be done as long as circumstances can be carefully controlled.

Medium format is not so flexible. Straddling as it does the gigantic gap between large and miniature formats, roll film equipment requires a hybrid of techniques from both ends of the spectrum in order to maximize results. The most obvious difference between

35mm and 6 X 4.5, 6 X 6, or 6 X 7 is that the larger image sizes require longer focal length lenses with greater covering power. (Unfortunately, these longer lenses usually have smaller maximum apertures.) A typical normal lens for 6 X 7 for example is an f4.5/110mm. Assuming it could project a large enough image to cover the whole frame, a 85mm Nikkor, a short tele on my Nikon F3, would create a slightly wide-angle image on a 6 X 7 negative.

Depth of field is a function of f-stop, but it is also a function of focal length and magnification. For the same image magnification and at the same aperture, a 110mm 'normal' lens for 6 X 7 will exhibit the same depth of field as a 110mm short tele on a 35mm camera. However, for the same camera-to-subject distance the 110mm lens on the smaller format will cover less subject area than the 110mm lens on the larger format. When the subject-to-camera distance is the same, a shorter focal length lens is necessary in order to cover the same subject area on the smaller format—the shorter focal length lens on the 35 will yield noticeably greater depth of field and consequently greater apparent resolution. Stopping down the lens on the medium format camera to equalize the depth of field effect will be expensive, exposure-wise.

As well, compared to sleek 35mm cameras, the bulkier medium format cameras are indisputably awkward. An accessory hand-grip makes things more manageable but the heavier, boxier, roll-film machines cannot be reliably hand-held for the same long exposures. The bottom line of f1.4 at $1/30$sec. for my Nikon corresponds to f4 at $1/125$sec. for my Hasselblad.

To achieve the best results from medium format it is necessary to slow right down; broad daylight or bright electronic flash will allow consistent hand-held results but everything else needs a tripod. The selection of roll film format cameras forces the photographer to adopt a more methodical regimen. It sounds paradoxical, but self-discipline leads to greater freedom. Once the basics of camera steadiness and relatively small working apertures are satisfied the medium format worker can do things that 35mm can only parody.

There is a roundness, a smoothness, and a silkiness to medium format photographs because each silver halide grain is not fighting for its own place in the sun. Sharpness in 35mm is being able to see the clearly defined edges of everything while larger images promote an appreciation of the insides of everything. There is a tangible peace of mind associated with the knowledge that the smooth tonal scale and the wonderful detail will not be disrupted by magnification.

Mechanical Considerations

Optical systems should not move while images are being made. In picture taking, this means no camera movement whatever. In print making, this means the enlarger should be rock-steady.

It is very tempting to shoot with hand-held cameras but this temptation must be resisted if you want consistently sharp results. Only young people who practice meditation and never drink coffee can hope to hold a camera steady, critically steady, for any longer than $1/30$th of a second.

The tripod is the most important photographic accessory but when you must work with a hand-held camera, make sure you maintain an easy but solid grip. Before each exposure, let your breath be slow and even. Don't 'clench'; clenching makes you vibrate. Relax, then squeeze. This technique is required for all but the very fastest shutter speeds.

Subject Motion

If slow exposures are dictated by circumstances beyond your control, image degradation due to subject motion can occur whether or not the camera is mounted on a tripod. There are, however, a couple of non-photographic techniques that can improve results.

First, study motion. In every action of a repetitive nature there is a place of transition where, momentarily, the object is at rest. A hand goes up, but just at the top of the curve, before the beginning of the descent, it stops. A sharp photograph can be made at that exact moment. You must be quick; don't laugh when I tell you how to get that way. It's simple, really. You must be physically fit. Exercise hard for twenty minutes every other day. Eat simple foods and avoid caffeine and nicotine. Meditation and Yoga are helpful; a body at peace with itself is steady and reliable.

Focus

Make the best of your equipment by focusing carefully. It is easy to pass over the significance of this critical procedure because of the apparent ease with which SLR microprism screens snap in and out of focus. Unfortunately, the tiny elements in the microprism grid are carefully ground to a certain angle which can be truly accurate for only one focal length of lens. If the plain ground-glass collar and the microprism disagree on the point of precise focus, the ground-glass will be correct. Special screens for very short or very long lenses are available for some cameras. When focussing view cameras, always use a magnifying glasses or a loupe. Have your eyes checked regularly.

3. Optics and Photographic Point-of-View

The Biological Lens

Human vision is nature's almost perfect response to the visible portion of the electromagnetic spectrum. I say almost perfect because as spectacular as the system might be, there are a couple of flaws; the lens of the eye is not interchangeable without surgical intervention and for all practical purposes it has a fixed focal length.

Fifty millimeters (two inches) is the approximate focal length of the human eye. The lens element is a truly amazing creation. Its 'automatic diaphragm', the iris, changes the effective f-stop from about f5.6 in dim light to approximately f22 in bright light. Quick corrections are made according to relative brightness of different objects within a scene, thus allowing us to 'see' a tonal range

much wider than present-day photographic technology can accommodate. More amazing still is the fact that focusing is accomplished by actually changing the shape of the lens itself. This very useful mechanical process goes on continually and quite fast, yielding the illusion of almost infinite depth of field. Focus corrections are made spontaneously as one's attention shifts between different objects within the field of view. Overall angle of acceptance is very nearly 180° around an area of high resolution of approximately 40°.

So-called 'normal' lenses in photography are related to this special concentrated area of ordinary vision in that they have nearly the same angle of acceptance. The focal length of a normal lens is determined by the length of the diagonal drawn from corner to corner across the format being considered. The reason is that the comfortable viewing angle for most people is also about equal to the diagonal of the print. From this distance, the exact perspective will be assured by making the photograph with a lens having a focal length equal to the film's diagonal. For the 35mm rectangle, the standard focal length works out to be 43.266mm, but most manufacturers use 50 or 55mm. (Photographs made with wide-angle lenses are nearly always viewed from too far away for exact perspective, which is why it is often wrongly assumed that they distort.)

It's a coincidence that the favored normal lens for the 35mm format and the human eye have nearly the same focal length yet these similar focal length lenses don't see the world in the same way. This is because the brain, like the computer that can generate a full color map of Jupiter from a few electronic clues, processes the data relayed along the optic nerve from the eye and then reconstructs and image (the image we see mentally) so that everything looks O.K. We are conditioned from childhood to expect the visual world to follow certain rules of perspective and it is one of the brain's main functions to enforce these rules. That's why optical illusions are possible,; the brain, attempting to keep things in some kind of order, may be tricked. This was demonstrated in a dramatic experiment in which the participants wore special glasses which made everything appear upside down. Within a couple of weeks of constantly wearing these glasses, the subjects of the experiment reported that the world had righted itself and everything appeared normal. Upon removal of the reversing spectacles, everything looked upside down. It took another couple of weeks without the lenses for things to come right side up again.

I've made an effort here to illustrate some of the properties of human vision because the selection and use of various focal length lenses in photography is profoundly influenced by our conditioned physiological and psychological seeing. Some lenses, like the moderate telephoto in the portrait situation, are used to 'put the world right' according to our optical expectations. Other lenses, such as the fish-eye, are used to shock and surprise because the images they yield are so spectacularly different from what our poor brains keep trying to see. We use the range of optics to satisfy or tease our visual programming.

Point of View

It's easy to think of a wide-angle lens as a device to cram more stuff into the frame without having to move back or a telephoto as a device for getting close to the subject without moving forward. I won't deny that the 'mechanics' of lens selection are significant but I insist on emphasizing that the various focal lengths offer more than just a different angle of view. In fact, they each offer a different point of view, both esthetically and sociologically.

Sociologically? Indeed. Using the 35mm format as a basis for analysis, it's fair to say that a full-figure photograph of your average human made with a 50mm lens would require a separation of about eight feet between photographer and the subject. This is just barely within the range of normal conversational voice levels in a quiet room. A 90mm would stretch this figure to 14-16 feet. A 135mm would push it to 20-24 feet and voice communication between subject and

photographer would be limited to shouting. Also, at the longer distances, the visual behavioral clues of expression and body language are similarly diminished and confused. Switching to wide-angle optics moves the photographer and the subject to within five feet of each other; personal territories definitely intersect at such close proximity and many intimate channels of communication begin to operate. Directions may be given in a whisper, a twitch of the head or a raised eyebrow signals a new posture or perspective. This is sociology, the naked ape syndrome of photography. Watch a photographer at work with people and you'll be able to name his or her favorite lens according to the distance he prefers to put between himself and his subject.

Wide-Angle Lenses

My work is a mix of studio, photojournalistic/editorial, and publicity photography. As far as the people I work for are concerned, the most popular type of portrait is the *environmental* portrait; a photograph which places and individual within his or her milieu. It emphasizes the character of the subject by including information about expression, posture, clothes, and physical surroundings all at once. For this work, a moderate wide-angle is not only an asset but a necessity, at least in normal-size living spaces and offices. The shooting distance for a relaxed portrait of someone seated at a desk, say, allows a pleasing view of the features of the face while important objects in the foreground and the background may still be included. Compositional options may be fine-tuned without a lot of fuss because the wide-angle puts one close enough to the subject to allow quite significant alterations in framing with only a small amount of movement; repositioning the camera a foot or two up or down, left or right, reveals very different points of view. On a purely mechanical level, the moderate wide-angle makes working with portable electronic flash a very speedy operation. Most camera-mountable flash units provide an adequate field of coverage without attachments, and the short distances involved allow energy-conserving thyristor units to recycle in only a few seconds.

A normal lens or short tele is required to shoot people from the waist up without including a lot of environmental features because the distortion introduced by moving close with a wide-angle lens can make the photograph clumsy and unflattering. However, this effect might be desirable in some circumstances. A few modern journalists of cynical bent rely on this characteristic of wide-angle optics to make their subjects look vaguely awkward and ill at ease before the camera.

So-called *perspective distortion* is both the curse and the blessing of wide-angle work. The term perspective distortion, however, has very little meaning apart from the brain's response to the optical phenomena of nature. The eye actually sees parallel vertical lines of a building converging just as the camera does. The eye sees nearby small objects as large and faraway large objects as small, just as the camera does. Yet, unlike film, which simply records what the lens presents, our brains interpret and reconstruct the images streaming in from outside. The brain wants to see verticals that don't converge. The brain knows that the bee on the flower is smaller than the farmhouse at the other end of the field. By collecting the light coming off these objects on a two-dimensional surface and then presenting the flat image out of context, we are working relative to our optical preconditioning. In real life situations, the brain tries to correct apparent visual anomalies, and, up to a point, succeeds while a photograph can only looks how it looks.

The perspective offered by very-wide to ultra-wide (28-17mm for 35mm cameras) can push visual tension right to the limits of tolerance. We will accept a rather odd-looking photograph when there is no choice in the matter; a fish-eye picture of the inside of space capsule, for example. In fact, wide-angle affects are often appreciated in dramatic views of buildings or natural panoramas. However, people and familiar objects pictured close up by extreme wide-angle lenses will never look 'natural'.

The commercial photographer has in the wide-angle view a spectacular tool for presenting the wares of the market place in an interesting and exciting way. Like all good things in life, though, this techniques suffers when used in excess. Not only do we grow tired of grotesque caricatures of people, but super-elongated automobiles and girls with legs that go on forever begin to lose their visual excitement after awhile.

On a somewhat more sinister note, the common use of very wide optics in photojournalism can change what might have been an impartial witness to historically significant events into a sensationalist representation. Through a 24mm lens, an upraised arm looks menacing, the arrogant look unbearably corrupt, while the weak and needy look irretrievably lost. Such imagery is effective up to a point. Beyond that point, established by good taste, the power of the photojournalist is eroded as his or her audience becomes visually jaded.

Telephoto Lenses

The wide-angles are clearly the right tools in certain situations but continuous facile employment of perspective distortion means that the photographer has surrendered the content of his or her images in favor of form. When the design of the photograph is a consequence of the lens characteristics alone, the power of the imagery will decrease over time. Just like the folks with the upside down glasses, we get used to sensational points of view. When this happens, our collective visual consciousness cries out for more natural perspectives and photographs in which form and content strike a harmonious balance.

Except for special circumstances with certain shaped faces and very special lighting, the moderate telephotos (85 to 135mm for 35mm cameras) are necessary for pleasing 'head and shoulders' portraiture. These lenses put enough distance between camera and subject to render nose, chin, and ears in suitable proportions. They are long enough to give subjects a fair deal visually, yet short enough to keep the photographer within the critical psychic circle of influence so as to allow the development of a working rapport.

A lens of longer focal length, say 180mm or beyond, is not quite as fine a tool for portraying the human face. This, too, is a problem of 'perspective'. Where short focal lengths tend to emphasize the features closest to the camera (giving a swollen, bulging look) the distances encountered with long lenses tend to flatten facial contours resulting in an image with noticeable lack of depth.

In photographing products the drama and exaggeration of the wide-angle approach is generally bypassed in favor of the more straightforward view offered by the longer lenses;their clear and undistorted presentation allows the innate elegance of the pictured objects to carry the show.

Since 35mm and medium format systems have a very limited choice of lenses offering perspective control, the long focal length lenses are necessary to help render parallel vertical and horizontal lines properly. Things appear correctly rectilinear only when photographed absolutely dead-on by shorter lenses. Without perspective control, objects photographed from below look to be tilted away from the camera, while objects photographed from above look to be tilted toward the camera. This happens because at short distances and at an elevated point of view the top of an object is closer to the lens than the bottom. The top therefore is rendered larger on the negative and the print looks top heavy. A long lens, however, puts the camera far enough away to make the difference between the top of the object and the camera and the bottom of the object and the camera insignificant. This balances the perspective and makes the picture feel right.

Aside from aesthetic considerations, there are many circumstances when the simple factor of image magnification alone is the basis for choosing a long lens. If mechanical or geographical barriers separate photographer and subject, telephotos will pull in a decent image size. The degree of magnification is directly proportional to the increase in focal length. Thus at the same camera-to-subject distance, a 200mm lens yields and image of four times the size of a 50mm lens.

The inevitable limiting factor is that as image size increases, so does the significance of focusing error and camera movement. Depth of field is a function of aperture size, which in turn is a function of focal length. The longer the focal length the shallower the depth of field at a given f-stop, all else being equal. At moderately wide apertures and close distances this may be a matter of inches or even fractions of inches.

As focal lengths stretch, it becomes increasingly difficult to hand-hold tele lenses without a loss of resolution due to the magnification of camera motion. A rule of thumb is to never use a shutter speed slower that the reciprocal of the focal length of the lens being used, e.g., for a 135mm use $1/125$sec, for a 500mm use $1/500$sec.

As we move up the scale of focal length past the medium teles *compression* of natural perspective begins to dominate in a way that is opposite and complimentary to the *expansion* of perspective yielded by short lenses. To encompass a given object we must move farther and farther away; the scene visible in the finder starts to bunch up and a view of fields, foothills and mountains seems to grow out of one plane. Similarly, blocks of city skyscrapers begin to look like pancake-thin copies of themselves pasted onto poster-board. Sports freaks and voyeurs simply accept this fact of super-tele life; creative photographers make the most of it by watching for creative juxtapositions of objects normally seen as greatly separated. Sometimes the combination of extremely long lenses and air pollution or thermally induced turbulence will introduce odd distortions or color shifts. Like the compression effect, such optical mutations can be photographically interesting; if not, they may be reduced somewhat by polarizing, UV (ultra-violet) or color correction filters.

4. Perspective Control and View Camera Basics

The Merriam-Webster dictionary defines perspective as "*the art of painting and drawing so that objects represented have apparent depth and distance.......a view of things (as objects or events) in their true relationship and relative importance."*

We have seen how 'point of view' and the selection of lenses are used to manipulate the emotional and technical aspects of photographic 'perspective'. In fact, it is a photographer's prerogative to choose how reality is to be represented in two dimensions; the view camera has been a part of photography from almost the very beginning, and since its introduction it has remained the premier tool whenever total perspective control is essential. Eventually electronic image processing will supersede the photo/mechanical sophistication of the view camera, but for now, and certainly for the near future, no professional photographer doing even a moderately wide range of business can expect to function without it.

Most 35mm and medium format cameras are rigidly constructed so that the lens and the film are always held in a particular alignment to one another; although the lens is focused by varying its distance from the film, the mechanism by which it is moved will have been carefully designed so that the *axis of the lens* always maintains exactly the same orientation relative to the *film plane*. Thus, the lens and the film may not always be the same distance apart, but in all conventional solid-body cameras a line drawn through the middle of the lens will always be perfectly perpendicular to the film plane and perfectly centered within the image area. View cameras are designed to be similarly rigid and precise. However, the alignment between the lens and the film plane is not fixed but instead may be adjusted and then locked in position. These adjustments (or *movements*) make the view camera a powerful and versatile photographic tool.

The modern view camera is constructed from a modular system of interlocking parts chosen according to the requirements of various types of work, but the basic configuration typically consists of a rigid bar or tube (the *monorail*) on which are mounted front and back *standards* linked by a flexible light-tight *bellows*. (The *flat-bed* camera and the *field* camera are alternate configurations which are more portable but less adjustable.)

The 'standards' are sophisticated supports for a lens and a focusing ground-glass/film holder. They're built to allow all the 'movements' necessary for complete image control. They can be moved forward and backward (*focus and magnification*), up and down (*rise/fall*) and side to side (*shift*). They can be rotated around a vertical axis (*swing*) as well as tilted forward or backward around a horizontal axis (*tilt*). On fancy view cameras the movements are achieved by manipulating precision geared mechanisms with finely calibrated vernier dials while less expensive versions use friction dampened sliding controls. All view cameras have some method of freezing the adjustments (*lock*) so that nothing changes just before or during the actual exposure.

View camera movements have two main functions: control of perspective distortion and focus control. A typical 'table-top' product photo might require a slight rise plus a backward tilt of the rear standard to center the object in the frame and restore a rectilinear look in addition to a forward tilt of the front standard to optimize the focus. A street-level wide-angle view of a tall building might require a perfectly vertical rear standard (confirmed by the built-in bubble level) to keep everything parallel as well as a substantial rise on the front standard to bring the top of the building into the field of view. The variations are subtle and endless and magnificently effective.

Lenses for View Cameras

Solid body cameras need lenses that will just cover the frame corner to corner, but view camera movements work only if the *image circle* is big enough to accommodate an off-axis optical displacement which can exceed the dimensions of the film by fifty or even one hundred percent. Lenses with good coverage and high resolution at the edges of the field are difficult to make and consequently expensive to buy. It is encouraging to note, however, that truly excellent lenses, particularly wide-angles and longer teles, are readily available today whereas even ten years ago they were very hard to come by at any price.

Front Rise and Fall

When the camera is level and pointed at a tall subject, part of the subject will not be visible in the finder. Tilting the camera upwards will bring the whole subject into view, but the vertical lines of subject will appear to converge. If the camera is again leveled, raising the lens will extend the field of view sufficiently to include the whole subject while allowing the vertical lines to stay properly parallel. Front falls are used in a similar way when the subject extends below the uncorrected field of view.

Front and Rear Shifts

Displacing the lens horizontally accommodates very wide subjects in the same way that front rise and fall accommodates very tall subjects. Sometimes a dead-on rectilinear view cannot be achieved because the perfect camera position is blocked by an obstacle; in such awkward situations shifting the lens will allow an off-center camera location while still maintaining perspective integrity. This is very useful for architectural interiors. Bothersome reflections can often be eliminated in this way, as well.

Front Swings and Tilts

Lenses are designed so that the plane of focus is perpendicular to the lens axis. Focus problems arise whenever the plane of focus is not parallel to the subject plane. Such a misalignment occurs when the camera must be tilted to encompass a tall subject, for example. In a rigid body camera the focus error which results can be minimized only by stopping down the lens to increase depth of field, but this approach is limited in effectiveness. View camera movements allow the axis of the lens, and thus the plane of focus, to be conveniently manipulated. Front swings and tilts are considered the most valuable controls on the view camera because depth of focus can be controlled without changing aperture. Close and distant subjects (on the same plane) may be reproduced sharply without altering perspective by simply tilting the lensboard; the degree of focus correction possible greatly exceeds any increase in depth of field from simply stopping down the lens.

Back Tilts and Swings

Movements of the back standard are really movements of the *film plane*. To preserve correct perspective, the subject and the film plane must be parallel. Back swings and tilts are used to maintain this critical relationship when the camera must be tilted or angled to accommodate a particularly wide or tall subject which cannot be included even with fully extended front rise, fall or shift. In such a case appropriate front tilt and swings are used to restore proper focus.

Focusing the View Camera

On a monorail-type view camera both front and rear standards may be used for focusing although fine focusing should be done using the film-plane focus adjustment. Since magnification is a function of lens-to-subject distance, front standard movements will affect image size but this may go unnoticed with distant subjects. 'Flat-bed' or 'field' cameras do not usually allow back focusing, so the whole camera must be moved to maintain exact image size in those situations where this is critical.

Focusing is accomplished by viewing a reversed and inverted image on a ground-glass screen. The image is often dark and hard to see, particularly with wide angle lenses. Various manufacturers offer space-age laser-etched screens which are significantly brighter and easier to use. A loupe or flip-down jeweler's magnifier is indispensable as is a large, light proof focusing cloth. A few patches of velcro on the edge of the focussing cloth and around the top and sides of the back standard will also make life easier, particularly in a breeze. Both the cloth and the loupe may be replaced by a *reflex finder* with a binocular magnifier/viewfinder for easier focusing in tight or dimly lit situations. The vagaries of focusing a view camera under difficult circumstances often make Polaroid tests for focus and composition indispensable.

5. How to Select a Particular Format

Many 35mm systems offer a wide range of accessories but roll film equipment encompasses more or less every innovation in modern photography, although you may have to spend $25,000 and acquire several different cameras to achieve total flexibility. One can obtain super-wide, super-tele, macro, micro, perspective-control, and panoramic lenses and cameras. You can get quick change backs for 70mm long rolls, Polaroid proofs and ground glass focusing at the film plane. Some medium format cameras offer the swings and tilts of view cameras and even adapters to accommodate 4 X 5 film.

Unfortunately, there are limitations; the most critical being speed of operation. There are some professionals who have sufficiently intimidating reputations so as to be able to demand enough time to work without distracting haste. Those of us not so privileged must cope with the many idiosyncrasies of roll film machines while hustling around in a photographic frenzy. For example, many cameras still lack interlocking shutter cocking film advance levers and its entirely possible to expose the same frame several times. I've missed photographs because I forgot to remove the darkslide from a rapidly changed film back.

Most medium format cameras are very well built but there is no getting around the fact that they are noisy. A motor drive relieves some physical effort but generates enough noise to limit the usefulness of roll film cameras on assignments where both rapid shooting and low noise are essential. Stopping to load film every ten or twelve shots is a pain in the neck, yet switching to 220 or 70mm long rolls is an expensive way to extend shooting time. There is a problem in finding a lab to handle the long lengths of film as well.

View cameras require long set-up times and they are both expensive and painfully slow to operate. Nevertheless, they are sometimes indispensable.

I have worked out a rough guide to help chose between formats. To begin with, I always choose 35mm in low-light fast-moving situations, in situations where 35mm transparencies are required for slide shows, and in situations which require quiet, unobtrusive shooting. If, however, in low-light situations speed of operation is not so critical and I am allowed some measure of control over light levels, I will switch to a 6 X 6 SLR on a tripod. Most magazine or publicity work is shot on 35mm slide film. However for relatively stationary or detailed subjects I switch to medium format, again on a tripod. All my work with color negative is done on roll film, unless I know in advance that small prints will be satisfactory.

All complicated photography which demands Polaroid testing, all work which requires both color and b&w simultaneously, and 90% of my studio work is done with medium format cameras. Many jobs which the client expects to see shot in 4 X 5 can be successfully shot on roll film and then duped to 4 X 5 or even 8 X 10. As I mentioned earlier, some clients will specify medium format just to avoid the inconvenience of having to view small 35mm proofs or transparencies.

Large format is called for whenever perspective controls are an absolute must, when focus controls for extended depth of field are required, or for those times when a client (for whatever reason) personally demands big negatives or transparencies. The argument for using 4" X 5" to obtain higher resolution has been eroded by the introduction of films like Ektar 25 or Technical Pan.

6. Image Composition/Design

I do not feel competent to advise anyone on how to go about creating a well structured image. I have no formal training in design, and no conscious design technique. I know I take cues from my clients and from the visual output of others, and then react intuitively to make something which apparently has some commercial value. How or why this works is quite beyond my ability to understand. I can only recommend you try the same approach and see if it works.

A precise but diplomatic interrogation of your clients will yield a surprising amount of detail about how they wan their photographs to look: pay attention, and provide what is asked of you. Similarly, maintain an active curiosity about what is going on in the visual world around you: advertising art, the 'fine ' arts, as well as film and editorial illustration are constantly expanding our visual literacy. Become a student of the work of your inspired colleagues and experiment with the techniques that you find appealing. Let your own style evolve naturally.

15.

Optimizing Commercial Work

Introduction

Every photographer evolves a unique working style and a personalized technique for dealing with the amazing variety of commercial assignments. This chapter is not intended to prevent or diminish the value of such development. On the contrary, by offering some practical advice on how to deal with each of the categories of professional work listed in Chapter Two I want to provide a technical and aesthetic foundation upon which to build an efficient business. In Chapter Six I introduced the *Ninety Percent Rule* and the *Law of Extraordinary Effort*; now I want to animate these two basic principals by applying them to examples of real-life photographic tasks.

Studio Product Photography

Job Definition and Expectations

There are three physical categories for studio product photography: pictures of objects which will sit happily on a table-top, pictures of objects which are to big for a table but small enough for the floor, and pictures of objects which are too big for the studio. I

generally deal with objects from the first category, although a small percentage of work involves the second category. I have to rent a big studio from a local TV station once or twice a year to shoot a car or a big industrial machine under controlled conditions.

Usually I will first hear of a particular job over the phone. The work begins with trying to discover what level of photographic sophistication is expected by the client and whether or not the budget can support his or her expectations. If the job is straightforward a face-to-face meeting is not necessary. A big budget or a sophisticated shot usually requires a trip to the clients office, although some people prefer to meet at the studio. In almost every case a detailed layout or at least a sketch is provided; don't make any commitments without first seeing some kind of drawing or sample photo to narrow down the possibilities. It is unwise to take on work on the basis of the message, "I'm sending down a 'thingamajig'. Do what you can with it."

Every object to be photographed has special attributes which are significant to the client. The preliminary discussion must uncover what these attributes are and how they are to be featured. It is advantageous to determine what lighting, format, and background the client expects and to argue civilly for any variations that might make the job easier or better without compromising those expectations.

Film and Equipment

I choose small format equipment for product work only when 35mm slides are required or for close-up work of very tiny objects like coins. (The Micro-Nikkor f2.8/55mm lens is very easy to use and very sharp.) I prefer Kodak Ektachrome EPY Professional (balanced for tungsten light, ISO 50) for slides and I have had very good results with the new Kodak Ektar 25 for very fine grain 35mm color negatives, even under incandescent light. I favor Ilford Pan F (Rated at EI25, slightly under-developed for contrast control in Kodak DK-50 diluted 1:1) for black and white. Because of its very high contrast Kodak Technical Pan Film is much more difficult to work with than Pan F but it is worth the effort when exceptionally detailed b&w work must be done in 35mm. (Specifications, instructions for contrast control, and a special developer for Technical Pan are available from Kodak.)

My instinct, and the choice dictated by the Ninety Percent Rule, is to use medium format for product work whenever possible. A reflex finder with a built-in meter prism plus the interchangeable film backs make my 6 X 6 SLR fast, convenient and inexpensive to operate. I have ended up with a Hasselblad system after extensive experimentation; I find it slightly idiosyncratic but very reliable mechanically. The lenses are exceptional. I have even grown used to the square format, which at first I considered wasteful (most photographs are rectangular) but I have grown to appreciate the convenience of never having to hold the camera sideways.

Most product photos will be reproduced to fit a standard $8^1/2$" X 11" page: blowing up a 6 X 6 negative or transparency to this size is not a problem. My preferred film for this work: Kodak EPY120 for transparencies and Kodak Vericolor VPS II Type L (tungsten balanced and suitable for long exposure times) for color negatives. Ilford FP4 (rated at EI64, slightly under-developed in DK-50 1:1) will handle most black and white work, although I will switch to Pan F when exceptionally fine grain results are required. I use Polaroid 669 for testing with color negative film, Polaroid 668 with reversal films, and Polaroid Type 664 (ISO 100) for testing in black and white. (Type 664 is a perfect exposure match for 100ISO transparency materials.) Type 665 produces a fine-grain negative which is sometimes useful if a b&w enlargement must be pulled in rush; the developer residue and *anti-halation* (flare reducing) coating must be removed (I coax all the goop off with a stream of water from a vinyl hose) and then the film can be fixed (agitate the film in the tray of paper fixer for one minute) and dried conventionally before printing.

The main drawback to my medium format system for product photography is the lack of adjustable perspective control. Virtually all product photographs are shot at a slightly elevated camera position, so the vertical lines of the subject appear to be diverge at the top of the image. I find that in many cases this may be remedied adequately by using a long lens (at least 150mm for 6 X 6 format) to increase subject to camera distance.

Because most of my work is shot on color negative and processed in my own darkroom, there another simple technique I can use to correct perspective; tilting the easel when making enlargements is very similar in effect to tilting or swinging the rear standard of a view camera and offers a valuable degree of correction for diverging or converging parallels. Eliminating distortion from typical product photos requires one side of my 11 X 14 easel to be raised about an inch. The resulting side-to-side disparity in focus can be corrected by stopping down the enlarger lens to f16 or so. (Some enlargers have tilting negative stages and lens mounts to deal with this problem.)

There is no question that the 4 X 5 view camera offers maximum photographic quality and control. The considerable extra effort and expense involved is a fair trade-off when first class work is expected and intended. A well-made 4 X 5 transparency is virtually the industry standard for the ultimate in technical performance, at least in the eyes of most clients and color-separators. I choose 4 X 5 whenever depth of field or perspective must be perfectly controlled or when the final shot is to be reproduced larger than 8½" X 11" (i.e. a billboard, or a double-page spread in a magazine). Fifty percent of the time, however, I work in large format simply because the client expects it.

I use mostly Kodak Vericolor II Type L for 4 X 5 color negatives and Ektachrome 6117 (tungsten) for color transparencies. Ilford FP4 makes truly lovely large format black and white negatives. Polaroid 668, 669, and 665 films are available in 4 X 5 as Polaroid Type 58, 59, and 55. The negative from Type 55 is retrieved the same way as described for Type 665, although the larger negative has a more stubborn anti-halation layer that requires a longer rinse (up to four minutes) to remove. The Polaroid negative is quite good and will certainly do for any photo which is to be reproduced on newsprint or in a smallish magazine ad; however this material has such a wide tonal scale that sometimes contrast can be too low, particularly with a light colored subject and background.

A quick but crisp b&w negative can be made by exposing 4 X 5 FP4 at EI25 and then processing by hand in Ilfospeed Paper Developer for ninety seconds at 68°F with constant gentle agitation followed by a thirty second rinse in running water, and a one minute fix in Edwal Quick-Fix. A fifteen second final wash, a dip in Photo-Flo, and a two minute blast with the hair dryer delivers a printable negative in well under ten minutes.

Backgrounds

Generally a background color or texture will be requested, or at least suggested by the client. For simple table-top work, smooth colored paper or plastic sheets are commonly used for backgrounds; some materials are available already imprinted with a graduated density of color to achieve a contemporary look without having to fuss with the lighting.

Larger objects can be set on nine foot or eleven foot wide *seamless paper* which comes in thirty-six foot lengths and a variety of colors. This stuff is expensive (about $60 per roll

in my area) and fragile. I find it simpler just to paint the studio cove whenever I need a wide background. I can cover my 15 X 15 X 13 foot shooting space with one gallon of decent latex paint in about half an hour; drying time is about two hours.

Many different surfaces of plastic-laminate (Arborite/Formica) are available in 4 X 8ft sheets as are paper-laminate boards and wallboard. Some of the high-gloss or more heavily textured surfaces will require a polarizing filter to cut down unwanted reflections. You will find it convenient to shorten the sheets to 4 X 6ft. for storage and handling.

Photographs of products on pure white backgrounds are requested quite often. A white background makes *close-cutting* easier. Close-cutting is a mechanical process done by the (non-photographic) printer which requires the preparation of a thin red or orange plastic overlay, called a *rubylith*. A sheet of rubylith material is laid over the photograph and a hole is very carefully cut by tracing the outline of the product's image with a fine razor knife. The resulting *mask* is used to completely eliminate all background density during photo/mechanical reproduction of the image.

A product photographed on a white background has a more contemporary look if it appears to have a small shadow. This slight shading, called a *drop-shadow*, is not all that easy to achieve. In order to keep the background pure white, such photos are often close-cut and the drop-shadow is later added later by a retoucher, but this doesn't always look quite right.

There is an easy darkroom technique which preserves both a natural looking drop-shadow and a clean white background. The product in question is shot against a white background; it should be lit to advantage but still have a pleasing shadow. The test strips and test prints are made in the normal way, however, the final print is exposed through a paper *dodging mask* made by cutting a hole in a test print of the photograph. The hole is cut with a razor knife by following along the outer contour of the image (just like a rubylith). Cut around the shadow as if it was a part of the object. Paper masking will eliminate all trace of background tone in color or b&w prints. The mask must be kept moving during the exposure for the drop-shadow to have a soft edge. This technique takes about ten minutes to do and costs less than a dollar.

If the object must be photographed in a messy situation or if the background is visible through openings in the object, a retoucher can paint out, or *opaque*, the negative. He or she applies a light-blocking paint directly to the surface of the negative with a very fine brush. Retouchers prefer to work on 4" X 5" or larger negatives, but uncomplicated shapes can be successfully opaqued on medium format as well. My retoucher charges $25 per negative for this treatment. I charge $25 for paper-masking, as well.

A pure black background is not called for very often, but there are a couple of variations on deep black that can be quite dramatic. The first requires only black seamless and one additional light; the light is filtered to some appropriate color (filter 'gels' which can withstand high temperatures are available from theatrical or cinematic lighting supply houses) and focused behind the subject to form a spot of light with diffused (*feathered*) edges. What results is a very vivid background tone which fades through richer, darker color until it goes to black.

The second variation has an even more contemporary look and works very well with objects which have an interesting surface texture. The product is placed on a clean, unscratched sheet of glossy black acrylic plastic (plexiglass) which has itself been placed beside a perpendicular white card or white painted wall. A diffused spot of light is directed at the white reflector wall/card; its position is adjusted until the camera picks up the reflection of the light on the black plastic as a feathered 'halo' around the subject. An attenuated reflection of the subject will also be visible. The overall effect is quietly elegant particularly for jewelry, glassware and industrial items made of polished metal.

Lighting

In Chapter Eight I introduced the two basic approaches to studio lighting: the first is a broad soft-light which simulates daylight from a large window or sky-light, while the second is a highly 'orchestrated' combination of several small and large sources, each focused and directed so as to enhance or highlight one particular attribute of the subject.

The ersatz-daylight method is by far the easiest approach to product photography, the most common configuration being a single soft-light positioned above and partly behind the subject; a white card is positioned below the camera to reflect light from the overhead source back into the scene in order to 'open up' (*fill*) the shadows. This arrangement gives a pleasing, gently sculptured look to the subject as well as a light foreground which gradually fades into a darker (or black) background. Scaled-down and scaled-up versions of this lighting setup are used to photograph everything from jewelry to food to cars.

I have already suggested a couple of ways to animate a plain background. Adding a third lamp, in this case a slightly diffused 'hard' light positioned behind and above the subject, will provide a *rim light* effect which greatly enhances the illusion of depth by separating the subject from the background. The third light can be fifty to one hundred percent brighter than the main light and adds a feeling of 'three-dimensionality' by emphasizing the shape and surface texture of the subject. Ninety percent of product work can be lit in this way.

The basic three light arrangement must be augmented with additional hardware when shooting either a complicated object or a still life which involves several different objects with a variety of textures and reflectivity. This is the cross-over point between simple and complex lighting. I usually start with a soft-light above or at one side. Different parts of the set are treated different ways; the lighting is built-up, layer by layer, with small spotlights (*baby spots* or *kickers*) and larger lights (like the Lowel DP's) which may be softened with diffusers and/or feathered with barn-doors or tinfoil hoods (*snoots*). Mirror fragments are positioned with putty or plasticene just outside the field of view in order to reflect slivers of light into areas that are too tiny be lit directly. Sometimes paper or tinfoil reflectors are cut to size and taped to the back of glassware and bottles to brighten-up their texture or contents. Similarly, light can be directed upwards through a hole in the set to achieve an even more startling effect with translucent objects. In this work you make your own rules; there are no secret formulas, however the Law of Extraordinary Effort begins to operate as you start attending to the subtleties of lighting in an imaginative way.

Props and Support

Chapter Eleven explored the many support services available to commercial photographers. You must decide for yourself if the budget and the level of sophistication of a particular job justifies calling for outside help.

Early on you will likely be willing to find or make all the props needed for elaborate product shots yourself but as your time becomes more valuable this will seem less and less appealing. Quite often clients can be enlisted to help in this area. Usually the client will supply the product to be photographed and it is likely that some related objects and possibly a background material can be supplied at the same time. For example, if you have been asked to photograph a can of paint perhaps the client has easy access to paintbrushes, stirring sticks, paint trays, etc., and will supply them to you for use as props. The same client might have a used painter's drop-cloth which would make an interesting background. All you have to do is ask.

Setting up the Studio for Product Work

I have a copy stand with a motorized shooting platform built into one wall of the studio. It's very handy for 'table-top' shots of very small products because the finger-tip control over the height of the shooting stage allows the selection of a comfortable working height. The platform is only two feet square, so for larger objects I extend its size by clamping on a larger piece of plywood. The edge closest to the camera is supported from underneath with a small light stand once the working height has been determined. A useful alternate is to make a small shooting table with a *Black & Decker Workmate*, a very versatile portable work-stand available at any hardware store.

Larger objects are shot on a makeshift table which consists of a sheet of $3/4$" plywood laid over a couple of Work-Mates or simple collapsible saw-horses. Objects to big for such a table go directly on the floor.

As I mentioned in Chapter Seven, some sort of lighting grid suspended from the studio ceiling makes complicated lighting much less difficult by eliminating the clutter of light-stands and wires. If such an arrangement is not possible, I recommend that in addition to several conventional light-stands you obtain one heavy-duty stand and a *light-boom* such as the one manufactured by Manfrotto. The boom will suspend the main-light above the set and allow precise manual remote control over its orientation. Actually, even with a ceiling grid, there are many situations where the boom will be indispensable for precisely locating a critical light or reflector.

After having created a couple of fancy lighting setups you will recognize the significance of my earlier suggestion to equip the shooting space with several independently fused switched outlets in strategic locations. Lacking such a luxury, make sure that only industrial-strength extension cords with reliable connectors are used to supply the electricity for those power-hungry incandescent lamps. I will repeat my earlier warning that quartz-halogen lights are fire hazards. A tightly focussed beam from a 1000 watt lamp can easily ignite paper, cardboard, cloth or wood. Keep an extinguisher nearby.

Remember that expensive quartz lights will fail if jarred sharply while operating. It is a good idea to secure light-stand legs and power cables to the floor with gaffer tape.

All product photography with tungsten lights will involve sufficiently long exposure times to warrant a sturdy camera support. Life is much easier if a studio camera stand is used for this important purpose rather than the ubiquitous tripod. On location the tripod is a practical tool because it is light-weight and compact. In the studio, the main function of a camera support is to keep everything steady while allowing complete freedom of movement when necessary. Studio stands are designed with locking wheels for ease of travel around the shooting area and they have counter-balanced camera supports which facilitate quick and precise height adjustment. A good studio-stand is a worthwhile investment, particularly for careful work with 4 X 5 equipment.

Editorial Photography

Definitions and Expectations

Photojournalism is not included within the province of commercial photographers because of the popular notion that news is not a product to be bought and sold. Photojournalists, therefore, are supposed to be removed in some way from the corrupting influences of the marketplace. Editorial photography (the kissing cousin to photojournalism) is very much a part of the business world in that it supports and delivers two clearly defined products: entertainment and information. Photographers who work for magazine art directors are expected to be sensitive to both editorial policy and design philosophy so as to produce work which fits into an ongoing format. Creativity, originality and insight are expected and appreciated as long as the style of the publication is not compromised. The editorial photographer is an instrument of cultural propaganda, and as such, must go out into the world and extract from it images that suit a particular ideology. Diplomacy is as important as photographic technique.

Film and Equipment

The 'look' of a magazine is the responsibility of the *art director*, or AD. It is important to realize that photography, despite the fact that it may sometimes take up more space than the written work, is only one of several components; the *writer*, together with his or her *story editor*, determines the thrust and tone of the article, the art director will have specific ideas as to how the article can be reinforced visually, and the photographer is expected to quickly produce stylish images that will enhance those ideas.

Normally you will consult with the AD over the phone and a layout and a few relevant *tearsheets* (printed samples of work the magazine has previously published) will be sent to you by courier. In very tight situations, a quick sketch may be 'faxed'. It is important to study the tearsheets in order to fully understand what style of work is expected. It is prudent to obtain some back issues of the magazine for the same reason. Sometimes you will speak directly to the writer or editor in order to get a clearer idea of the purpose of their story, but always remember your client is the art director.

Always find out exactly what time-frame you will be expected to accommodate. Deadlines are very, very important in the magazine business. Not all art directors have a clear understanding of photography so they sometimes make demands without regard to the technicalities: have enough presence of mind to avoid dead-end situations. Right from the beginning of negotiations be realistic about deadlines and straightforward about limitations imposed by the medium itself.

Sometimes you will be asked to take care of processing, but very often undeveloped exposed film must be sent to the client by direct messenger. Good exposure technique will reduce the risk of a technical embarrassment; always bracket at least $\pm^2/_3$ stop with reversal film.

Virtually all color photographs reproduced in magazines come from 35mm or $2^1/_4$" X $2^1/_4$" slides. Events which must be documented on the run, such as political meetings or campaigns, sports, and the performing arts, can be shot on 35mm, but cover shots and important portraits will likely be requested on medium format. Some magazine work is done in black & white.

Most of the editorial work I do is shot with ISO 100 Kodak Ektachrome EPP; half on roll-film, and half on 35mm. Fast-moving subjects require higher-speed films, and even grainy super-fast emulsions are acceptable if important images cannot be made any other way. The selection of equipment varies according to the subject matter and the time available for shooting. Some sensitive 'reportage' situations require very discreet 35mm work with available light and long lenses while an environmental portrait of a businessman or politician might call for some heavy-duty lighting and the Hasselblad. Exotic editorial illustrations are sometimes shot on 4 X 5, as are most photographs intended for publication in architectural magazines. Expect to spend more time arranging access to people and places then actually shooting.

Locations and Backgrounds

Some editorial assignments involve studio and location still-life work and the techniques will be similar to those used for product photography. The selection of backgrounds, however, will require a slightly different approach; in editorial work the **context** is just as important as the subject. For example, an agricultural story might require a photo illustrating a particular kind of grain; the AD would likely prefer a shot of a sunburnt, callused hand holding the seeds in front of some interestingly textured sacks or farm machinery rather than a slick-looking seamless back-drop.

Unless isolation of the subject serves the purpose of the story, editorial portraiture is similarly contextual. Businessmen or women are photographed in their working environment, typically an office or factory, scientist will be shot in their labs, athletes in the gym or on the playing field. Often such portraits will include other people, and your job will be to illustrate some sort of working relationship. If your diplomatic skills are good you will generally be quite free to orchestrate the photograph to suit yourself. Be selective about the background elements that are included in the photographs, and chose areas and objects that are editorially significant but also geometrically pleasing. Unless there is some purpose in doing otherwise, try to line up the camera so that vertical lines in rooms, buildings and other structures appear vertical in the photos.

Lighting and Shooting Technique

Editorial work involves photography of both people and objects so electronic flash is more useful than incandescent lighting. Nevertheless, don't forgo a tripod because many situations can be shot successfully with available light.

Magazine assignments must be done quickly because of tight deadlines and because the subjects of the photos often have little time to spare for posing. Consequently, I have developed a very compact lighting kit that is easy to carry and simple to set up and tear down. I've permanently attached a 400ws flash generator with a large easy-to-grip handle to one leg of a wheeled, collapsible light-stand on which is also mounted a fan-cooled flash-head with an extra-bright (500 watt) quartz model-light. A small tripod, a 72" silver/white umbrella, and a heavy-duty extension cord are secured to the light-stand with a bungee cord (a strong elastic strap with hooks at each end). In addition to two cameras bodies, lenses, and film, I carry in my camera bag a flashmeter, a replacement model-lamp, and a remote infrared trigger which allows cordless flash-synch. In the car I pack a back-up portable flash, a 100' extension cord, and a folding reflector which I occasionally use to help fill in harsh shadows. If a light-colored wall or ceiling is not conveniently located for bounce-flash, the large umbrella is a very useful and attractively broad light source with soft shadows. It also collapses quickly for easy movement through doorways. The short flash duration and the remote trigger system allow fast and convenient hand-held shooting in either 35mm or $2^1/_4$ X $2^1/_4$ format. At 400ws the flash is usually bright enough to overpower the ambient light so color balance is not a problem.

In some circumstances, for example a portrait which includes a relatively dim computer screen, I put the camera on the tripod, and shoot by available light. Sometimes it is easier to simply turn off the room lights and use the model-lamp as the main source. If the room is lit by fluorescent lights a *30M (magenta) gelatin filter* (available in various sizes from Kodak) will usually correct the greenish color-caste for Ektachrome daylight film. Usually no filtration is required with daylight film under mercury-vapor lamps, although I have used as much as 30R (red) in some locations. Yellow sodium-vapor lamps, ordinary tungsten fixtures and the model-lamp by itself all work fine with unfiltered tungsten-balanced Ektachrome.

From time to time a shot of a person or an important object within a large fluorescently lit room requires *balanced flash,* a combination of available light and filtered electronic flash. In this technique, the camera is placed on the tripod and a 30M filter is used over the lens. A 30G (green) gel is positioned over the flash-head in order to match the color temperature of the flash to that of the ambient fluorescents. The camera aperture must be adjusted to give the correct flash exposure, and the shutter speed is adjusted to accommodate the fluorescents. A typical exposure for 100ISO Ektachrome might be f11 at $^1/_4$sec. (With a little coaching, people are quite good at staying still for up to one second.) No color correction is necessary when using this technique to balance flash and daylight or when shooting in black and white. Unfiltered balanced flash is commonly used to preserve a natural look when working in a room with large windows and an interesting view of the outside.

The majority of editorial clients will be satisfied with sharp, well-exposed slides which show what they asked for consequently ninety percent of editorial assignments can be shot with the imaginative use of a single flash in combination with the available light. Nevertheless, any extraordinary effort will be immediately noticed. Magazine art directors are very talented people but they are constantly frustrated by the hassle of having to find competent photographers in distant places that can be trusted to do even marginally acceptable work. Competent work, delivered on time, is very much appreciated. If you go farther and produce a few clever variations in lighting and composition in addition to fulfilling the basic requirements, you will delight your clients and assure your place in an exciting market. This may require hauling around a more elaborate lighting kit or some diplomatic begging for more time from busy people but it will be well worth the effort.

Support

There are two kinds of support in editorial work. The first kind should come from clients. Magazines spotlight intense, controversial, and very contemporary people and issues. Getting close enough fast enough and produce timely photographs is not always easy. If clients are not prepared to make introductory calls or help you work through the inevitable glitches, much time will be wasted and the effectiveness of the photography can be compromised. Unfortunately, some editorial clients fade into the background after the initial telephone contact; they feel they are buying an aggressive 'point-man' and a hot-shot photographer in one stroke. By taking such an unsupportive tack clients are avoiding their own 'homework' and demanding a service which they don't really pay for. Should the AD, the writer, or the editor refuse to help arrange access to difficult people or locations, try and persuade them to free up a lesser personage, perhaps a *research assistant* or even a secretary, to do a little work on the telephone in aid of your project.

In the case of particularly troublesome clients that you wish not to offend, you must do all the legwork yourself or hire an assistant to do it for you. Happily, that's not the only type of support that an assistant can render; some enthusiastic help on location can mean the deference between ordinary and extraordinary photography. An intelligent and self-motivated assistant can not only arrange the necessary approvals in advance of a complicated shoot, but also have the appropriate equipment in place before you arrive and then tear it all down after you're done. You won't have to search for cameras, lenses and loaded film backs during the shoot either, so the distractions will be at a minimum. Busy subjects will appreciate the fact that someone is on hand to take care of the technical details and will consequently relate to you as more of an equal; the better the rapport, the better your work can be.

In the Studio

Editorial still-life is of course technically very similar to ordinary product photography, however stylistically it needs to be somewhat bolder. The AD will normally have some definite suggestions, but when it is left up to you, study what has been published previously and then make an imaginative leap of faith.

When people are to be photographed in the studio, have everything prepared ahead of time so that they will not be inconvenienced or irritated. Clothes and accessories should be discussed in advance, but have them bring extra, just in case. Most subjects (even businessmen) are soothed and relaxed by the attentions of a hair/make-up stylist.

Magazine clients expect the studio portraits they commission to be stronger and more exotic than conventional portraiture. This might mean specially painted backdrops or high-contrast lighting or simply an unusual point of view. Sometimes conflicts can develop because the approach which best serves the editorial purpose may not always be the most flattering to the subject. It takes some skill to smooth ruffled feathers and you might have to deflect a little flak on behalf of your client in such circumstances; this is not an occupation for the squeamish. As a rule I avoid working for those art directors who expect me to be unkind on their behalf.

Rates

Every magazine has its own payment schedule; either a day-rate or page-rate, plus expenses. Magazines are very forthright about rates and rather inflexible; you will not have to guess what your work is worth to them. Editorial assignments for national magazines pay about half of what is typically paid for commercial advertising photography in big cities.

National magazines will pay $400 to $500 plus expenses such as film, processing, and travel for a typical assignment which might involve a day's work yielding anywhere from one to five specific images. Expect fifty percent more for a cover. Local magazines pay about half the national rates, or even less, and they are usually more than willing to trade advertising space in exchange for photographic services.

Annual Reports and Executive Portraiture

Definitions and Expectations

Working directly for corporations is much like editorial photography. There is a similar mix of studio product shots, location portraiture and industrial views, however the financial stakes are higher; rates are often double what is paid for editorial assignments. The philosophical approach is unashamedly partisan, with the emphasis on a stridently positive presentation.

The work will be assigned by an independent designer retained by the corporation, by an advertising agency art director, or by someone in-house, perhaps an executive-assistant in charge of *public relations* (PR). In the first two instances, all the familiar rules of working with visually-literate professionals apply, but in the case of the in-house art director, some extra attention is required. Corporations look carefully at each other's annual reports and a particularly lavish production by IBM or Xerox will inspire many enthusiastic PR people in smaller firms. Since they are often unaware of the real costs and effort involved, my first question to such people is always, "Are you working with a designer?". If the answer is negative, I try to convince them of the advantages of hiring a professional designer, and I recommend one or two or three of my designer clients who might be suitable.

Should the professional design route be rejected, the job will involve a lot more than photography. If the client recognizes and respects good work and is willing to take some advice, the project can be good fun and professionally stimulating, although it is unlikely that any non-photographic 'design' services can be billed directly. When the client is unable to make decisions based on photographic realities, or if every aspect of the work must be 'approved' by someone higher-up in the corporate structure, the assignment can be a nightmare of false-starts and re-shoots. It is difficult, but prudent, to determine in advance exactly who will be evaluating the photography and what criterion will apply. A policy should be developed to deal with re-shoots and cancellations requested by the client or the client's superiors. Tact is of the essence as corporate egos can be monumental.

Deadlines are just as important in annual report work as for editorial work. Businesses are obliged by law to produce financial information at specific points in their accounting cycle; make certain that corporate clients are aware how long it will take to produce decent photography. If clients ask for additional work during the course of the project, they should be clearly told how delivery times will be affected.

Film and Equipment

The tools of choice for annual report photography are virtually identical to what one would select to do good editorial shooting, however higher budgets and longer lead-times make larger format and slower films the favorites. That is not to say that 35mm is unacceptable, but simply that all small format work must be technically first-class.

I have found that corporate assignments which originate out-of-town must be shot on transparency film. On the other hand, annual reports which are designed and printed locally can often be shot on color negative, with the big selling point being the economic advantage of having prints made to size for *gang-separation*. The photo-mechanical process for color printing requires the preparation of three individual black and white 'separations' which represent the cyan, yellow, and magenta components of the image to be reproduced. In *four color printing* these three colors, plus black, are laid down one at a time with different inks.

Nowadays, separations are made electronically on a precision *laser scanner*. Color prints or color transparencies can be accommodated with the flick of a switch. The typical industrial-size scanner will accept images up to twenty-four inches square. The separations are made the same size as the final size for reproduction. Significant savings are realized if several small images are separated together (gang-separated) rather than just one at a time. Because color balance and size are adjusted during the separation process, the individual images to be gang-separated must be *color-matched* and sized proportionally (i.e. all photographs made to 100% of the final reproduction size, all 150% of the final size, etc.); this is easy to accomplish with color prints.

Lighting and Shooting Technique

Generally speaking, corporate work proceeds at a more dignified and deliberate pace than editorial shooting. There will be more time and more co-operation because the client will have a fairly clear notion that your purpose in being in his or her office or factory is beneficial. Some individuals, for their own mysterious reasons, resent any sort of interruption but as a rule a pleasant, considerate attitude will make shooting in the workplace a morale-raiser for everyone.

You will have enough time to work, but you will still be expected to work efficiently. Both executives and production workers have busy schedules so time-out for photography costs the money. A shot involving a machine inside a manufacturing plant might temporarily shut down an entire assembly line and idle a dozen or more workers. As I mentioned earlier, annual reports must (to be blunt about it) glorify corporate activity and this often demands more sophisticated lighting and a some 'set' preparation. In an industrial situation this involves transporting and setting-up a couple of lightstands, umbrellas, and a big power-pack, cleaning-up grimy machines and floors, as well as keeping an eye out for safety hazards; this is not a one-man or one-woman deal. An assistant is just plain necessary and it is definitely inefficient to try to do this sort of work without help.

My assistant and I work as team to move, set up, and tear down equipment. We have found that a collapsible two-wheeled dolly is very handy for transporting heavy gear through corporate offices and factories. The flash generator is strapped in at the bottom for balance, with camera and film bags on top. A tripod, two light-weight wheeled light-stands and two umbrellas are attached to the back with elastic cords. We carry long extension cords in crank operated *wire-caddies* (available at hardware stores).

A typical corporate/industrial scenario begins with the selection of a day, or days, for photography. This might be arranged after a walking tour of the facility a few days earlier, but usually the site is previewed the morning of the shoot and a logical shooting schedule is mapped out at that time. The client, be it a PR person or a designer, will then tell people when they will be needed for pictures and what preparation their work-area requires. Even the *CEO*, (chief executive officer), needs to clean up his desk.

Some industrial installations are just too big to light, but most machinery-shots involve people so the scale is more manageable. I usually talk to whoever is to be in the photo at the same time as I am setting up the lighting; just a breezy patter, to set a relaxed mood. Typically a main light, most often a 72" umbrella, is placed slightly to one side of the subject and angled carefully to also light the background machinery. A second light, also a fairly big umbrella, is positioned somewhere behind and above the subject to provide some rim/back-light on both the person and his or her tools. Care must be taken to avoid distracting reflections from shiny metal surfaces.

While I have been arranging the lighting, my assistant will have found a power outlet, checked up on the location of the circuit-breakers, connected the flash generator, and begun to clean up the shooting area. (We carry paper towels and spray cleaner with us.) The scene is metered with a flashmeter, and a Polaroid test is taken as standard procedure. If the worker is doing some other task while we set up, my assistant stands-in for the test. The real subject is actually needed only for the few minutes during which two or three

rolls of film are fired-off. Exposures are bracketed ±^{2}/$_3$ of a stop for transparency film, and not bracketed at all for negative film. When I'm satisfied that I have a good shot, all the stuff is wheeled 'tout ensemble' to the next location.

White-collar corporate work unfolds in exactly the same way, except that site clean-up consists of rearranging office furniture and accessories rather than scrubbing grease off machines. Very busy executives and the CEO will have been informed well in advance of the session, but you can expect only ten to fifteen minutes of their undivided attention for the actual shooting. Group shots are even worse; the behavioral age of people in groups seems to decrease in inverse proportion to the number of people involved. Sometimes one has to be quite stern. Call in the most senior people just before you're ready to shoot; they are usually the most impatient and their appearance has a disciplinary effect on their colleagues.

Portraits of CEO's and other heavy-hitters require special attention. Whether they are male or female they must appear to be strong, honest, bold, sensitive, kind, generous, intelligent, healthy and attractive. This is not always easy to achieve. The environmental elements must be carefully chosen; good taste and a harmonious balance of textures is important. Watch out for objects in the background which might appear to 'grow' out of the top of a head, such as vertical seams in walls or pole-lamps. Even the jazziest offices have lots of silly 'collectables' laying around; avoid including anything shabby, worn, or vulgar. Clothing should be conservative and properly fitted. Hair should be neat without any 'stray' strands. A little pancake make-up will disguise most facial blemishes.

There are a number of sturdy-looking postures which will work for ^{3}/$_4$ length portraits but whatever the pose, make certain that the subject's back is straight; this will contribute to a look of sincerity and alertness. Men should keep their hands away from the crotch, women should make sure that their legs and necklines are organized in some dignified way. A slight forward lean, combined with a warm expression gives either gender a look of quiet strength. Slight diffusion is sometimes very effective in some 'informal' working portraits. Something to hold makes people feel and look more 'in charge'; try pens, eyeglasses, business related books and folders or even one of the firm's products if the scale is appropriate. The mechanical aspects of 'holding something' (i.e. the position of fingers and arms) should appear natural and unobtrusive.

Lighting for executive portraits may be somewhat unconventional for younger individuals or companies; strong side-light combined with a hard, bright rim light adds energy to an executive portrait. Older executives and conservative firms eschew drama in favor of a more 'classic' look.

Support

Your assistant is your main helper, but it is necessary to have a corporate heavy-weight somewhere in the background to call on in case of difficulty. This person will most likely be the executive immediately superior to the PR person who is your escort at the site and he or she should be the one to put pressure on any uncooperative types. Every job will have a tense moment or two when access to some important person or location is unexpectedly blocked; life is much easier if the political clout is on your side.

Public Relations Photography

PR photography is a hybrid of editorial and corporate work; a super-charged version of the indefatigable optimism common to all annual reports combined with an accelerated editorial technique. Budgets are smaller, and most assignments focus on one-time 'events' such as press conferences, awards presentations or trade shows.

The results of PR photography are either handed out as 'souvenir' prints to the participants in the special events, published in the corporate newsletter or included as part of a press-release aimed at magazines or newspapers. This type of photography is commonly shot on color negative, from which both color and b&w prints can be pulled. The occasional slide might be copied from a print or else made directly from the negative by a color lab. The latter method is technically superior so it is preferred when the slide is intended for reproduction. The former is very quick and usually satisfactory, for a slide which will appear only in an audio-visual (AV) or video presentation.

Elaborate PR work is technically very similar to annual report photography. Most often, however, simple flash-on-camera lighting and a 28/90mm zoom lens on a 35mm camera loaded with Vericolor III Type S film will do the trick. When large proofs are required I shoot Kodak Vericolor 400 in medium format. Many of the events which must be recorded in this work occur in small rooms, so bounce flash can be used to upgrade the quality of light. A small flash-mounted soft-box can make the light more flattering if the room is large. PR 'events' usually require the photographer to wear a suite and tie.

Audio-Visual Presentations

AV work is another hybrid style. It embraces many of the techniques of product, editorial and public relations photography. Only recently, all audio-visual shows were 35mm slide shows, but now video presentations are almost as popular. Generally speaking, the electronic media works best for small groups so there is still a considerable demand for conventional photography. Many video presentations are, in fact, based on electronic reproduction and manipulation of 35mm slides.Shooting for AV is much like making a movie. The work is scripted and a detailed shot list, or *story-board*, will be provided. Some studio photos will be necessary, but since AV shows are usually intended to sell a service, or to teach someone how to perform a service, there will be a greater proportion of location shooting.

Most AV budgets are on the slim side, so you will be expected to work quickly. The slides do not have to look as slick as those

103

intended for a magazine or an annual report, but on-camera flash lighting will not do. One umbrella/flash-head on a rolling light stand will be satisfactory, however, as will zoom lenses and a moderately fast film, such as Ektachrome 200. From time to time some extra lighting may be required for complicated shots, but most often, a single light and/or available light will suffice. (Fluorescent lighting should be corrected with a 30M filter, as discussed earlier.)

Because AV presentations are supposed to be shot according to a predetermined plan, the production company will usually have one or two people accompany the photographer on location. Often these people are willing to 'assist' during the shooting, so an 'official' assistant will likely be unnecessary; tactfully inquire ahead of time if, in fact, this will be the case.

Slide shows tend to be 'quick and dirty' projects, with long work days and relatively low remuneration, sometimes only a couple of hundred dollars per day. On the plus side, you will come in contact with many business people whom you may wish to contact in the future (provided there is no objection from the AV firm), and you will get a thorough technical work-out. The production people, being highly skilled in location diplomacy, know how to organize things efficiently so watching them in operation will be a valuable learning experience. AV shows require hundreds of slides so a certain degree of experimentation is welcome and a few reshoots are not unexpected.

Catalog Photography

Almost all catalog work will be done in the studio. There is a tremendous range of quality and budgets to match. Many studios survive on annual 'bread and butter' catalog accounts.

The most basic catalogs are shot in black and white. Relatively high contrast prints with plain white backgrounds are favored for reproduction on newsprint. It is not unusual to shoot a couple of dozen objects, perhaps packaged food or hardware items, with virtu-ally the same lighting and camera position. Such consistency is actually preferred and most catalog shots are routinely retouched to eliminate distracting reflections or shadows that result because of the constraints imposed on the lighting. Sometimes 4 X 5 Polaroids are satisfactory as 'final' prints. Rapid turn-around and very short deadlines are the norm. Retouching is usually the client's responsibility.

In my area, low-budget studios charge as little as $25 per shot; a photographer working for $15 per hour might be expected to produce forty or fifty pictures in eight hours. This is basically the rock-bottom of commercial photography.

Moving upward on the catalog scale takes us into color books with higher production values. A more sophisticated approach is needed, with a more individual treatment of each item. The point of view might be more or less the same for every shot, and one background color or texture might be used throughout as a stylistic device. All the photography is expected to tastefully demonstrate the important attributes of the product being sold.

Rates here start at about $400 per page, with anything from one to ten photographs, each shot to exact size for gang-separation, per page. A major catalog could be two hundred pages, so sometimes the photography will be split between several studios. Because many catalogs feature light-colored objects such as jewelry, tools and chrome appliances, transparencies are preferred, so an 8" X 10" view camera is indispensable. Catalog clients will expect any photographer that takes on their work to accommodate all items, big or small. A large studio with a loading dock to handle truck-loads of merchandise, including appliances and furniture, is a necessity.

Smaller scale specialty catalogs are more manageable for the one-man or one-woman operation. Such pieces are produced by some of the high-profile retail chain stores or even well-heeled industrial supply houses of various kinds. All that is required, aside from the basic skills for high-quality product photography, is a sympathetic approach to the needs of the target market and a willingness to learn enough about the specialized products to shoot them in an imaginative but appropriate context. Usually a designer will be involved before the photographer, but if not, the client should at least be informed of the value of professional design and provided with a couple of names. Sometimes the photography will involve one relatively contemporary background, say high-gloss black plexiglass, used in several slightly different ways with an assortment of products. Sometimes more elaborate sets must be built and propped, perhaps weathered barnwood shelves for fancy kitchen utensils or chrome-wire grids for computer hardware.

Color Balance Considerations

As a rule catalogue photographs will be reproduced side-by-side and slight variations in color balance will be painfully obvious and quite distracting so consistent color balance is a subtle but important consideration. It is therefore extremely important to stick to one emulsion batch and the same processing lab when shooting a multi-shot job. Similarly, it is best to use the same lighting fixtures and bulbs throughout, as the color temperature of both bulbs and reflectors can change over time. The color response characteristics of film, particularly reversal film, changes with temperature, so make certain that whatever material is taken from the freezer has enough time to warm up to room temperature. A fifty sheet box of 4 X 5 film will need at least four hours to get from $-10°F$ to $+70°F$.

Should several white objects, such as running shoes or dinnerware, have to be shot on transparency film with different color backgrounds, the objects will pick up a color-caste from the background and no two whites will look the same. This is awfully unprofessional looking, and it is worth some effort to talk the client or designer into selecting a single color for all the shots. If this is impossible, however, some improvement can be affected by raising the objects off the background by an inch or two. Changing the angle of the object relative to the plane of the background surface can also reduce color contam-

ination. As a last resort, each photo can be filtered slightly to bring all the whites to one color. This will require some testing and a selection of Kodak *gelatin* color correction (CC) filters. Obviously, it is much easier to fix the color by individually balancing prints made from color negatives.

Copywork

Some types of photography are not very glamorous, and copywork is a good example; the skills required are very simple, the time involved is negligible, and the necessary equipment is inexpensive. Nevertheless, refusing work because it is too 'ordinary' is like throwing away all your pocket change at the end of the day; it's just not sensible.

Copywork (or 'flatwork') is the reproduction of some existing two-dimensional image through photographic means. The image to be reproduced could be anything: a photographic slide or print, an architectural rendering, or even an illustration from a book or magazine. The copy itself might end up as a 35mm slide, an 8" X 10" print, or a wall size mural. The basic criteria are sharpness, color fidelity and contrast control. There are a few simple tricks that can make the work easier.

Lighting

I prefer tungsten light for copy work; a bright, continuous source speeds up both focusing and lining up the camera. A little care must be taken with heat-sensitive originals, but usually there is no problem.

The basic arrangement for flatwork places the camera exactly perpendicular to the material being copied and lights are positioned at 45° on either side of the camera in order to project an even field of illumination. A single light is perfectly acceptable for copy work as long it can be adjusted for uniform brightness over the whole image area; the focusing capability of the Lowel DP lamp is very handy in this regard.

When the material to be photographed is not perfectly flat, changing the angle of the light will sometimes eliminate unwanted reflections and *hot-spots* but some shiny, irregular surfaces (an oil-painting, for example) cannot be accommodated in this way. In such difficult cases the only remedy is *polarization*.

How Polarizers Work

Consider light as composed of energized particles, called 'photons', which vibrate as they travel along an otherwise straight path. The *frequency* (the number of vibrations per second) determine the color of the light. The plane of the vibrations relative to the direction of travel determines the *polarity* of the light. Generally, the polarization of light is more or less random, which is to say that the photons vibrate in any and all directions. A *polarizing filter* has a wonderful ability to transmit only those photons which are vibrating in one particular plane. The particular plane is called the *axis of polarization*. Two polarizing filters placed so that their respective axes of polarization are oriented at 90° to one another will be perfectly opaque to all light. (This property may be invoked electrically in certain materials. *Liquid crystal displays*, or LCD's, operate on this principle.)

Many materials reflect or absorb light of only one polarity. For photographic purposes the reflectivity of such materials may be reduced by controlling the polarity of the illumination. Polarizing filters for lights are available in heat resistant sheets through suppliers of theatrical lighting equipment. Polarizing filters suitable for use with photographic lenses are made of optical quality glass and are available at any camera store. Virtually all troublesome reflections may be removed when both the copy-camera and the copy-lights are polarized.

Lenses

There is no such thing as a 'perfect' optical system, and each photographic lens will excel at some particular task. Most lenses for general shooting, including wide-angle, normal, and telephoto types, are designed to be used in situations where the size of the subject exceeds the size of the image at the film plane by a factor of approximately ten to one. In addition, their performance is optimized for distant subjects. This means that for precise copying of small images a special purpose lens is required. My 55mm Micro-Nikkor is such a lens. For the larger formats, lenses specifically designed for copy work are designated as *process lenses* or *apochromatic (apo) lenses*. They are usually quite expensive. In most circumstances, however, any good quality 'taking' lens will do a reasonable job if the image to be copied is 8" X 10" or larger, and if the lens aperture is set two or three stops smaller than maximum. Stopping down in this way increased depth of field and reduces many *aberrations* (optical deficiencies) that exist a maximum aperture, while avoiding image degradation which occurs as a result of *diffraction* at the very small apertures.

Mechanical Considerations

As I mentioned, the camera must always be positioned exactly perpendicular the surface of the material being copied. Of course it must be held very still for maximum definition. The most reliable method of achieving this precise condition is to use a copystand, which in it's simplest form has a baseboard and a column much like an enlarger's. The camera is attached to the column by way of a mounting-plate which may be adjusted for height with a knob. Two (sometimes four) lights are permanently attached to the baseboard at the prescribed 45° angle.

Such a setup works fine for most copywork, but when shooting a lot of different size originals the constant variation of camera height can be hard on the back. I prefer to have the camera at a fixed level which allows me to keep my back straight, so I built a copystand with an adjustable baseboard. The copystand is suitable for originals up to 24 X 36" but for really big drawings and posters I find it is more convenient to tape them to the back wall of the studio and line up the camera with a spirit level. In Chapter Seven I described how I mounted the ceiling-lights in my shooting space to work as copy-lighting. A wheeled studio-stand makes it easy to change the position of the camera.

Film, Format and Technique

The selection of film and format depends on the intended use of the copy-photo. Vericolor Type L negative film is so very good that I am able to handle most of my copy work with the Hasselblad; I frequently use copy negatives produced with this way to make multiple 8 X 10's of architectural renderings. To copy artwork or graphics that will end up as large display panels or Duratrans posters in bus shelters, I always use 4 X 5 Vericolor L. I make very presentable copy slides from color prints and drawings with the 55mm Micro-Nikkor and Kodak EPY tungsten balanced Ektachrome. In this case I use a gray-card in combination with the camera's built-in meter to determine the starting exposure. Extreme close-up work, with an image to subject ratio of 1:2 or less, will require some exposure compensation. This is automatically taken into account with BTL (behind-the-lens) meters, but for 4 X 5 I start with an incident light meter reading and then confirm with a Polaroid test.

Excellent duplicate transparencies can be made very inexpensively at any professional lab, but from time to time I make them myself by inverting my Chromega enlarger's color head and shooting Ektachrome EPY in my Nikon. The Micro-Nikkor must be used with an *extension tube* (a carefully made cylinder which fits between the lens and the camera body to permit close focusing) for the necessary 1:1 magnification. EPY is sufficiently sharp for this purpose but copy slides from anything harder than moderately contrasty originals tend to be unattractively harsh. I have found that contrast may be modified by introducing some *controlled flare*. For low-contrast originals I mask off the part of enlarger light source not covered by the slide itself but for high-contrast originals I omit the masking because the subtle flare produced by the spill-light has exactly the right contrast-reducing effect.

Color Fidelity

As we have seen, sharpness is a photo-mechanical problem which is resolved by keeping the camera properly aligned and very steady, by focusing accurately, and by using a fine-grain film. Maintaining color fidelity, however, is a matter of understanding the *spectral response of photographic materials*, rather than something which can be accomplished by a particular technique.

It is necessary to understand that color *fidelity* is not the same as color *balance*. Correct color balance is a rather subjective and imprecise term which describes a print or slide which has no overall color bias; when grays are gray, and skies are blue, and grass is green, and skin looks 'normal', color balance is said to be 'neutral'. On the other hand, color fidelity has to do with accuracy and implies that the film, and film processing, as well as the enlarging paper and paper processing will respond in a linear and predictable manner to a full palette of color. In other words, true color fidelity is achieved only when all colors are reproduced on photographic materials exactly as they appear in reality. Unfortunately, this serendipitous state of affairs will never happen because the color we see in prints and slides is generated by organic dyes which are physically limited in their ability to imitate the real world. An extreme but cogent example; a fluorescent yellow tennis ball will never look anything but a dull yellow-green when photographed because the colors in a print or a slide can only be a chemical approximation of 'real' colors. Ektachrome will never glow in the dark.

All this can be expressed in numbers with graphs of spectral sensitivities and responses, but the bottom line is simply that photographic materials are not honest about some colors. This can be very bothersome for precision copy work, particularly architectural renderings, where color fidelity is extremely important.

Problems arise when certain paints and inks trigger the wrong response; one type of green used by a certain manufacturer of popular felt-pens reads as yellow with Ektachrome and lavender with Vericolor Type L and Ektaprint paper. The probable explanation of this is the addition of ultraviolet or infrared optical brighteners to various pigments and dyes. These brighteners are often present even in photographic papers. Sometimes the solution is to switch films, for example Fujichrome Professional handles many blues and greens much differently than Ektachrome and Vericolor.

Any client who expects copy-prints which closely match their originals should be informed of the limitations of the medium. Comprehensive testing is the only way to achieve totally predictable results. Once the value of color-testing is understood, the artists who produce renderings and perspectives that are intended to be copied will usually try and select colors according to how well they photograph. Photographers are not responsible for photography's technological shortcomings as long as clients are kept well informed.

Contrast Control

In Chapter Twelve I described the value of contrast-masking for difficult negatives. This technique may also be used for controlling excessive contrast in copy-work, although such an inconvenient and expensive approach should be considered only as a last resort.

Every copy-photo will pick up a little contrast, and in the case of some soft, pastel-like originals (such as old faded photographs) this is not an alarming situation. When contrast does become intrusive, the introduction of controlled flare (described earlier in relation to slide duplicating) is the easiest remedy. This technique can be used with reflective originals by simply using a white background rather than black.

Although conventional practice officially precludes the manipulation of contrast in color materials by chemical means, I have found that both Ektachrome and Vericolor films respond well to slight changes in processing. With color negative materials a reduction of fifteen seconds in the first developer can induce a significant drop in contrast without any particularly noticeable color shifts; the slight drop in density may be corrected by increasing the exposure by 25%. Transparency materials behave the same way although a slight decrease in maximum density (D-max) can be expected; development

must be reduced by forty-five seconds. Contrast can be increased by extending developing times. Variations of more than ±15sec. for negatives and ±45sec. for transparencies are not recommended.

Rates

Usually I charge $35 for a single 6 X 6 or 4 X 5 copy negative, but offer a reduction if several are to be made at the same time from similar sized originals. I charge $10 for a 35mm copy slide from originals 16" X 24" or less in size, and $25 for slides of larger originals. A 4 X 5 copy transparency is worth $55. Prints from copy negatives are billed the same way as prints from ordinary negatives.

Copy work is often required in a hurry, particularly by architects and real-estate developers. 'Life and death' situations may require working extended hours or even all night long. I apply a *rush fee* of 25% to 100% over and above the regular costs in such circumstances.

Architectural Photography

Definitions and Expectations

There are five basic categories for architectural photography, namely exterior views, interior views, documentation and dramatization of architectural models, 'progress photos', and copywork. The studio work (models and copying) is just a another variation of conventional practice, but the location work of shooting actual buildings inside and out involves several more specialized skills which I will discuss in detail shortly. All my previous comments on copy work apply to architectural renderings, perspectives, and line-drawings of various types; as a rule architects are particularly interested in accuracy of color.

The thrust of architectural work is to sell, promote, or document the work of architects, interior designers, and developers. Everything depends on making whatever is to be photographed look very good. The same skills are of value to heritage preservers, city planners, engineers, and landscape architects.

All architectural photography demands that the photographer be empathetic to the many nuances of architectural style. Every architect and every architectural firm has their own design rationale. Only through extended conversation with the client will the subtleties of the various design philosophies be understood. Many architects, accustomed to producing pretty renderings of their buildings with idealized skies and uncluttered surroundings, are blissfully unaware of the realities of location photography. It is therefore just as important to inform them of what is and what is not possible as it is for them to explain what they expect from you.

Film and Equipment

Although there is a great deal of work that is best done on 35mm format, the industry standard is the 4 X 5 view camera. Architectural photography requires perspective and focus controls and a full range of lenses, particularly wide-angles. A sturdy but 'luggable' tripod is a necessity, as is a lightweight but strong carrying-case for lenses and film. A 'bag' bellows for use with wide angle lenses, a Polaroid film-back, an incident or 'spot' light meter, polarizing filters to fit all lenses, a darkcloth (and a magnifying loupe) or reflex finder, and a professional bellows-type lens shade are also basic requirements. Each lens should have it's own cable release.

The Schneider Super-Angulon 47mm f8 or f5.6 lens is the widest lens available for 4 X 5. It doesn't quite cover the corners of the format, however, so no vertical or horizontal displacements are possible. I carry one for use in really tight situations. Most wide angle work involves a 65mm or 75mm plus a 90mm, with the 90mm being the workhorse.

For details or shooting at a distance, a 150mm and a 250mm are sufficiently long. From time to time a 360mm might be called for but this is an expensive luxury that may be satisfactorily emulated by simply cropping the 4 X 5 negative or transparency.

All wide angle lenses suffer from an un-avoidable condition called *edge fall-off* which means that the intensity of the image-forming light is greater at the center of coverage, and less at the edges. This is not a really overwhelming problem when shooting on color negative film because the change in density can be accommodated when the prints are made. Unfortunately the narrower latitude of slide films accentuates the fall-off to an unacceptable degree when vertical or lateral shifts are used.

The solution to the problem is a simple but expensive accessory called a *center-graduated neutral density filter*. Essentially a piece of optical glass with a fuzzy gray spot in the middle, this filter is designed to balance the light over the whole image area. As with any filter placed over wide angle lenses, there is some loss of coverage. The Schneider filters are in the $500 range, but I have found that the $300 Fuji 77mm graduated filter intended for the FUJI G617 Camera works fine. I use a 77-67mm step-down adapter ring to attach the filter to my 75mm lens. The same filter fits the back element of my 90mm.

I have a rigid plywood/metal-clad case for my lenses, film, lightmeter, Polaroid back and filters. For local location shoots the camera stays mounted on the tripod and travels in the back seat of the car or over my shoulder with the dark cloth as a 'shoulder-pad'. Inside the case the various objects are separated by thin foam-covered dividers.

Medium format equipment plays only a limited role in architectural work because of the lack of lens movements. (Special purpose panoramic camera or cameras with some shift and rise capability are available, but at astronomical prices.) However, some architectural shots, such as simple interiors or small-building exteriors can be done with conventional lenses. The economies and convenience of roll-film may be realized by using a *roll-film back* with a 4 X 5 view camera. This clever device can be fitted instead of regular 4 X 5 film holders; some roll-adapters will accommodate multiple formats, although 6 X 7cm is typical. A template must be used to mark off the smaller image area on the ground-glass.

Many architectural clients have a need for 35mm transparencies. I use a couple of

Nikon F3's and a wide assortment of lenses. Outdoors it is possible to shot without a tripod, but indoors, and for critical exteriors, a tripod is mandatory.

The 28mm Nikkor-PC Lens allows a remarkable degree of shift and rise. It is wide enough for most interior and exterior applications where perspective corrections are required. (The 24mm PC lens from Olympus is an excellent optic with a wide field of view, however it does not have as wide a range of movements as the Nikkor 28mm PC.) Because of the mechanical complications, PC (perspective-control) lenses do not have automatic diaphragms so the f-stop must be set by hand which slows things down a little; sometimes a tripod is necessary to maintain precise framing alignment in dim light/small f-stop situations. A 20mm *rectilinear* wide angle lens (which maintains straight verticals and horizontals, as opposed to a distorting 'fish-eye') does the job of the 47mm in 4 X 5. For dramatic close-ups and compressed perspective effects I have a 300mm tele. The 28mm-90mm zoom is the lens I use most when shooting for slide presentations.

Film for architectural work varies with the conditions and the client, however the vast majority of my 4 X 5 work is done with Kodak Vericolor Type III VPS however for tungsten or sodium vapor light, as well as for very long exposures at night, I will switch to VPS Type L. Lately I have been experimenting with Vericolor 400 in large format, and I have been very pleased with the results; shorter exposures are always welcome. For transparency shooting in 4 X 5 I prefer Kodak Ektachrome, balanced for tungsten or daylight as required. Polaroid tests are generally made on Polaroid Type 555, a 400ISO b&w film which comes in an eight exposure pack. I prefer this instant film because the eight-shot pack is very convenient to carry and use. The long-scale image develops in just thirty seconds and it is a reliable indicator of Vericolor's response. Colour negatives shot on 4 X 5 material are so rich in detail that special previsions for b&w are unnecessary; I print directly onto Panalure paper when black and white enlargements are requested.

Vericolor Type S and Type L are also fine for medium format applications. I don't think I have ever shot transparencies of architectural subjects on roll film although I have used 120 Ilford FP4 and Pan F for b&w.

Small format architectural photography has very recently had an incredible shot in the arm with the introduction of Kodak Ektar 25 color negative film. This 35mm material represents the ultimate in fine grain and resolution and some are saying that it rivals the legendary Kodachrome 25. When all the technical precautions for preserving sharpness are scrupulously followed, Ektar 25 is capable of results almost as good as 4 X 5. I believe that it will have a significant role to play in the production of professional portfolios for those architects that cannot afford the expense of full-scale large format documentation.

I favor the Kodak Ektachromes for 35mm slides because of the convenience of in-house E-6 processing. Lately I have been trying out the new Fujichrome Professional slide film (also processed E-6) and I find it does a better job than the Kodak material with foliage greens and sky blue. Kodak has recently introduced several new Ektachromes (EPX and EPZ, for example) that provide other alternatives. For really careful work I use the slowest films available. Often my clients like me to produce a series of preliminary 35mm 'snapshots' and then go back and reshoot selected images on 4 X 5. For these hand-held 'quick and dirty' assignments the higher-speed films like Ektachrome 400 are more than satisfactory. My standard for copy work remains EPY Tungsten Ektachrome. From time to time black & white slides of line-drawings are requested and I have found that Kodak Technical Pan Film processed for high-contrast does an excellent job; most architects are not bothered by the reversal of tones but for those that are I use Polaroid 35mm High-Contrast Reversal Film.

Technique

Exterior Views

Most people think of architectural photography as being photographs of the outsides of buildings and certainly location shooting of completed and landscaped projects is a major aspect of the work. The majority of such photographs are made by daylight although some dramatic results can be achieved with artificial lighting at night. In either case, after the job has been discussed with the client, the actual site must be visited to determine the best vantage point and the best time of day to do the photography.

It may save some grief later on if the client comes on the scouting trip and participates in the resolution of some of the problems. Architectural photography is related to photojournalism in the sense that the conditions under which the job is performed are not controlled. It is important for the client to understand the limitations imposed by the orientation of the building and its situation in relation to other structures and the landscaping. In some cases, even the time of year is significant. Where I live, buildings which face north receive direct sunlight for only a short period during the summertime. Seasonal variations in the density and color of foliage must also be taken into account.

Although I am getting quite skilled at predicting how buildings will look at different times of the day, I still make several visits to check exactly when the sun will be shining at the perfect angle to maximize the appearance of important design elements or textures. Some urban downtown areas are so crowded that sunlight might penetrate the concrete clutter for only minutes at a time. If I am to photograph several buildings at once, I make a schedule indicating the best shooting positions marked off in twenty minute intervals starting from a little before sunrise and ending a little after sunrise.

If the only decent vantage points from which to shoot are located on private property such as the roofs or fire-escapes of adjacent buildings permission from owners or managers must be obtained beforehand, particularly if late or very early shooting is anticipated. In some after-hours situations a security guard or custodian will have to be hired. This is a time consuming process, and it is a good idea to convince the client to take care of it if possible. If that can't be arranged, however, make it clear that the time spent over such arrangements will be billed at some reasonable rate and then have your assistant do the phoning. If the shooting locations are not at ground level, an assistant will be required to help move the gear, as well.

I can't tell you how to deal with the aesthetic aspects of the work except to say that architects view their projects in the same way that most people view their children; some heavy thinking is required in order to produce photographs they will find acceptable. Fortunately nature supplies an infinite variety of lighting and sky conditions, so once the geometry (composition) of the shot is determined, it is just a matter of waiting for the other variables to line up in some appropriate way. In fact, patience is the main attribute of good architectural photographers. (While waiting for the sun to come around or for clouds to waft into position, walk around the site and pick up any bits of litter that might clutter up your image although co-operative clients will have arranged for a major clean-up the day before the shoot.)

Every city has an airport with some kind of aeronautical weather service listed in the phone book. Usually whoever answers the phone will be quite generous with information about cloud conditions and wind, the two main elements which affect photography. It is very difficult to keep a bellows type camera steady in a breeze, even with a heavy-duty tripod, and of course the sky and clouds will be the 'background' for all outdoor photography. Cloud conditions also determine the 'quality' of sunlight (i.e. color, specularity, direction), the critical factor in daytime work.

Direct sun at an appropriate angle makes most architectural design in stone, concrete, and wood come alive, while diffused light is often the kiss of death. I take pictures of buildings under overcast skies or under shaded conditions only if there is no other option. I might be forced to work with poor light if clients have called me in the wrong time of the year, if the building is completely surrounded by other tall structures, or when deadlines are tight and the weather is bad. Low contrast light makes colors 'mushy' and reduces apparent resolution which in turn yields a weak and unflattering impression. One remedy is to push-process the film, just like for low-contrast copywork, to give a little more 'snap'. This technique goes a long way to restoring a look of solidity and strength, unfortunately the skies remain deadly white or dull gray. For some important jobs, I have a retoucher airbrush in a nice blue sky. This is not an expensive process because the geometric silhouette of a building is simple for the artist to deal with. Another approach is to switch to black and white material, if the client is willing, which allows much greater contrast control. Shooting at night will sometimes allow exciting photographs of structures which happen to look less dramatic in the available daylight. Color negative film is a logical choice for nighttime photography because of it's wide exposure latitude and it's ability to accommodated a wide range of color temperatures. The best photograph might be made with a carefully timed combination of twilight and artificial light (street-lights or flood-lights).

Sometimes direct sun is avoided for aesthetic reasons having to do with the texture of the building's exterior. Some glass, tile, and metal clad buildings look best reflecting the luscious colors of a sunset, a sunrise, or a 'pre-sunrise' or 'post-sunset'.

Once the aesthetic considerations have been dealt with, the simple mechanical steps of location work with large format equipment must be attended to. The procedure is more or less a methodical routine which must be repeated over and over; the intention is to establish an efficient pattern in order to produce predictable results.

As I described, for local location shoots I prefer to carry the camera mounted on a tripod over my shoulder with everything else in a lightweight case. Once a suitable camera location has been found, I set down the case and set up the camera at the appropriate height. Most architectural exterior views are made at eye-level, which yields a 'natural' perspective and makes operating the camera physically easier. Some fine-tuning will of course be necessary so a tripod with a gear driven center pole is very handy. A tripod with the capability to disengage or extend

secondary leg supports to allow very low vantage points is useful as well. Whatever the height and location, care must be taken to ensure the tripod will not slip. The camera should be carefully leveled with the built in bubble indicators. (A small mirror is handy for viewing the shutter and aperture controls when the camera is positioned awkwardly.) For really awkward camera positions I use a very heavy-duty camera mount made out of a spare tripod head and a large pair of *Vise-Grip Pliers*.

The right lens must then be selected and secured on the camera. All movements should be 'zeroed' before setting up the controls for the shot. You will find that the most commonly used movements are front rise and horizontal shifts, which allow the image to be 'centered' while maintaining vertical and horizontal perspective. Occasionally the lensboard will be tilted forward a little to maintain focus all the way from the foreground. With extreme rise the lens board may be tilted backward very slightly to maintain coverage. A slight swing will do the same thing in the case of extreme sideways shifts.

Check the focus with a loupe, particularly when using wide angle lenses (which tend to project an annoyingly dim image). After the image is framed, corrected, and focused, the final camera adjustment is the correct positioning of the lens shade; large format lenses have an amazingly wide angle of acceptance, so extra care must be taken to prevent stray sunlight or bright reflections from striking the front lens element at odd angles.

Next, a meter reading is taken and a decision made on the f-stop, bearing in mind that lenses for large format are 'optimized' for best optical performance at around f22. As a final check, a Polaroid test is exposed, processed and evaluated. (Always carry a small plastic bag for the Polaroid litter.) If you are working on-site with your client, it is prudent to view the Polaroids together, and explain the reasons for selecting such-and-such a camera position, lens, time-of-day, etc. If the Polaroid is satisfactory, make the exposure on conventional film. I always expose two 4 X 5 negatives (i.e. both sides of a film holder) for each shot. The two pieces of film are processed separately, thus minimizing the chances of chemical or mechanical damage. It is virtually impossible to eliminate dust on location; hopefully, one of the two negatives will stay 'clean'.

The film holders should be placed in the case with the dark-slide tabs up; after the exposure they should be replaced with the tabs down. Some care must be taken to avoid shifting the darkslides inadvertently; if you are a worrier, use masking tape to secure them.

Precision 35mm architectural work proceeds in much the same way as for 4 X 5, except that it is a little trickier to level the camera without a built-in bubble indicator. (If you find this task difficult, bubble-levels are available which mount on the accessory shoe.) When shooting slides the lack of Polaroid capability must be compensated for by framing very carefully and by $\pm1^1/_3$ and $\pm^1/_3$ stop exposure bracketing. Although clients won't be able to see instant test-prints, they will find the bright and life-like viewfinder of an SLR much easier to read compared to the dark, up-side-down and reversed image on a 4 X 5's ground glass.

Slides made as photographic 'notes' can be shot quickly and informally with fast film and a hand-held camera. I still bracket, but only ±1 stop on either side of the exposure suggested by the BTL meter. Density and color are less important with this kind of work because what is required is simply a rough preview of the point-of-view and the available lighting.

Interior Views

Shooting indoors is more complex than outdoor photography because working space is limited and lighting conditions are often problematic. Scouting the location is the first job after speaking with the client, and again, it is advantageous to have the client on hand for the 'walk-through' so that any access or logistical glitches can be worked out cooperatively well before the shoot.

Shooting by available light is the simplest and fastest way to handle interiors. A pleasing color balance is not difficult to achieve if only one source provides the primary illumination. Interior spaces without windows are simpler to deal with than spaces that combine artificial and natural light. Lighting headaches arise when sources of different color-temperature are mixed because photographic film exaggerates discrepancies which are automatically accommodated by the human eye and brain.

Often modern offices have no windows at all, just banks of fluorescent fixtures in the ceiling. Sometimes tungsten 'pot' lights provide visual accents but these are normally switched separately so they can be turned off during the photography. If the tungsten lights are wired to dimmers, it is possible to reduce them down to a faint, more photogenic, glow. Overhead fixtures equipped with plastic diffusers provide broad and consistent lighting, but to prevent flare it is important to mask-off any bright sources outside the image area with a lens shade or flag.

Offices and other spaces which combine fluorescents and daylight require more work. If the windows have blinds and if the room lights are bright, closing down the blinds will at least make color photography possible. Unfortunately, the windows and their immediate surroundings will appear quite magenta because the overall color balance must be adjusted to eliminate the green caste characteristic of fluorescents. Waiting 'till it gets dark outside will eliminate the problem, but if the client insists on pictures which include some natural light a more sophisticated approach will be necessary. If the windows are accessible and not too big, they may be masked with large colored gels which are available from theatrical or cinematic supply houses. Alternatively, the lighting fixtures may be filtered to match the daylight. (Preformed 'filter-tubes' can be slipped over fluorescent lamps or appropriately sized sheets may be laid down on top of the plastic diffusers.) Finally, the fluorescents may be switched off and the interior lit entirely by balanced electronic flash. Obviously, any lighting approach other than available light entails a significant investment in time and equipment.

The geometry of interior shots is largely determined by the so-called 'wide angle distortion' produced by short focal length lenses. The exaggerated perspective which results when wide angle lenses are used in confined spaces is, in fact, unavoidable, although it can be minimized by carefully positioning the camera and by very carefully arranging the position of any objects in the foreground. Such things as chairs, plants, floor-lamps and tables must be moved around just inches at a time to achieve the most tasteful, or simply the least jarring, effect; Polaroid tests are more or less obligatory for compositional fine tuning.

Exposures indoors are typically very long (15 to 120sec, at f32) so the film of choice is Kodak Vericolor Type L. VPS or Vericolor 400 are useful for available-daylight with or without flash fill. Ektachrome indoors on large format is an expensive proposition. To save both time and money I try to test the lighting and determine exposure and filtration on 35mm slide film before going to 4 X 5.

Progress Photos and Mechanical Documentation

Making a visual record of a building under construction or documenting engineering details of existing structures is not necessarily the most creative of photographic activities but, like copy work, it is a straightforward and lucrative commercial activity.

Progress photos may be requested by architects, engineers, contractors, developers, building owners or even the bank which is financing the project. Through 1988/89 I documented the construction of a very large office tower; my client, the contractor, received monthly disbursements from the developer of one or two million dollars based (in part) on photographic evidence of work completed. I received $400 per month to make photographs every two weeks from three pre-determined vantage points. The shooting took only half an hour each time and only one roll of 120 color negative film; three 8 X 10's were made from each of three negatives.

The main requirement for documentary shooting is accuracy. The exact degree of detail to be recorded depends on the final use of the photos. For example, my contractor client wanted to show only the major structural elements of a steel and glass skyscraper, something easily photographed from a distance. In another situation, an architect needed photographs to defend himself in a lawsuit which hinged on some improperly installed cedar siding; in that case the request was for close-up photos showing the exact condition of the defective materials.

Color is not always required in this work, but any prints must retain very high resolution. Whether b&w or color, all prints must be dated, and negatives filed for easy access. Medium format equipment is a suitable choice for documentation of details and for shooting progress photos that do not require perspective control. (My high-rise shots were not corrected for parallel verticals.)

Architectural Models

There are three interrelated factors which determine the photographic approach to architectural models: scale, point of view, and the degree to which real-life conditions are simulated. The most sophisticated models cost several thousand dollars and are large, highly detailed, and meant to be examined at every angle form 'street-level' to 'bird's-eye'. Miniature cars, trees, people, and even plexiglass 'water' contribute to a very realistic appearance. At the other end of the scale are unpainted and unadorned assemblies made of foam-core or cardboard which are intended to represent only a building's basic shape.

Depending on the scale and the fragility of the model, photography may take place on location or in the studio. I prefer the controlled conditions of the studio because I can do a better job with less effort: after all, a model is only an exotic 'product'. As a rule architectural models are expected to be lit in a way that mimics sunlight; this is easy with a boom-mounted slightly diffused tungsten light and some large reflector cards to fill in the shadows. Ask the architect from what general direction he wants the 'sunshine' to come; such things are incorporated in the site-plan specifications when the building is designed.

Several different vantage points or points-of-view may be required. The street level view is the trickiest to carry off convincingly. The center of the lens will be just a fraction of an inch off the 'ground' in order to duplicate an eye-level perspective and miniature obstacles, such as elements of the 'landscape' and other 'buildings', are sometimes more difficult to deal with than their real-life equivalents. Nevertheless, the same camera movements are required to maintain the parallelism of vertical and horizontal lines. Front tilts and swings are very useful since depth-of-field becomes a problem with extreme close-up work.

A technique that adds credibility to color photos of models is the creation of an artificial 'sky' as background. This is easily done by painting the studio cove blue or by taping a length of seamless paper to a wall. A tone that's slightly denser than the real sky works well if it is lit from the bottom to give a graduated effect. Once in a while I get ambitious and make cotton-batten 'clouds', which look surprisingly realistic when shot slightly out-of-focus. To achieve a highly dramatic ambience I project a slide of an exotic sky condition, such as a sunset, onto a white backdrop behind the model.

Photographing the Performing Arts

Definitions and Expectations

The performing arts include theater, dance, film, TV and live music of all kinds. The design and content of the pictures must harmonize with the aesthetic intentions of each performance and still be strong enough to hold up on a theater marquee, a performer's portfolio, or in a newspaper advertisement. The very existence of some cultural institutions we take for granted may in part depend on the photography which is used to support funding applications to government and philanthropic agencies. Photography plays a role in developing an educated audience through clever advertising and visual out-reach programs.

The traditional promotional vehicle for the performing arts is the 8 X 10 b&w glossy, but 35mm slides and color prints are very much in demand, as well. The b&w 8x10's end up in performers' portfolios and newspaper ads while the slides are used for TV promotion, ads in four-color magazines, and fund-raising or educational AV shows. Color prints are sent to newspapers and magazines as well, but more commonly they are used for lobby or window displays.

The key to successful performing arts photography is the understanding that virtually everyone in the entertainment business is 'sensitive' about something. Tact, discretion, and the ability to work unobtrusively are the critical skills. It is true that there is some need for aggression whenever the photographer is expected to manage some aspect of the proceedings, such as a *photo-call* (a photo-call is to theater what a photo-opportunity is to politics), but whatever direction is given must be couched in diplomatic language.

Performing arts institutions are divided organizationally into administrative and artistic camps. Usually the public-relations section of the administration hires a photographer and the photos are selected from contact sheets by people whose work is publicity. The appearance and staging of the production are the responsibility of the *artistic director* and his or her colleagues, the lighting and set designers. It is the function of the director to set up the appropriate mood and pacing of the show, so his interpretation of the work being presented determines the type of photographs which may be produced. All this adds up to a dilemma. The production photographs must satisfy the flashier, more expansive tastes of the publicity people, but at the same time they are expected to truly represent the subtleties and nuances that the director has built in to the show. Some consultations with both groups are necessary; they must understand that producing such photographs under typically difficult technical conditions requires their cooperation, a reasonable length of time, and quite a bit of film. (Two or three usable images from a thirty-six exposure roll is not unreasonable.)

Well established companies expect to pay normal commercial rates for good photography but some high-profile cultural organizations and smaller performing arts companies are financially strapped. Barter arrangements which exchange photographic services for tickets and/or advertising in programs are not uncommon. Just like working gratis for charities, working for reduced rates on behalf of the local theater, symphony, or opera company will expand one's reputation while supporting positive aspects of community.

Technical Considerations

In the Theater

Making good pictures in the theatrical environment does not present overwhelming difficulties. The "better-living-through-chemistry" people have surpassed themselves recently with the creation of exceptional new high-speed emulsions. Even so, it is the work of the lighting designer which ultimately sets the technical limits.

Contemporary theatrical lighting instruments generally employ a one or two kilowatt 3200°K quartz-halogen lamp as the active element. Although color temperature changes toward red/orange as these units are dimmed, all color slide films balanced for tungsten work well for the stage. Nevertheless, I have found it convenient to shoot mostly with a 'daylight' film, Kodak Ektapress 400 or 1600 35mm, from which I make color prints, b&w prints, and the occasional 35mm slide.

There is no 'standard' color temperature or flesh tone on the stage. Lighting designers use colored gels, diffraction screens, special reflectors and a variety of lenses and masks to create and then subtly alter the visual mood. It is necessary to keep in mind the aims of both the artistic director and the lighting designer when evaluating color balance. In several years I have never found it necessary to resort to filtration. In almost every case, alterations in color balance are registered in a pleasing fashion by today's films.

There are two photographically significant approaches to theatrical lighting design, the first of which creates a basic, all-encompassing mood for a particular scene. By selecting appropriate filtration, intensity, and location for each lighting instrument, the designer sets up a visual 'baseline', so to speak, from which the audience may experience what it is they have come to see. Here, there are no obvious 'effects', no heavy handed manipulation of color or brightness for the sake of demonstrating technical virtuosity. What effects there are, are introduced by skillfully modulating the various elements making up the overall quality of the light falling on the set. What is required to carry off this approach effectively is basically an equal measure of restraint, sensitivity and good taste. The results can be very beautiful and the lighting values can be easily accommodated by current films.

It is much more difficult to work with lighting of the second type in which all the same lighting tricks are applied, but more intensely; in these situations a collection of strong effects are scattered across the stage. Lots of hard side-lighting, sharply focused lights overhead, and follow-spots are used for emphasis so the general impact is harshness. When visual moods are constructed from a series of excessive visual effects tied together, photography can barely keep up. Exposures bounce all over the place, and the too-wide brightness range causes facial highlights and dark backgrounds to disappear off their respective edges of the density spectrum.

All this has led me to the following conclusions: 1. It is very important to watch at least one rehearsal in order to anticipate changes in lighting and *blocking* (the physical position of the performers on the stage). 2. Push processing is not a solution to dim lighting because contrast becomes unmanageable. It is better to shoot film at the rated speed while paying careful attention to those techniques outlined in the section in Chapter Twelve dealing with sharpness.

The most accurate instrument to measure light for stage photography is the spotmeter. It is slower than the BTL meter but it is infallible at a distance. For b&w, color negative, and slide films a direct reading off a facial highlight with the meter set at on-half the film's rated ISO will guarantee an acceptable exposure. Once a feel for the lighting changes is acquired, the camera's built in meter can be used to quickly 'guesstimate' the exposure for fast changing situations.

I use the Nikon F3 and 28, 35, 50, 105, 200, and 300mm lenses. I use the telephotos on a tripod, and only when I am forced to work away from the stage (as in opera where it is necessary to shoot over the orchestra pit). I much prefer to work with shorter lenses right at the edge of the stage; that way I have a greater choice of shooting angles. Early on I worked with Leica rangefinder cameras because they were so quiet, but now I rely on motorized Nikons because they are faster to focus. In the last ten years even actors have become habituated to the whir and clank of motor-driven SLR cameras so I get very few complaints about excessive noise. (A few free prints will smooth the most ruffled feathers although discretion is still advisable when shooting very quiet dramatic scenes.) For set shots and cast photos I use the Hasselblad loaded with Vericolor 400.

I never use flash for shooting any theatrical performance, although I do carry a portable unit with me to take care of the inevitable 'head-shots' required for programs and lobby displays. Sometimes its possible to set up photographic lighting for Rock 'n Roll concerts because the overwhelming visual effects used by the performers themselves are not diminished by the occasional flash from a strobe.

Film and TV

Shooting on a TV or motion picture set involves a slightly different technique because there is no continuous performance (except for the rare 'live' show), just a series of short rehearsals which alternate with on-camera 'takes'. The drill here is to stay out of the way of the technical people while shooting discretely from behind the film/TV cameras during the brief rehearsal periods.

Some extremely cooperative directors will allow the principal performers time to set up scenes just for the still camera but most often budget and time restraints don't allow this luxury.

In TV work the *floor director* knows where and how much time will be allowed for stills; this is the contact person who will point you to the right place at the right time to get the necessary shots. In film, a *production assistant* will have the same responsibility. In film or TV, absolutely no noise or movement is permitted while the cameras are running. Violations will not be tolerated for a second, but a considerate and patient photographer will be recognized immediately and usually accommodated. If the set is particularly tense because of missed deadlines or the bad behavior of some incorrigible actor, extra sensitivity, and perhaps a thicker skin will be required.

Backgrounds and Props

Backgrounds and props are provided by non-photographic professionals and are not originally intended to be used for photos. Be aware that at any film or TV location the exact position of these elements on the set is critical in order to maintain *continuity* from scene to scene. Should you actually be allowed on the set don't move anything before checking with the floor director or the production assistant. Probably a union worker will have to move anything that needs rearranging. On stage, the lighting will determine how much of the set will be visible; a disparity of three or four f-stops between facial highlights and background detail is not unusual. This will be beyond the capability of slide film to record, but b&w and color-negative films will just manage it. Film and TV sets are more evenly lit so incorporating background elements is much easier and looks more natural. The main value in working as close to the performers as possible is the facility with which photogenic elements of the set may be selected by changing camera position.

Food and Fashion Photography

Definitions and Expectations

Both food and fashion photography are actually exotic forms of product photography. The food photographer makes attractive photographs of food. The fashion photographer makes inspiring photographs of clothing. The operating principal is good taste. Every aspect of the work, from the selection and preparation of the model/ingredients through to presentation and lighting, is geared to evoke an involuntary response: "this food tastes good" or "these clothes look great". Unless the photographer is very unusual, the specialized expertise that supports this work has to be obtained from outside. In some areas professional food/fashion/hair/makeup stylists can be hired, but failing that, talented amateurs can be recruited (see Chapter 11). The degree of refinement and sophistication will be limited by the budget, the deadline, and the imagination of whoever does the styling and finds the props. The food/fashion client usually has very specific ideas of how the presentation should look. As I described in Chapter 7, some kitchen/dressing-room facilities are required. Rates vary between those paid for editorial work, and those paid for the fanciest of commercial illustration photography, depending on the end use.

Lighting and Backgrounds

My earlier comments about product photography apply to shooting both food and fashion. Soft light works in some circumstances and hard light is favored in others. Warm-colored hard light with very soft fill is often used to simulate daylight streaming through a window. Electronic flash makes sense for both genres: fashion involves people and food is perishable so short exposures are desirable in either case.

Film and Equipment for Food

Generally food is expected to be photographed in fine detail so slow emulsions and large formats are favored. Transparency film works best to capture the delicate highlights in liquids, the translucent greens of leafy vegetables and the subtle textures of meat, bread, or pastry. Medium format is acceptable for simple setups, like shooting straight down on a single plate, but the corrections and large film area of 4 X 5 are required for most assignments.

Film and Equipment for Fashion

Fashion photography began with a formal technical approach, but today it has evolved to the point where a wide array of styles and techniques are used freely. Magazines, catalogs, and point-of-sale posters are reproduced from super-sharp 8" X 10" transparencies, color Xerox copies of grainy super-speed 35mm negs, or anything in between. The most common configuration is a motorized medium format SLR loaded with a fine-grain transparency film, such as Kodak Ektachrome EPP in combination with powerful, rapid-fire electronic flash directed through large softboxes. The texture and detail of clothes, accessories, skin and hair are easily recorded with this kind of artillery.

Advertising Illustration and Stock Photography

Definitions and Expectations

Advertising illustration and stock photography have something in common: they both draw on the techniques, the equipment, and the materials regularly used in pursuing work of each and every category already described. Stock houses and advertising agencies expect competent photographers to be able to generate images of any kind, anywhere, any time. Of course they consider variations in style and preferences, but once an assignment or request is agreed to, the photographer is expected to deliver original and technically excellent work.

Four main differences distinguish these two 'jack-of-all-trades' genres from each other. First, stock photography inevitably has a long lead-time but advertising clients are always in a hurry. Second, stock shooting may entail creating dozens, or even hundreds, of thematically related images, while advertising illustration calls for only a few images at time, and often only one. Third, the advertising agency is the client and end user so it pays directly; stock houses are *photographic brokers* who sublet images to dozens of clients so they pay more slowly and only after deducting a sizable percentage. Finally, the income from an advertising image is typically a one-time proposition, while stock photos can generate money for years.

Selling Stock

Stock agencies supply existing images to clients who come to them with specific needs. Consequently, the agencies must maintain large well organized libraries of strong photos dealing with many topics. Photographers are chosen on the basis of an imaginative portfolio and the proven ability to produce. In fact, a certain minimum number of new images are demanded each year. The agency will have a list of current popular subjects, for example, 'the environment', 'teenagers', or 'bio-technology', and photographers must by themselves arrange, produce, and finance self-assignments which will generate exciting images to suit. Any and all formats are used but the final product is inevitably either a 35mm or 4" X 5" duplicate transparency. Income will be a percentage of sales, with the rule of thumb being that each decent photograph can earn approximately $10 per year: so, 1000 images might generate $10,000 every twelve months. This is a field for self-motivated people.

Aerial Photography

There are some things that cannot be adequately photographed from the ground. These might include buildings and large construction projects, industrial sites, agricultural scenes, geographical topography, even entire cities and towns. The solution is to get up high in a helicopter or small plane. This does not have to be an expensive production undertaken by experts only—like other photographic techniques that seem intimidating at first, aerial photography can be straightforward and economical if the proper preparations are made in advance.

It is wise to start organizing an aerial shoot at least a week or two beforehand. Air traffic is tightly controlled by many regulations so pilots will need a few days to obtain the necessary permission from regulatory bodies to fly low, especially in urban areas. Generally it is not too difficult to arrange to fly at fifteen hundred feet or higher, but to get lower involves a fair amount of red tape.

The yellow pages of the phone book or a few calls to local television news producers will yield a list of flyers experienced in working with a cameraman. Call ahead and arrange to inspect the plane or helicopter. Generally a door or window can be removed for unobstructed shooting. Some aircraft have removable panels in the floor. Take along your equipment. As you sit in the passenger seat familiarize yourself with the limitations imposed by the structure of the aircraft and the safety harness you will be required to use. Discuss with the pilot how you will communicate during the flight (a headset or hand signals will be necessary under some conditions) and what maneuvers can be safely carried out while airborne.

Photographic preparations begin with deciding the time of day to shoot. Dust and smog reduce contrast, so strong side-lighting is often important to increase contrast and subject definition. This means early morning or late afternoon/early evening is usually best. The air is cleaner in the morning, but the evening light is sometimes more interesting as a result of the coloration that atmospheric contaminants produce.

Film and format are dictated by mechanical limitations—aircraft are always moving, so quick and easy operation is the rule. Small or medium format motor-driven cameras are best. If you can rent a small gyroscopic stabilizer that screws into the tripod socket of the camera you will be able to control the major gremlin of aerial work—vibration. Helicopters are particularly bad but turbulence can disturb even the most stable craft. Fast shutter speeds are necessary to counter both mechanical vibration and horizontal movement through the air. It is best to stick to the highest shutter speeds available. Apertures can be wide, since depth of field is not a problem: in fact, it is sensible to actually tape focussing rings at the 'infinity' position. Shooting on the fly requires the photographer to 'pan' the camera—i.e., keep the subject framed in the viewfinder by shifting in the direction opposite to that of the movement of the aircraft. Higher contrast films like Ektacolor Gold, Vericolor HC, or the slower Ektachromes are the best choices. Ultra-violet filters help improve haze penetration and increase color saturation.

All this might sound exotic to the beginner, but it is usually a lot of fun if properly planned. Costs can be kept reasonably low by making certain that your arrangements can be changed at no cost and at short notice in accordance with the weather. Plan your flight so that time in the air is minimized—the helicopter service I use actually charges by the minute! Plan your shooting angles ahead of time and work out a sensible flight pattern with the pilot on the ground. Take along spare equipment as insurance against breakdowns in the air. Check with your insurance agent to make sure you are covered for aerial work.

The costs vary according to the type of aircraft. I prefer small helicopters because of their maneuverability—in my area they rent for about $300 per hour. With a cooperative pilot I can fly from the airport to downtown, shoot half a dozen different views of a building or an industrial site, and be back at the airport in about forty five minutes. A small plane is cheaper—$75 to $150 per hour—but considerably less flexible in the air. The same assignment might take up to an hour and a half in a plane. A good way of reducing costs is to solicit work from more than one client—it is easy to shoot half a dozen different sites during the same session. Many people consider aerial photography prohibitively expensive, so an offer of some reasonable priced shots is difficult to resist.

Remuneration for aerial work is higher than regular commercial work because clients recognize that both costs and risks are greater. A rule of thumb—double your normal hourly or day rates. Earnings are further enhanced by print sales—aerial views are striking if properly done, so large display prints are often requested. 'Commuting' time in the air can be put to good use by shooting 35mm slides for stock.

School and Team Photography

Earlier I described a simple method for making multiple prints. Having mastered this technique, you will find that any market that requires lots of prints from the same negative is a very lucrative market. School and team photography is one of these photographic gold mines—once you have established a clientele they will want you back year after year. Schools and community sports groups are everywhere and the technical requirements for shooting are minimal. This work may not be exotic, but it will keep you in contact with the community and it will pay the bills.

My advice is to stick to medium format for this work—the increased definition will set your work apart from most of the low-ball competition. No artificial lighting is required outdoors in decent weather. Indoors take the trouble to use a couple of electronic flash units high up (to avoid reflections from eyeglasses) and on either side of the camera about 45°—if you have lights that are powerful enough to bounce from the ceiling or from a couple of big umbrellas, all the better. If shooting space permits try to abstain from extreme wide angle lenses since they introduce unflattering distortion at the edges of the frame. Watch for reflections from glossy painted walls or windows behind the groups.

On the business side, you will find it a nightmare to deal with each team or class separately. It is always better to make an arrangement with one reliable person within the organization—trade cash or photographic services (extra prints, a personal or family portrait) in exchange for them organizing the schedule, handling the print orders, and collecting the money. It is reasonable to provide decent sized proofs in advance but it is prudent to collect the money at the time of the print order.

Many school and team markets are already served by mass-production portrait specialists. The only way into the market is by competitive pricing and improved service—an excellent 'carrot' is to offer to produce gratis a dozen or so carefully orchestrated images to illustrate the school yearbook. Shooting the school play or Christmas pageant is another irresistible gift. The community club or amateur athletic association might need portraits of their board of directors or volunteers: be generous and friendly and new business will come your way.

Hobby and Special Interest Groups

Many people participate in activities outside of work, school and family. These groups range in sophistication from model airplane clubs all the way to national-level political organizations. In every case an appropriate photograph is considered a valued tool or memento, but organizing really good photography is commonly neglected and the work is done by the nearest amateur. It is a simple matter to make your services known to the organizers. Watch the local newspapers for announcements of upcoming events such as craft fairs, meetings, conventions, and fundraisers—there will always be a telephone number and a name to call so it is really a simple matter to follow up on the telephone. You will be surprised how many groups will be surprised at the services a reasonably priced professional can offer them. Your most effective selling tool will be offers of no-charge photos of special events or special people in exchange for access to the membership. The profitable areas will be multiple print sales of group photos plus well executed 'product' photos of whatever the membership is interested in: i.e., model airplanes, arts and crafts, antique cars. Secondary markets for the same images might be local or regional newspapers or specialty magazines and newsletters. Many groups on the local level are strongly interconnected with like-minded groups on the national or international level. Take good care of everyone and you will be pleasantly surprised as your market naturally expands.

Boudoir Photography

Many mystical traditions warn that it is unsafe to pursue the secrets of the cosmos until one is at least forty years old and has acquired a good measure of both maturity and wisdom. The same proviso applies to those would pursue this most intimate realm of specialized portraiture.

Boudoir photography is a novelty in the commercial photography world, unless you happen to be working for such publications as *Playboy Magazine*, in which case we are talking about very big business. I will leave matters of taste to individuals and their customers, but let's assume that something a little less explicit than the aforementioned publication is typical for local 'glamor' shooting. It is safe to say that in any urban area there is some market for this kind of work—generally speaking fun, good taste, and soft lighting are combined in the making of images that are playfully seductive. The subjects are almost always women, and the photos are inevitably gifts for boyfriends or spouses. Such work, when undertaken discretely and in good taste, is not undesirable as a sideline or speciality within a commercial photography practice. However, I recommend against shooting images involving nudity for magazines—the potential for messy misinterpretations is not worth the trouble. In any case, the presence of a third mature person in the studio during the shoot will provide a measure of protection against unsavory rumors, etc.

Practically speaking all the techniques of 'Hollywood' portraiture apply here. Everyone you shoot will have special features—legs, face, hair, body—that should be enhanced and/or exalted photographically. Studying how the masters do it is probably the quickest route to technical and aesthetic control—many excellent books have been published on the subject. Some sessions will go better if a friend, spouse, or parent is present during the shoot, some will not. Sensitivity to the fears and desires of the subject is of course the key to success.

Rates for this work are substantially higher than normal portraiture—the preparations beforehand and the typically challenging shooting conditions warrant the extra charge. You will find that those who seek out such photographs are extremely happy to reward consideration, professionalism, sensitivity and tact.

Models' and Actors' Portfolios

Shooting photos of people who make their livings via their appearance lies somewhere on the middle of the scale between executive portraiture and boudoir photography. Anyone who expects to excel in this work should have a real appreciation for people and an ability to tune into nuances of character and personality.

The model's portfolio and the actors 'head shot' are photographs not often seen by the general public: they are, instead, the internal currency of the fashion and theater worlds. Consequently, photographers who want to work in these areas cannot usually find advice in books or professional seminars. My advice is to directly approach talent-finders in the model agencies and casting or public relations people in live-theater companies. Explain that you are interested in acquiring work in this area, and show them your best portrait efforts with the explanation that you would like to tailor your skills to suite the specifics of their businesses. Usually they will respond positively—after all, good portfolios and head shots will only make their lives easier. Be brief: these people are usually very busy. If you make a good impression you can expect to be shown typical photographs which in all likelihood you will feel quite capable of emulating: if this is so, make an offer of a costs-only session for a model or actor. If this works out satisfactorily more referrals will inevitably follow.

Rates for this work are typically modest, certainly at the local level, but as your reputation expands rates can climb quite satisfactorily. After all, the bottom line is that your good photographs will help get people work. Typical low-budget sessions might attract $25 to $75 plus prints, more sophisticated sessions might attract $100 to $250, plus film, processing, and prints. There is also a decent buck to be made in the production of multiple prints, particularly if you are willing to generate a high-contrast negative and burn in names and addresses. (People expect to pay between $25 and $50 for this service.) There is a good chance that a year or two of low-budget shooting will lead to more highly paid fashion

work for catalogs and magazines, in the case of models' portfolios, or higher-profile publicity stills and production photography, in the case of actors' portfolios.

Legal/Security/Insurance/Accident Photography

Attention to detail and a minimum of equipment will go a long way in this business. Essentially the job requires documentation of physical conditions as they exist—or existed—in the real world. Everyone in the insurance and legal fields has a need for clear photographs (often, but not necessarily in color) whenever disputes of various kinds arise. Those who own objects and property that must be insured also benefit from a photographic record. This is not glamourous work, but for the persistent and the methodical in search of extra income it pays to advertise your professional capabilities to the major legal and insurance firms in your area. Small ads in local papers will start the ball rolling with private citizens. Upscale retail (furniture, cars, furs, jewelry, etc.) stores might be willing to give out your business cards to well healed customers making major purchases in exchange for photos for there own purposes.

Technically the requirements are straightforward—decent 35mm equipment, fine grain film, and slightly-off-camera electronic flash will handle most situations. A macro-lens is useful for shooting coins, stamps, or jewelry. Most customers will be satisfied with machine made $3^1/2$" X 5" prints, although the occasional client will need 8 X 10's as supporting documentation in court or arbitration proceedings.

There is one consideration in this work that must not be overlooked: accurate notes. All negatives and prints must be carefully documented for shooting date and location and other particulars as specified by the client. The new data backs are a relatively inexpensive way to take care of some of the paperwork, but there is no substitute for written records.

Rates vary all over the scale, but a starting place might be $50 per hour plus a 50%

markup on drugstore photo-finishing rates for your area. Heavy duty legal work for a large firm might bring in $150 per hour plus expenses. You will be worth more as you become fluent in 'legaleze' and the protocol around various kinds of litigation.

Small Magazines and Weekly Newspapers

In the section on editorial photography I outlined the standard of work expected by national and international magazines. Now I would like to discuss an accessible local market that permits the aspiring photojournalist or editorial shooter to learn and earn at the same time.

Every community supports one or more small weekly papers dedicated to reporting on local political, economic and cultural events. Where advertising revenues will support the expense, these newsprint tabloids evolve into modest glossy magazines featuring some color photography. The realities of their markets dictate very tiny budgets for photography and this fact is a blessing in disguise for ambitious young photographers.

Anyone who takes the trouble to bring in printable photos of the events that interest these publications has virtual guarantee of publication plus enough money to recover shooting costs. This is an easy way to break through the classic paradox of big-time publishing which says no assignments without experience, but no experience without assignments. Working for small papers and magazines hones photo-journalistic reflexes and technical skills while building credibility and access to local 'movers and shakers'. Good work submitted on speculation will lead to one-shot assignments and eventually feature stories. After a couple of years of conscientious shooting you will have an armload of tear sheets and samples—possibly enough to warrant the trust of some nervous editor at the assignment desk of a big city paper or national magazine. Another advantage—the weeklies usually have wide circulation and are typically willing to trade advertising space for photographs: this means that you can promote and expand other aspects of your commercial photography business while you train for wider horizons.

People and Pet Portraiture

This book is mostly about commercial photography—a business that in some circles has a fairly exotic reputation. There is a certain caché to shooting celebrities, politicians, and other exotic 'products', but ordinary portraiture has charms of its own. The work takes patience and affection for regular human beings but if your disposition is suitable you can rest assured there will always be customers. If the career path outlined in the section on small magazines and weekly newspapers appeals, portraiture is a manageable business to run simultaneously. This is because photojournalism requires flexibility in scheduling in order to respond to unfolding events. Portraiture—unlike a regular 'day-job'- is a practice where you can set your own schedule: as long as you mention the possibility beforehand, should things have to be rearranged at short notice they will not be offended.

Another plus: portrait income is derived largely from the sale of a number of relatively pricey prints. Darkroom work is easy money.

As is the case for a number of photographic specialities, there are many excellent books available on portrait technique and marketing. Kodak publishes a very useful pamphlet that by itself covers all conventional practices.

Dealing Directly with Printers

In most-high profile commercial photography the chain of people interposed between the producer of photographs and the final user includes a designer or advertising agency creative director. Nowadays this traditional path is no longer automatically chosen. Some buyers of photography choose to retain more control over expenses and aesthetic matters by taking their work directly to printers. This scenario leaves a very interesting door open for ambitious photographers.

Just like the magazine and periodical publishers, printers come in all sizes. Just like small magazine and periodical publishers the smaller printing outfits are willing to try relatively unknown photographers that can demonstrate basic skills and enthusiasm. The same general course of events will play out over a couple of years of catering to local concerns, only the upper limit on fees at the end of the apprenticeship period is considerably higher. This is because periodicals, even on an international scale, have limited budgets for editorial shooting. In direct contrast, printers use photography as components in commercial rather than journalistic projects so they can afford higher input costs. In a working environment which bypasses the substantial fees of designers and agencies, financial restrictions are even less severe.

All this means that the opportunities which flow from direct association with printers can be substantial. The projects which result from successful collaborations of this kind can be lucrative and as technically sophisticated as any agency extravaganza. A further advantage—working closely with printers will provide immediate feedback about what photographic solutions work in print, and why. This knowledge is invaluable to those who want to do the very best work at any level.

The 'BIG' Shot

As I've already mentioned, advertising illustration encompasses virtually every photographic skill. Ninety percent of commercial photography is simply the intelligent and consistent application of straightforward technique. However, from time to time, and with increasing frequency as one's reputation grows, producers of advertisers come looking for the 'big' shot, that particularly outstanding image which flows from a combination of imagination and technical virtuosity. A recent example was the central element of a national campaign for a major airline. The 'evolution' of this assignment involved the cooperative efforts of several people.

The original idea was a response to Canadian Pacific Airline's desire to contribute financially to worthy cultural institutions. The campaign, entitled 'The Art of Flying', was intended to inform travelers of the fact that, for a certain length of time, CP Air would donate $5 from every ticket sold to performing arts groups. CP's advertising agency is a Canadian firm with offices across the country. The first meetings took place in Vancouver where CP's head office is located, however the original creative solution came from the art director at the agency's office in central Canada.

The campaign would involve a number of elements, notably direct mail brochures, four-color print ads in national magazines, and backlit posters for airports. The AD envisioned a still photograph as the main graphic element. She wanted a romantic, delicate image of a pastel-colored surrealistic room with arched windows, a parquet floor and a clear blue sky for a ceiling. Various items symbolic of the performing arts were to be 'floating/flying' gracefully through this room; thus, 'The Art of Flying'.

A color 'comp', or rendering, was produced and the idea was immediately accepted. There was 'political' pressure to produce the photo in Vancouver. Nevertheless, of Winnipeg, and the fact that the campaign was to be tested first in central Canada, brought the work to Winnipeg, my home town.

There was some concern that the image was going to be extremely difficult to produce. The AD envisioned a fairly large set, perhaps six feet wide, which would have to be built from scratch and then photographed with an extreme wide angle lens to achieve the exaggerated perspective. The floating objects would be shot separately and stripped in electronically. The AD didn't know how the undulating ribbons she wanted could be incorporated.

I attended a meeting to see the 'comp' and to discuss the technicalities. It took only a few minutes for me to realize that it would be difficult to create an image which invoked a feeling of flying by assembling components photographed at different times. I asked for a day or two to come up with an alternative and an estimate of costs.

From my experience shooting the performing arts I knew that set makers often created rooms with odd proportions and I reasoned that a small room could be built to scale using the same methods. If the various props could somehow be suspended invisibly the whole thing could be lit and photographed together as one convincing illusion. I wasn't yet certain how to deal with the ribbons, but I was quite sure that a single image was the best approach. I called the master prop-maker at the Manitoba Theater Center. He agreed to build a room-to-scale for under $800. It would be about three feet wide and would incorporate the perspective effect we needed. The back wall of the model would be $3/4$" plywood so that it would support stiff wires from which I proposed to hang the props.

During another meeting I convinced the AD that a single photo would work. The savings on electronic stripping alone would amount to two or three thousand dollars, which she appreciated. A mask, a ballet slipper, an ornate picture frame and a violin were chosen to be the 'floating' elements; the problem of their relative sizes was not resolved until I remembered having seen very small ($1/16$ scale) violins which were used by young children studying the Suzuki Violin Method. The art director had a picture frame made up specially to match, and a child's ballet slipper

was found next. An appropriate mask was located at a toy store and some pretty sequins were glued on by the AD.

My assistant came up with a clever idea for the floating ribbons. He suggested that two identical ribbons be sewed together, back to back, over a slightly smaller strip of thin sheet metal. They could then be coiled and looped gracefully through the other props and still retain whatever shape was required. The art director did the sewing herself!

The miniature set was commissioned and constructed. It arrived in about a week and I had very little trouble mounting the four main props to stiff wire projecting from the back wall, as planned. The AD came to the studio and together we placed the ribbons. From the camera position none of the supporting wires were visible, and the 'floating' objects looked absolutely magical. The lighting took about an hour to organize and the photo was made on Kodak VPS Type III 4 X 5 film. A 16" X 20" color print was retouched to correct some small imperfections in the set. All the print materials for the campaign were derived from the retouched enlargement.

The campaign was a huge success. Besides pleasing the client it won a prestigious national award.

16.

Finding Affordable and Functional Equipment

How to Determine What You Really Need

In Chapter 12 I put forward the proposition that the goal of photographic efficiency is to consistently maintain high standards in the simplest, quickest, and most economical way possible. Choosing sophisticated tools with which to undertake the craft of commercial photography is a delicate and complicated task involving a careful trade-off between simplicity, speed of operation, and cost. The often irresistible temptation is to acquire the most modern toys available, despite their heavy prices, while clinging to the rationale that the investment will be recouped by way of increased productivity. Sometimes this is the wise choice, but more often it is not. Restraint and photographic cleverness will generally permit the creation of a highly saleable product, so long as certain basic requirements are met.

The first step in acquiring tools should be an analysis of the nature of the work you intend to do. If you intend to specialize right from the beginning the process is straightforward and the mix of tools immediately apparent. For example, someone who is interested specifically in editorial work or photographing the performing arts needs a good 35mm outfit and two or three decent electronic flash units with appropriate reflectors. However, in commercial photography 'general practice' things aren't so simple. Perhaps one's expectation is to be involved in advertising illustration, public relations or audio-visual work, plus some corporate annual report or industrial photography. The selection of equipment in this case becomes a pretty costly exercise. In addition, most beginners will be uncertain of what constitutes the necessities and this uncertainty is typically accompanied by the impulse to buy too much stuff.

During the discussions in previous chapters equipment needs for specific tasks have already been sketched out. In considering what to buy be brutally realistic: suppress the urge to buy equipment in anticipation of work that you hope will come your way. This means that in the early stages of your business, discipline yourself to use whatever tools you already own to tackle your assignments. When you reach the limits of your own equipment, rent or borrow. After of few cycles of working in this manner it will become very clear what are, and what are not, necessities.

New or Used?

Avoid buying anything new, at least at the beginning of your career. Good used equipment is easy to find in any city. By concentrating on 'pre-owned' tools you will automatically eliminate two odious traps—first, the latest whiz-bang gadgets will not be readily available second hand, so you cannot be seduced by the purveyors of the newest (the most expensive), or the fanciest (the most complicated): you will much more likely buy only what you actually need rather than what the industry flacks say you need. Second, selecting used over new will help you keep some distance from the 'cult of equipment', that sad group of materialistic photographers who substitute jazzy machines for good work: the patina of age enhances an appreciation of functionality while diminishing the temptation to exalt technological status symbols.

How and Where to Buy

Shopping for good used equipment takes a little longer than simply plunking down big dollars at the local professional supply house. Still, there is no reason not to check out the camera stores in your area to see what they have accepted as 'trade-ins'. This equipment will likely have been mechanically refurbished, or at least inspected, before being offered for sale, and will usually be covered by a thirty, sixty, or ninety day guarantee. Expect prices to be 25% to 50% less than new stuff.

'Want ads' placed by individuals in local newspapers and photographic magazines are another source. Prices will inevitably be 20% to 30% lower than those typical over the counter at the retail stores, but expect no guarantees of any kind. Usually a vendor will be willing to allow you to run off a quick roll of film; a small deposit will hold the item while the tests are developed and examined. After a few transactions of this sort you will become quite expert at recognizing signs of abuse, such as interior dirt, loose or scratched lens elements, as well as sloppy or nonfunctional controls. (Really expensive items should be checked out by a competent service technician.) I have found that most people who own professional level photo gear are very careful with it so, generally speaking, the used market is a reliable source of serviceable equipment.

Specialty items are usually available used through the two or three page advertisements placed in the big photography magazines by mail-order houses. I have purchased both new and used over the telephone (using a credit card) and have always found the service to be quick and honest. Warrantee repairs are a pain in the neck, since whatever needs fixing has to be shipped back and forth across the country. Nevertheless, good prices and the proliferation of quick courier services such a Federal Express make this less of a chore than it used to be.

Finally, there is some justification for buying at least some equipment over the counter at your local supplier. Everyone lives in a 'community', and a community requires local participation in order to flourish. As a local business it is sensible to patronize other local businesses to ensure a healthy micro-economy and general goodwill. Mutual support is an insurance against those stressful times when extended credit or an emergency equipment loan can forestall disaster. Price-wise, local merchants are sensitive to competitive pressures from the national chains and mail-order suppliers: although local retailers cannot match deep-discount prices because of higher overhead and lower volumes, a little good-natured bargaining will often save five to fifteen percent. Sometimes contra agreements can be negotiated which trade photographic services, testimonials, or in-store 'workshops' for more substantial reductions. It never hurts to ask.

Large Format Mythology

Large format systems can generally be used to generate higher quality results than smaller formats, so long as other variables (such as light levels and subject movement) are well controlled. This idea is often sufficient incentive to propel the beginner into the camera store. Large format camera systems generally cost more to acquire and operate than do small format systems. This idea is often sufficient incentive to propel the beginner into the bank.

I believe that for most commercial purposes big cameras, (i.e. 4 X 5 or larger), can be bypassed in favor of medium format, or even miniature (35mm) format, so long as the best of modern films are used in conjunction with the techniques described in Chapter 12. This contradicts the popular mythology that would have a typical commercial studio equipped with a comprehensive arsenal from all three formats. In this day and age, it is only the extensive perspective controls of view cameras that make them technically irreplaceable for certain specialized tasks. Therefore, I make the following recommendation: unless you have a special interest (and a ready market) in architectural photography or very sophisticated product photography, delay the investment in large format equipment as long as possible.

When the need becomes real, the focus and perspective controls needed for product work can be had relatively cheaply. Large format systems are typically modular in construction. The basic camera consists of a monorail, two standards (one for the focussing ground-glass/film back and one for the lensboard) and a light-proof bellows to connect them. You will need a few sheet film holders and a lens of about 250mm focal length and sufficient coverage to permit the necessary movements. A Polaroid back is a tremendous help, as well. This set-up will take care of fully 90% of large format studio work. Those who venture outside the studio will need a 90mm wide angle and a polarizing filter. Later it will be found useful to add lenses of shorter (47mm, 75mm) and possibly longer (150mm, 360mm) focal lengths.

When the time comes, it makes sense to choose lenses made by the same manufacturer so that characteristics such as color transmission and contrast are consistent, al-though this is not in any way an absolute necessity. Only those who end up devoting most of their career to super-quality large format shooting will inevitably invest in one of the upscale view camera systems and a complete set of matched lenses.

The Truth About Automation

We live in a world revolutionized by electronics. Cameras have not escaped. Auto-film indexing, auto-focus, auto-exposure, and automatic flash synch are common in cameras of all price ranges. There are two advantages to these remarkable developments which benefit the aspiring commercial photographer. First, the new cameras have displaced many excellent non-automatic/quasi-mechanical cameras and these older machines are now readily available second-hand. Second, the prices of older cameras have been significantly lowered because of the influx of the (supposedly) more desirable automatics.

I believe that automation has virtually no role to play in commercial work. True, cameras that focus and determine exposure all by themselves can speed up work in fast breaking situations, such as those found in photo-journalism or other documentary pursuits, but in almost every other circumstance there is plenty of time to think before shooting. Commercial photography is, at the core, an exercise in control. Control is based on sober thinking. Machines think, in a way. But machine thoughts are not yet a viable substitute for human thoughts, at least for photographic professionals.

There are problems associated with each type of automation. For example, auto-exposure cameras will do a decent job of estimating an appropriate setting for each frame exposed. In commercial work the basic exposure situation usually remains the same throughout the shoot, although the framing will be slightly different. However, as the framing changes, automatic cameras will compensate with small exposure adjustments; not a problem when the film is to be printed by another automatic machine. Unfortunately, in the non-automatic darkroom each frame will have to be tested individually before being printed: this is very time consuming and makes the creation of a set of matched prints a real ordeal since color balance can change subtly with exposure changes. Contact proof sheets made from film shot with auto-exposure cameras look unprofessional, since every frame has a slightly different density. Similarly, auto-indexing cameras preclude adjusting film speed for personalized exposure indices, while auto-focus cameras sometimes react too slowly or simply pick the wrong subject to focus on.

Equipment Modification

Professionals use their tools so much that they become intimately aware of any design flaws. Some shortcomings are inherent in the basic construction and must be tolerated, however other deficiencies are easily corrected with the resulting benefit being greater efficiency. Consider these examples:

The Nikon F3 came from the factory with a manually operated momentary contact switch to turn on a miniature incandescent lamp which, in turn, illuminates the liquid-crystal exposure readout and the f-stop numbers on the lens barrel. Since I have a number of clients in the performing arts, I often found myself shooting in dark surroundings. Constantly depressing the switch became a real inconvenience, so I had a technician bypass the switch entirely and rewire the camera so that the viewfinder was illuminated whenever the camera was on. This was a simple and inexpensive change, but it has saved lots of grief.

A similar approach solved a problem with my large format system: I was able to use all my 4 X 5 lenses, except the 250mm, with the 'bag' (wide-angle) bellows on my view camera. This meant that I had to switch to a longer bellows whenever I wanted to use this particular lens. Inside the studio this was a minor hassle, but outside the studio it was more of a problem. I had to pack and carry extra gear, plus it took extra time to make the changeover whenever I switched lenses. Also,

changing bellows meant exposing the inside of the camera to the elements which inevitably led to dust marks on the film. My solution was to have a machine shop build an extension lens board for the 250mm lens. This board is the inverse of the 'recessed' boards commonly available for short focal length lenses. Recessed boards allow wide-angle lenses to be mounted an inch or so closer to the film-plane than flat boards. My 'extension' board allows the longer lens to be mounted $1^{1}/_{4}$" farther away from film plane, a condition that allows almost full movements without having to change bellows.

Modifying relatively new equipment will, of course, instantly void any warranties. Nevertheless, as your equipment ages and you become more familiar with it, the need to make a few changes will arise naturally. It takes a certain degree of courage to alter factory built machines, but the effort is worthwhile.

Maintenance and Repairs

Some professionals have their gear checked, cleaned, and repaired (if necessary) once every one or two years: this is a prudent practice, although not an absolutely necessary one, provided a few simple rules of preventative maintenance are followed. First keep your equipment clean and dry, since dust and moisture are the primary active agents in the destruction of optical and electronic apparatus. Second, avoid hard knocks, which inevitably induce misalignments that reduce sharpness and shorten the life of otherwise precisely mated moving parts. Both these precautions are more easily reinforced with the proper selection of equipment cases. I prefer well padded, water resistant nylon cases that open at the top as opposed to the hard-shell water-proof variety that open like suitcases: I find that soft cases provide plenty of protection while allowing rapid access on the job.

I don't bother with preventive maintenance, unless a piece of equipment has been accidentally banged around or exposed to some sort of hostile environment. Instead, I maintain a constant sensitivity to the mechanical feel and characteristic sound of everything I use, the intention being to notice right away if anything changes. Such mindfulness allows problems to be detected early and consequently reduces the heavy repair costs and inconvenient 'down-time' associated with serious failures.

Some repairs or modifications cannot be properly handled by local technicians. I am not shy about calling the service departments maintained by the major distributors. When I have technical problem which cannot be resolved near home, I telephone, ask directly for the service manager, and identify myself as a professional photographer. Not once have I received anything but courteous and efficient treatment. It is usually more expedient to ship damaged equipment by air courier yourself, rather than have a store do it for you. Distributors' addresses and phone numbers are available from your photographic retailer.

17.

Working Outside the Studio

Introduction

In medium sized cities, where specialization is more or less an impossibility, often much of the commercial photographer's work must take place on location away from the studio. This will include editorial, industrial, and audio-visual photography, together with executive portraiture, corporate brochures or annual reports and more. Advertising illustration involving a product that is extremely big, delicate, or valuable will have to be shot on location as well.

All this can be very trying but there are a few practical guidelines that will make the work flow more smoothly.

The following advice for intended for those who must undertake assignments anywhere within a few blocks to a few hundred miles away from home.

(Note: 'Travel' photographers and internationally oriented photojournalists cover a much wider and more exotic territory, but never having been involved in these occupations, I lack the expertise to counsel anyone interested in such work. Ken Haas has written a comprehensive guide to working around the globe called *The Location Photographer's Handbook*, published by Von Nostrand, New York.)

Location Work and the One-Person Operation

The traveling commercial photographer is a technical one-person-band totally responsible for selecting, transporting, erecting, and tearing down an appropriate collection of tools. Besides packing and using the gear, location shooters must guard against damage and theft, as well as insure that their work doesn't cause any undue wear and tear on the job-site itself, which could be anywhere from a fancy executive office to a high-tech scientific laboratory to a retail store full of valuable objéts d'art.

The only way to maintain one's composure under these circumstances is to plan ahead. Remember: life on the road can be hard at first, but the discipline and experience which comes from doing it all alone will prove invaluable as the scope of the work expands to the point where one or more assistants have to be managed efficiently.

Within Driving Range

Try to find out as much as possible about the place where you will be working. During the initial telephone contact with your client,

131

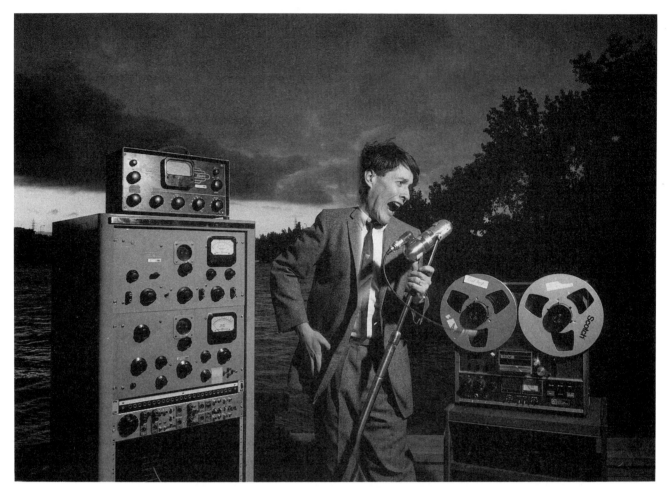

This high energy image was the result of a collaborative effort between myself, a graphic artist, the host of an off-the-wall FM radio show, and his producer. The client was actually the Canadian Broadcasting System—the project was to create a b&w postcard to be used by the host of Nightlines. *The radio people wanted an image that suggested the scope of the medium (I suggested the outdoor setting) plus the nature of the business (I suggested the vintage technical equipment). We set up on a riverside dock and I used a single electronic flash head with a small reflector to overbalance the evening sunlight for a highly stylized look. The old tape machines and the bulbous microphone were taken from storage in a CBC warehouse.*

The shot was originally intended to be more on the mellow side, but Ralph Ben-Murghi (the radio host) started to act up—I took one shot and knew I had what I wanted. The picture went all through the CBC bureaucracy before it got approval. Hasselblad, 60mm lens, Ilford FP4 film, electronic flash/daylight.

inquire about such things as ceiling height, the size and location of windows, the availability of electrical outlets, and the whereabouts of fuses or circuit-breakers. Determine the most efficient access from street level and the proximity of working elevators. If you are at all uncertain about the nature of the environment, make a quick personal visit.

Next, decide on how much equipment is required and how it is to be moved. A fair amount of straightforward location work can be well done with a selection of equipment that can be easily hand-carried by one person:

usually this means one camera bag containing a 35mm or medium format system, plus a compact lighting case that might contain two or three light-weight stands, flash units and umbrellas, as well as the necessary power cords. A more elaborate job might need a 4 X 5 kit, a high-power flash generator, three or four heavy duty stands and heads, and some cloth or paper background material: the bigger load can still be handled by one person if it is cleverly packed onto a two-wheel dolly and secured with elastic cords.

A really complicated job will call for lots

of heavy artillery but it will also require a photographer that is alert and well-rested. Use a messenger or courier service to transport the equipment: its cheap, and no special skills are needed just to lug stuff across town. Save your energy for setting up and shooting.

Finally, always make sure that adequate back-up equipment is close at hand. For example, if you are shooting with medium format cameras and electronic flash, keep a tripod, a 35mm kit with some fine-grain film, and a portable flash in the trunk of your car. It's always better to come away with something reasonably acceptable, rather than have to cancel a job because of lack of preparation.

Working Style on Location

An old Eskimo was asked what he considered to be the main survival technique for living in the high arctic. He answered simply, "Never sweat." The same advice applies to location photography.

The studio is a place where careful photographers exercise total control over their work, but away from the studio photographers are psychologically pressured to work less methodically. Most people, including clients, have virtually no knowledge about how commercial photography is properly done. On location, 'ordinary' people quickly grow impatient with the many small adjustments and arrangements that are the heart and soul of excellent photography. This impatience must be resisted by the photographer. A measured pace is the key to success.

Before the job begins, prepare your client with a reasonable estimate of the time the work will take. While shooting, keep clients and both non-professional and professional models informed about how long things will take overall, and approximately how long their individual involvement will be required for each shot. Calmly assume their co-operation, and thank them when it is offered. Don't lose your cool in the face of recalcitrant behavior: just keep pressing diplomatically for whatever time and help you need.

Working Out of Town

'Grief potential' escalates when you have to fly. Airplane travel usually means physical separation from one's equipment, and the increased risk of theft or accidental misdirection. Hotel rooms and rental cars are vulnerable in the same way. Don't advertise your valuables: make, or have made, some nondescript cases (locked, well padded $3/8$" plywood boxes are great) and avoid labeling the contents. Use your own name on baggage stubs, rather than your business name. Keep cases and gear covered or locked away in the rental car trunk. Check with your insurance agent to make sure your stuff is covered for travel by air in general, and 'mysterious disappearance' in particular. If equipment is lost while on location, phone your agent right away and report the loss. Rent whatever is necessary to complete your work, and keep all receipts plus a detailed account of the extra time you had to spend: you will be reimbursed if you have policy with a 'business interruption' clause.

Generally speaking, airlines will permit photographers to carry on a moderate compliment of equipment. Cameras, lenses, and film should be the priority. X-ray-proof bags for film are a waste of time, since carry-on luggage can be inspected by hand on request. When asking for this service, indicate that you are a professional photographer and have your business card and some other identification ready. It may require a few extra moments to explain that 4 X 5 film boxes can't be opened in daylight. Carry a ten sheet box with few pieces of film in it to demonstrate the construction and contents of the boxes you are trying to protect. Diplomacy is the key to success. (One sure fire way to beat the x-ray menace is to buy fresh film at your destination: its a little inconvenient, but it saves some grief at high-security airports.)

Many airlines provide special treatment for the luggage of first-class passengers. This is generally the best method to ensure that your equipment arrives at the right place at the right time. Convince your clients that the extra money is worth the reduced worry and that their photographer needs to arrive on location rested and unflustered.

When I travel, I take along a fairly sturdy but collapsible two wheeler to help make long airport treks more manageable. On jobs where several cases of equipment must be moved an assistant is a necessity, both in terms of security as well as basic energy considerations. Someone reliable should always have an eye on the equipment, even if this means eating in turns, and moving equipment in relays. When I travel with an assistant I prefer to rent a hatch-back for easy access to equipment, but when alone I prefer a car with a lockable trunk or a fully enclosed van. A few short lengths of light metal chain and two or three small 'keyed-alike' padlocks will go along way towards deterring pilfering when gear must be left unattended in hotel rooms or vehicles.

I have several friends who travel as representatives for various camera manufacturers, and I rely on their advice about decent hotels and restaurants. Generally the people you work for don't want to know the details of your accommodations, etc., although some corporate clients will have their local staff assist you in getting organized.

Up-to-date knowledge of the local weather conditions is critical for outdoor location work. The most reliable source will be the meteorologists at the airport, listed in the phone book under 'weather information, aviation'. On complicated jobs remember to allow at least a day for orientation and scouting. Architectural work in a strange city can be quite tricky to orchestrate, since navigation and sun-angles are dependent on one's knowledge of the local geography.

Work extending over several days should be processed on location to alleviate worry over the success of the shoot and to eliminate the possibility of accidental damage to unprocessed film while traveling. Check with the local Kodak representative to find the best professional lab available. (Save time and hassle by doing this at home before you set off.)

Reasonable Client Expectations

I've already suggested that first-class travel plus time allotted for orientation are virtual necessities. Unfortunately, some clients aren't so sure about the value of any sort of special treatment. It is necessary to set some limits on client's demands while on the location, or working conditions can quickly degenerate to unacceptable levels.

Perhaps the most easily abused parameter is the length of the working day. At home, an eight or nine hour period is naturally assumed to be the maximum for a specified 'day-rate', but out of town sometimes ten, twelve, or even fourteen hours are expected. This expectation is aggravated by the fact that extended days are sometimes necessary photographically for outdoor work, since the most pleasing light conditions usually occur around sunrise and sunset. Like all parameters of any assignment, it is best to discuss working hours before the job is underway. For your own peace of mind and physical health, ensure that there is adequate time for rest on any prolonged location shoot. Financial compensation for unavoidably long days should be part of your business arrangement.

How to deal with delays due to weather or other conditions beyond your control should be discussed beforehand, as well. One third or one half your normal day rate, plus expenses, is reasonable to expect for hold-overs and travel time. Similarly, any camera repairs or cleaning which are necessitated by adverse conditions (such as sand or salt spray) encountered on location should be considered: many clients will not object to such costs if they are factored in during the planning stages, but they will strenuously object after the fact.

Minding the Store

Some local work will inevitably be lost when you are out of town on assignment. If the absence is to be a lengthy one, it is considerate to inform your regular clients exactly how long, and arrange with a trustworthy professional colleague to be on standby while you are away. This is a prudent practice when you take a vacation as well.

Short trips can be managed by simply checking in a couple of times a day with your answer machine or service. When things are very active at home, use the hotel fax services (or bring your own machine along) to maintain 'visual' communications and carry on quoting. If all calls are answered promptly, most new work can be accommodated by careful scheduling.

I believe that it is unreasonable to expect long-distance charges unrelated to the job at hand to be considered a billable location expense.

Recovering Travel Costs

When quoting any location job, stipulate a satisfactory day-rate plus a reasonable estimate for expenses such as car rental, hotel, meals and film processing. It is a simple matter to keep receipts and provide photocopies when the final invoice is submitted. All such expenses are fully deductible at tax time.

18.

Computers, Electronic Imaging, and Telecommunications

Introduction

Computers are now an indispensable part of most businesses. Photographers working on their own have been some of the most stubborn holdouts—but I predict that the rising tide of automation will prove irresistible in the end.

Bookkeeping chores are often the first to be automated. Most photography businesses are relatively uncomplicated and using a computer for keeping the books might seem to be technological overkill, nevertheless there are a number of advantages. First, if you establish a regular routine for data entry, you will have everything you need to know about your business literally at your fingertips. The computer is an electronic cardboard box with the lovable ability to automatically organize the information put into it. There is tremendous peace of mind in knowing that every financial detail is safely stored away and instantly accessible. Second, computer generated invoices and financial reports engender respect in the other business people you will be dealing with. Bankers in particular respond wonderfully to the tidy and accurate printed lists of aged receivables so easily created by machine. Third, computers have multiple uses which are useful—even indispensable—in the photography business.

Word processing is very handy for all manner of business related communications. Desktop publishing applications and a good ink-jet or laser printer allow the production of sophisticated brochures, press-releases and illustrated proposals. Computer generated labels make direct mail advertising a snap. There are dedicated filing programs available to organize and access negatives and slides—such aids are indispensable if you intend to manage a stock photo file. There are even specialized data banks and user networks stocked with up-to-date technical and marketing information of special interest to photographers that may be accessed via long distance telephone. Finally, electronic imaging and image enhancement are rapidly encroaching on areas that have been traditionally dominated by conventional processes.

The dominant characteristic of the commercial photography business is the high speed at which things happen. Computers reduce response time and increase accuracy in all decision making. You will find that many of your clients are computerized and it is to your advantage to understand their language.

If you are not already computer-literate, find a friend who is. Most people involved with computers are very patient with beginners because very likely they were initiated by a knowledgeable friend themselves. Like all new technology, computers are intimidating only in the very beginning.

The Basic System

Computers come in two basic flavors these days—Apple and IBM. Although there are no Apple imitators, there are an incredible number of IBM 'clones' (computers that use programs designed for IBM-type systems), since IBM licenses its technology to many other manufacturers. The way things have evolved to date, Apple systems—specifically Apple Macintosh computers—are preferred by graphic artists, art directors, an other professionals concerned with the design of print media while IBM machines have been largely dedicated to business and accounting applications. Recently Apple and IBM have signed an historic agreement to intertwine their two technologies so the current distinction between them are sure to diminish in the future.

Currently both IBM and Mackintosh machines can be used for accounting and design although there are advantages and disadvantages associated with each technology which only a 'user' can explain. Making an informed purchase will involve some research.

Because of the proliferation of clones IBM machines are available at lower prices both new and used. Used machines can easily be had for between $500 and $1000. Sophisticated system can cost tens of thousands. The main determinant of price is the speed and memory capability of the particular machine. Happily there are many perfectly adequate bookkeeping programs that work quite well on simple machines. Matched with an inexpensive ($100–$200) dot-matrix printer a cheap IBM clone can automate any photography business. Dot-matrix printers are noisy

and relatively slow devices that use discrete dots of ink to build up the image of letters and numbers—although very readable, such output is not very sophisticated looking, particularly for important business letters or promotional materials. A low-end system can be upgraded when more cash is available by simply substituting a more expensive ink-jet (approx. $500) or laser (approx. $1000) printer. These devices can print a surprising variety of perfectly reproduced type and graphics much faster and much more quietly than a dot-matrix printer.

If the funds are available a better choice for someone interested in desktop publishing might be an Apple Macintosh—the graphics software for these machines is generally quicker and easier to use than that designed for IBM systems. Accounting chores may be handled on the Macintosh as well. Start-up costs will be substantially higher than for IBM type equipment. Elaborate Macintosh systems with huge amounts of memory are preferred for digital electronic image-enhancement.

Almost all computer systems are 'expandable' which means that memory and speed of operation can be enhanced by purchasing plug-in electronic modules. In other words, it is possible to start with relatively cheap and simple equipment and then upgrade as funds and performance requirements increase.

Accounting and Record Keeping

Keeping track of numbers was the first computer application dating all the way back to the days of room-sized vacuum-tube monsters. Today, every small business can afford an 'accountant-in-a-box' to make number crunching easier and more useful. Since bookkeeping chores are universal throughout the business world there are literally hundreds of software packages available to chose from—too many to attempt to review here. Generally speaking, however, they all handle the basic tasks. Invoicing, check-writing, inventory control, and automatic management of payables and receivables may all be computerized relatively painlessly as long as one has the self-discipline to devote a few minutes each day or a couple of hours each month to sit down and enter the appropriate data via the key-board. This work is amply rewarded by the satisfaction and peace of mind that comes with knowing exactly where you are financially at any given moment. Figuring taxes and making decisions on major purchases are much easier. You will find that relations with the bank are much more satisfactory if neatly printed computer-generated reports are available at the touch of a button.

Word Processing and Desktop Publishing

Computers have many applications beyond the domain of numbers. Even habitually non-verbal types like photographers must communicate in non-visual ways so it only makes sense to exploit micro-processor technology with word processing techniques. This book, for example, was written entirely on a portable IBM clone using a word processing program.

Simply speaking, all software devoted to helping writers—such as WordPerfect, Microsoft Word, or WordStar—makes a computer into an intelligent typewriter. By invoking simple commands with one or two keystrokes the electronically literate scribe can correct spelling and grammar, reposition words, phrases, or large blocks of text, as well as specify format controls like italics, bold print, and underlining. Many word processors will allow page layout to be previewed and manipulated. Some sophisticated software 'environments' permit graphic enhancements such as line drawings and photographs to be imported via an optical scanner while others permit editing several files or documents at the same time through the use of electronic 'windows' on the screen.

Its easy to see how creative computing can become an addictive occupation but for our purposes the computer as marketing tool is more than an intellectual plaything. Combined with a good printer, a computer becomes a miniature publishing plant—an effi-cient generator of highly-presentable print advertising.

Managing Your Image Library

Anyone who produces a lot of images quickly finds that storage and retrieval of slides and negatives can get out of hand without a good filing system. This situation is particularly annoying and wasteful for those who wish to resell commercially produced photographs to more than one client. In-house stock photography files are much more useful if all the images can be cataloged and properly cross-referenced so that photos with multiple uses are rapidly accessible.

Such a high state of organization can be approximated by meticulous people using convention methods but these days nothing comes close to a dedicated computer image management system. Even basic machines running inexpensive ($50—$200) software make personal stock photo management a breeze. A comprehensive image management package will permit the user to reference thousands of images by dozens of categories such as subject type, original client and application, season and location, technical criterion, previous sales, and much, much more. When actual photos or slides are pulled from storage to be sent out to buyers the programs can generate stick-on labels carrying pertinent data for shipping and captions. High-end hardware and software will accommodate photo-libraries in digital form so that images may be previewed on the screen and then transmitted electronically to potential buyers that are similarly equipped. These systems will also permit the transfer of digitized pictures into files for desk-top publishing and word processing.

In reality creative applications are limited only by the cost of the equipment and the imagination of the user. A recent example: Epix Corporation of Cleveland, Ohio has developed a system for electronic proofing for busy commercial studios. Negatives or transparencies are scanned and converted to still images visible on a video screen, completely bypassing the need for conventional paper proofs. Images can be manipulated and cropped , even arranged into electronic 'albums' to be used as selling tools with wedding, portrait and public relations clients.

Gould Trading in New York [7 East 17th Street, New York, NY 10003] offers an extensive collection of photo-related software.

Data Bases and Electronic Bill Boards

The previous discussion hints at the possibilities of computers as marketing and accounting tools—but there is more. Although they began as number crunchers and subsequently evolved into powerful manipulators of both words and images, computers are truly awe inspiring instruments for the storage and management of information.

A data bank is an electronic repository of intellectual knowledge—an electronic library accessible only via a machine. Your computer can be linked to massive, special purpose data banks through a *modem*—an electronic device that permits data transfer over the telephone lines. Some machines are can be equipped with a built-in modem while others operate quite happily with a stand-alone unit. Modems are not expensive but they come in a number of configurations: the ones that operate the fastest (i.e. more bits of data per second) cost the most money.

Data banks concerned with every face of human experience and knowledge—be it scientific, cultural, political—can be explored from the keyboard. Photography oriented data banks exist which index all manner of technical, management, travel, and marketing information. Users can electronically browse through the electronic library and then complete files may be 'down-loaded' directly from the data base into one's own computer memory. The breadth and depth of the information out there cannot adequately be described in a few words. Users subscribe by paying an annual fee, a usage fee based on the amount of time 'on line', plus any long-distance telephone charges.

Electronic bill boards are interactive data bases through which computer users exchange data and personal messages via the phone lines. Every commercial data base incorporates many specialized bill board systems that connect users to experts and teachers from specific fields. Billboards specific to the photography business allow clients to link up with photographers, photographers to link up with suppliers of equipment or purchasers of stock images, studio managers to link up with technical people from the photo industry . . . and on, and on. Electronic portfolios are viewed, assignments are assigned, equipment bought and sold, travel arrangements are made with a few keystrokes. Completed jobs can even be 'delivered' electronically anywhere in the world.

As with other applications, data base and billboard functions are more efficient with fast computers—slow machines accumulate higher usage fees and phone charges because they take longer to receive and transmit data.

Here is a list of info-lines for data bases and billboards of interest to the computerized photographer:

- America On Line (Kodak Forum) (800) 827-6364
- BIXnet (800) 227-2983
- Camera Eye (916) 361-1016
- Compuserve (Photoforum) (800) 848-8199
- Delphi (800) 695-4005
- Galacticomm (305) 583-5990
- GEnie (Photobase) (800) 638-9636
- Imagenet (401) 822-3060
- Media Line (619) 298-4027
- Omninet (214) 328-6909
- PhotoTalk (617) 472-8612
- Photocomm (415) 752-5615
- Photographica (916) 722-9187
- PhotoSource (715) 248-3800
- Photostar (703) 774-4667
- Skyland (704) 254-7800
- The Portrait Shoppe (916) 233-3791

Electronic Imaging and Electronic Image Manipulation

The biggest newspaper in my city recently built an new multi-million dollar building for their editorial offices and printing plant. The building was built without a photographic darkroom, yet this was not a design error, just a sign of the times. Photographers for the Winnipeg Free Press, using conventional 35mm SLR camera systems, shoot exclusively on color negative films. Exposed film is processed on a small C-41 processor: developing and drying take just a few minutes in the machine. Negatives are then digitized with an electronic scanner and transmitted through a computer network directly to a monitor on the desk of the photo editor. The editor uses electronic controls to manage contrast, density, color balance, and cropping—image content can also be modified but presumably things are not altered to the point where they distort the reality the photographer intended to capture. Next, the images are again electronically transferred, this time to the production room where plates for mechanical printing are prepared. In conversations with the photographers I learned that although they appreciate the speed and control electronic imaging permits, they miss the control they themselves used to exercise during conventional processing.

The scenario above is only one of the many circumstances in which computer technology is encroaching on familiar chemical/optical photographic processes. All the new technologies increase speed and reduce waste, but usually at the cost of quality. Conventional films and papers record information at a molecular level—because molecules of silver bromide are very tiny a piece of film can store a tremendous amount of data and image resolution will be extremely high. Since the electronic equivalent of photographic film uses much larger electronic sensors as the recording elements photographs produced electronically are significantly lower in resolution. This is why the Free Press photographers use conventional film instead of completely electronic cameras.

Once a conventional image is digitized in a high-quality scanner the game changes. The limit on photographic quality for photographs that exist solely as computer data files is a function of the memory capacity and the operating power (i.e. speed) of the 'host' computer. Small machines can cope with only very crude levels of resolution, while sophisticated systems costing upwards of $250,000 are essentially unlimited. As technology advances the gap between these extremes is narrowing so that anyone with $50,000 can expect to manipulate images that equal conventional photographs. The catch-22 is output—machines that can down-load high-resolution image files to electronic storage media (i.e. computer discs) are limited by the quality of digital printers when image files are printed out on paper. Super high quality digital printers output to photographic film—but they are extremely expensive. Kodak recently introduced a digital color printer which has broken pre-existing quality and price barriers—but at $30,000 it will not find a place in the office/darkrooms of many commercial photographers.

I think that high-end electronic photography and in-house electronic image manipulation will be inaccessible for most of us, at least for another few years. What will happen, though, is the option to have conventional images scanned and restructured at small production houses or custom labs, in much the same way that we get color laser copies at the quick-print shop. Consequently, it is necessary to understand digital photographic processes because they are even now very much integrated into the production of advertising and print-oriented news media. Technical, business, and ethical issues arise because the production of printed material is no longer an exercise in reproduction of existing photographs, rather it is, more and more, an exercise in the reproduction of manipulated photographs.

Photography and information now share a common digital language. This will pave the way for a brave new world of imaging with interactive books, instant news and many previously undreamed of applications. For example, the recent Gulf War was the first to be pictured electronically—some of the most compelling images were produced by automatic video cameras attached to high-tech weapons. Is photojournalism no longer trustworthy? Is photography destined to be a source of information or an entertainment vehicle? Who owns a manipulated image? Will individual photographers benefit from image manipulation, or just a few industry giants? Who is morally responsible for the impressions and feelings evoked by an altered image? Who is legally responsible? We have yet to find out.

Telecommunications

As we have seen, computers talk data and images over the telephone lines and over intra-office networks. The technology that was invented to facilitate this process has given us an invaluable communication tool—the fax (facsimile) machine.

Fax machines incorporate low resolution scanners for digitizing printed material. Incoming information is turned into hard copy via a thermal printer using special paper. Many units provide a copy function, as well. (Thermally activated paper fades in about six months but upscale fax machines use plain paper for permanent results.) Fax machines with telephone and answer machine built in are becoming more and more affordable. Your computer can perform fax machine functions with the installation of a communications card—files can be received, stored in memory and then printed out on your printer, while word-processed document files can be transmitted to another fax machine or computer without the use of paper. (Computer/fax technology requires a scanner for digitizing printed matter: the only other approach is to type the information from existing paper documents into your machine directly but this won't work with graphics or photographs.)

In just a few years fax has become an indispensable link between photographer and client: layouts are transmitted in seconds—bypassing expensive and time consuming couriers—and Polaroid tests are faxed back. I communicate with my publishers almost exclusively by fax machine, a method which is much cheaper than long-distance telephone. I now invoice my clients by fax because its cheaper than the cost of an envelope and a stamp and its more reliable than the mail.

Those of you who work in highly competitive markets may wish to reduce response time with other electronic communication devices. Cellular phones and pagers are highly portable, and relatively inexpensive—away from the studio they replace the functions of a secretary or an answering service at a fraction of the cost. Personally, I have avoided these machines because I find them distracting and depersonalizing—but I freely admit I have lost work and discouraged some potential clients because of this attitude. I rely on a remotely accessed answer machine and regular telephones when I'm away from the office.

19.

Beyond Photography

Introduction

Commercial photographers are resourceful people. It is interesting to consider, however, that the skills, experience, and equipment that animate a successful professional photography business are transferable to other enterprises. In fact, there are a number of convincing reasons for exploring alternate professional activities. In recessionary times a variety of ways to generate income can be a lifesaver, while in expansive times choosing from among a variety of disciplines can be stimulating, even inspiring. Here are a few suggestions:

Teaching

A Rationale

Professionals do not hatch out of eggs—sophisticated skills are learned somehow, somewhere. I learned by reading, by trial and error experimentation, and through the generosity of others with greater experience who had the willingness to share. For practicing professionals the benefits of teaching others are at least threefold: First, contact with enthusiastic students is refreshing. Second, the intellectual exercise of reframing basic principles in language that is comprehensible to others is illuminating and stimulating—

pumping mental iron, if you will. Third, some teaching is very lucrative. Lets examine these considerations one at a time.

Working photographers spend a great deal of time cloistered in studio or darkroom. Working relations with clients and suppliers tend to be intense and specifically business oriented. In fact, almost all interactions during the day—with models, assistants, sales reps, or customers—can be rather one-dimensional, especially when deadlines are tight. It is unfair to expect friends or family to be one's only pipeline to the real world but, happily, teaching others opens new doors. This is because students of photography are largely undamaged by the cut and thrust of competition in business. Consequently, their insights and enthusiasms are relatively undimmed.

Technique

If you are a at all enthusiastic and empathetic yourself, and if you take the time to learn a few teaching skills, you can expect to be effective and still have fun in a classroom setting. (Finding teaching venues will be discussed a little later.) I am married to an elementary school teacher and I have tried out a number of the techniques she has suggested—I now firmly believe that basic teaching skills work with people of all ages and all levels of sophistication.

How to do it? Well, there is a Chinese

proverb which states: I hear—I forget, I see—I remember, I do—I understand. Good teaching is just the imaginative application of telling, showing and doing. In a the classroom context this means incorporating techniques which address all the basic modes of learning: i.e. good verbal presentation (clear, informative), good visual presentation (useful drawings, illustrations and photographs), good physical props (real objects which students can handle) and lots of student/teacher interaction. Student involvement is promoted with methods such as question/answer, 'brainstorming' around central concepts, and role-playing (what if you were hired to shoot in the Arctic . . . ?).

Remember, boredom is the enemy of learning. Students will want to learn from real life examples; your personal experiences as a working professional are your most valuable teaching tools.

Teaching Opportunities

Actual teaching venues vary according to the motivation of the teacher. If interaction with other enthusiasts is one's main interest then offer your services to camera clubs and community centers. Cultural or charitable institutions will always have volunteers who do some sort of photography for newsletters or whatever—these people will be very grateful for advice and constructive criticism. In such circumstances one might receive a small gift or gratuity in exchange for technical advice, but the real reward will be the good feelings that come from community service.

More challenging and financially rewarding teaching opportunities exist at the community college, technical schools, and university were photography is being taught. Enlightened institutions recognize that long-time teaching staff cannot always keep up with the very latest technical developments. Often the practical aspects of operating a business are discussed only briefly in academic settings. Consequently, there is a need for reputable practicing professionals with good presentation skills—such people are asked to give lectures or seminars in the classroom in support of the existing curriculum. Fees for such work might be $25 to $500 depending on the time involved and intensity (i.e. level of sophistication) of the teaching.

Usually a straightforward proposal letter to the dean, principal, or director of an educational institution will result in a phone call or meeting during which the parameters of a short term teaching engagement are explored. Long term teaching positions typically require a formal degree or certificate of accreditation in the education field. However, If your part-time connection with the institution has been very successful then it may be possible to upgrade your own credentials at evening courses or during the summer.

Don't expect to make the same income teaching as shooting commercial photography, but remember all benefits are not measured in dollars.

The most lucrative of all teaching formats is definitely the professional development seminar. Success in this field requires that one's reputation and business practices are outstanding, even unique—and that other professionals in your field (or in related fields) will benefit from learning about your special approach to your work: much of the mystique associated with a successful teacher flows from a positive image of the teacher that exists in the mind of the student. If you have something special to offer start off by attracting small groups of students through newspaper advertising and one page instant-printed flyers distributed through photographic suppliers—the lectures/workshops can be held in your studio. For example, in my own studio I have taught architects and interior designers how to shoot their own projects (@$195 per person for a one day session) and I have taught aspiring professional photographers and advanced amateurs some of the nuts and bolts of real life business practices (same rates).

Writing and Photojournalism

Writing for Money

Commercial writing is very similar to commercial photography: in both instances carefully tuned communication skills are bought and sold. I say carefully tuned because in all cases buyers have very specific needs and criterion that their suppliers must understand and cater to—only the willing and the adaptable need apply. Also critical: a working grasp of the language, an appreciation of grammar, and an economical writing style.

My advice to anyone interested in writing about photography for money is to begin by carefully study existing published material and try to discern where your special interests and abilities fit into the larger picture.

Books and Magazines

Book and magazine publishers all have precise editorial policies. Some general categories are 'how-to', general interest, academic, niche-market, technical review: there are lots more. A useful way to explore the possibilities is through a book called *The Photographer's Market*, which lists book and periodical publishers by their area of interest. In addition to very practical technical and business advice there are samples of successful query letters and short personal essays from editors and publishers in which they tell what they want from writers. I am working on my fifth photography-related book—my first, and all subsequent publishers were sold by following the guidelines to professional writing practice I learned from reading *The Writer's Market*. Remember, it is not necessary to stick to photographic topics—any subject that requires lots of good photographic illustrations are possibilities, since writer-illustrators are very attractive to publishers.

Photojournalism

The book business is a slow business requiring a patient, methodical approach. If you are interested in quicker feedback and more excitement, consider taking responsibility for both the *photos* and the *journalism* in photojournalism. Earlier I dealt with breaking in to newspaper and magazine editorial photography—my advice was to start with local community-based weeklies and newsletters. My advice for breaking into photojournalism is essentially the same: start small and start local—assignments will be manageable and the editors will have time to critique your work. No big-city editor will consider your story ideas unless you have a substantial list of previously published prose. Even if you are an experienced editorial shooter already, you will be approaching former clients with a new product so you will be obliged to establish a track record. Small magazines and local papers are much more willing to take a chance on someone new—the financial rewards are significantly less, but the opportunities are greater.

Photographic Field Trips

Nothing comforts the photographically oriented tourist like the presence of a professional photographer. Field trips range in scope from jaunts through the local heritage district all the way to safaris in Africa. The skills involved are a combination of social director, travel agent and photographer-confessor. Acquire experience by starting small—I wasn't kidding about the heritage buildings. Offer your services to the historical society (or the naturalist society, or an environmental group) learn people skills and photographic patter. If you are suited to this work then a combination of word-of-mouth and increased self-confidence will lead to grander expeditions.

Renting Your Equipment and Studio

So far we have explored diversification in terms of professional and intellectual assets alone. However the typical commercial photographer owns a lot of stuff which other people will pay to use. Some costs are involved in becoming a supplier of rental equipment—special insurance charges, time lost making arrangements—but the benefits for someone willing to take on the extra responsibilities are worth considering in hard times. Equipment and facilities that might otherwise sit idle when assignments are scarce can earn hundreds of dollars per week if properly managed.

Rental rates are easily established by polling the competition—start lower and work up if the market is strong. My studio is a fairly modest room and I am able to get $125 for a day, camera and lighting gear not included. I don't usually rent equipment because of fears about wear and tear or theft. Possibly you will feel differently.

Photofinishing and Custom Printing

Earlier in the book I made a strong case for maintaining film and print processing facilities as part of a commercial photography business. If you followed that advice, and if the work proves easy and interesting, you might consider taking on outside photo-finishing jobs. Just like renting your studio or equipment, custom photo-finishing means coping with a degree of hassle, but scheduling inconvenience is insignificant if the additional income is significant. Following my methods for efficient darkroom practice will make processing profitable. The only real risk is taking on more work than can be reasonably managed while properly managing other responsibilities. Unlike the rental business where scheduling conflicts are tough to deal with, excess photo-finishing can simply be sent off to a custom lab. At worst, such a remedy might be a slightly less than break even proposition involving no loss of face for anyone.

Video and Film Production

Some of the most accomplished cinematographers and some of the most innovative producers of music and commercial videos are former still photographers. Its not hard to understand why this is so: at the peak of a high-profile career an expert still photographer has learned to manage all aspects of artificial light, learned to manage a team of highly individualistic creative people, learned how to manage substantial production costs, learned to sell abstract concepts to uncreative people and learned how to be consistently creative under severe physical and emotional stress: this sums up the requirements for successful film and video producers, as well.

In rare cases the shift from still to video is a natural extension, a kind of professional evolution. This happens when an upscale buyer of commercial photography—a supermarket chain, for example—asks their photographer if he or she will produce TV commercials that have a 'look' consistent with their photography-based print campaign. All beginning are not so grand, but the nature of the sea-change is the same. It is necessary to take all the skills so carefully acquired and extend them into the dynamic realms of time and movement and sound.

How to best accomplish the change and maintain one's professional standards requires some planning. Acquiring new skills means training; either school, apprenticeship, or just research and reading. I recommend university level film-making courses, especially those which emphasize commercial applications. Apprenticeship need not be entry level only—many reputable film companies regularly require high-quality skills and may be willing to trade services for training. Much can be learned by simply keeping ones's eyes open while on a film set or location shoot.

Hands-on experience begins with renting, borrowing, or buying and amateur type camcorder. After a month or two of experimentation rent some professional level video equipment and familiarize yourself with its potential.

Further preparation demands a slight reassessment of your 'supporting cast'. Consider the following: very good commercial still photography can be produced by an energetic person working alone. Film and video, on the other hand, is never a one-person endeavor. It is interesting to note that many of the professional support services employed by still photographers engaged in big-budget work are useful in the film and video business. In fact, your regular make-up stylist, prop-maker/finder, food stylist, location scout, and model agency will inevitably have experience working for your counterparts in the moving-picture business. That means they can help you by providing technical advice or simply by helping you connect with the other knowledgeable people necessary for the work. Additional support people—the 'film crew'—will deal with lighting, sound, costumes, logical continuity between scenes.

I don't think it is unreasonable to spend a year of diligent part-time work getting ready to launch a professional film or video career. As in other cases we have examined, volunteer work is a good entry point. Many well established charitable organizations have sufficient budgets to cover the production costs of TV commercials and educational films but still depend on volunteers to do the creative work. Schools and various cultural institutions are often in the same circumstances. Small, independent TV stations often have the same attitude toward aspiring film-makers as community newspapers have towards aspiring photojournalists. This means that one's first commercial efforts will have an audience. An added bonus—such stations will often provide loaner equipment, support staff, and editing facilities for promising freelancers with good story ideas and/or a creative approach to commercials. With a few video cassettes full of interesting work the upper limits are really only a matter of marketing.

Managing Other Photographers

Successful photographers find that after a certain point the business of photography becomes so familiar that their expertise become valuable to other working photographers. Since specialization is the rule in large urban centers, the possibility exists for well-connected pros to direct certain assignments to others working outside their specialty. I have met photographers who work out of a shared studio with several others: different temperaments and interests in such arrangements often lead one member of the informal collective into a managerial role. These services—professional courtesies really—do not generally involve a fee or commission. However, when coupled with a marketing effort and a clear-headed business plan the referral business is called *professional management* or *professional representation*. Fees are typically 25% or 40% of billings, after expenses are deducted. At rates like this it is fairly obvious that someone with entrepreneurial and management skills and an in-depth knowledge of the market can make a fair amount of money. The more aggressive among you can expect

to eclipse your incomes as photographers if market conditions are right.

I believe success in this field demands a financial version of the familiar 'golden rule'. By this I mean, keep in mind how you would like to be treated if your 'clients' were managing your affairs, and act accordingly.

Sales

Photographers seeking representation are not the only ones with an interest in the specialized business acumen of working photographers. Selling photographic products comes naturally to some shooters who might be disenchanted by the deadline pressures and intense personalities associated with the advertising business. In fact, some of my favorite photographers are in sales. I have dedicated this book to an old friend who was once a photographer and who is now the Minolta rep for the prairie provinces up here in Canada.

Commissioned sales people earn some of the highest incomes in North America—their earning potential is, strictly speaking, unlimited. In reality limits are set by macro-economic conditions and the competitiveness of the products they have to flog. Still, with a case full of innovative camera gear and a moderately healthy economic environment, six figure incomes are not uncommon.

Successful sales people are friendly, persistent, and good talkers. An internal marker of the sociable, outgoing personality may be persistent loneliness during those long, solitary hours in the studio—some salespeople are perfectly capable of meeting all the aesthetic, technical, and business demands of professional photography yet they miss the social interaction of doing deals face to face.

In the sales business perks and big bucks are associated with the best territories and respected product lines—neither of which are instantaneously attainable. The typical first step, however, is some experience behind the counter in a retail photo store. High performance in any sales position will move one upward and onward toward a managerial post or one of the coveted jobs as sales rep for a world famous manufacturer. Although the sales floor is one of the only true egalitarian arenas left in the western world, former professional photographers can expect their experience to be a real advantage.

Managing a Corporate or Institutional In-House Photo Department

Here is a true story: I have a friend who learned photography at a reputable technical college in London, England, and then returned home to Canada to shoot products for a big catalog house servicing a department store chain. He quickly realized that the road to independence and a fully equipped studio of his own would be long. After a year as a typical wage-earner my friend noticed an ad placed by a company in the 'careers' column of the local newspaper—they were seeking a photographer to manage the in-house photography department associated with their vast mining operation many hundreds of miles north of the Canada-US border, in the small one-industry town of Thompson, Manitoba.

A little investigation showed that the company had had very little response to the ad since most fully qualified photographers were not interested in living in a tiny community, particularly under arctic conditions. My friend applied for the position and, even though he was not exactly trained for it, he got the job and headed north.

The work was physically demanding and involved all kinds of photography: scientific documentation, public relations shots for the company newsletter, some advertising illustration, 'architectural' treatments of huge special-purpose structures, photojournalistic stories about mining operations and procedures, even executive portraiture. Through four years the young photographer labored at a wide variety of photographic tasks, upgrading his skills using excellent equipment that he was permitted to requisition as required.

All the while he saved his money—there was nowhere to spend it really—and he planned his return to the more cosmopolitan south. At the end of his four year contract he returned to his home city with enough cash in hand to purchase a house and a fully equipped commercial studio. One of his first projects was a successful exhibition of the wonderful large format black and white portraits of hard-rock miners that he had made a mile underground in his spare time! Now he does commercial photography at a leisurely pace during six months of the year, taking on only those projects which interest him.

Not all corporate connections are such a perfect fit, but this story dramatically illustrates the point that in exchange for some restrictions on personal freedom it is possible to make some money, acquire some experience, and build for the future. Institutional environments demand a degree of tact, a willingness to accommodate orders from 'above', and the self-discipline to do good work under sometimes emotionally sterile conditions. Even so, when the market for freelance shooters is tight, an in-house photography position can look mighty attractive. If your temperament fits the corporate profile there is no shame in making a career of this work, either.

The Community Advocate

Most of the alternate occupations I have discussed in this chapter are attractive because they have the potential to increase a commercial photographer's income. I have suggested several times that community service work is an excellent way to build up credible experience and a decent portfolio: this is true, of course, but I feel it is appropriate to talk about social responsibility as well. At the risk of sounding preachy, I want to say that those of us who regularly sell our skills in the marketplace also have the opportunity to make a contribution that extends beyond the strictly financial. I think it is only right to help others by volunteering our professional services to those agencies who do good in the community.

Working in a highly competitive field we tend to forget how valuable we are to those who can't afford the stiff rates we must charge our commercial clients. For the past several years I have produced photographs on a volunteer basis that the local Children's Hospital Research Foundation has used for fund-raising and community education. The work takes just an hour or two every other month, but the professional and personal satisfaction cannot really be measured.

20.

Professional Development

Introduction

It is human nature to resist change. In the business world, resistance to change manifests as a reluctance to alter traditional practice: having worked out a methodology that has proven profitable in the recent past the instinctive urge is to hold fast and do the same thing over and over again. I recommend that this approach be avoided if continued success under current market conditions is expected. I don't advice abandoning what works, but I do mean that continued success is dependent on learning. I assume that there must have been long periods in the past when conditions were stable and it would have been prudent to cling to tradition: nowadays stability is not common, so we must be quick and learn to adapt.

Happily we live not only in a time of change, but in a time of rapid dissemination of knowledge. Information which a hundred years ago would have been horded by learnéd societies dominated by the aristocratic classes is today available through a constant flow of books, magazines and public seminars. Computer networks, electronic mail and satellite television bring us what we need, so long as we are receptive and at the same time discriminating—it is neces-

sary to intelligently discard junk-data from the truly useful.

Start a Professional Association

Optometrists do not seem to have any trouble forming groups dedicated to professional development—why not photographers? In my town none of the good shooters belong to national organizations—we are all a bunch of strong-headed eccentrics, I guess. Yet a couple of years ago I felt the need to exchange information in a non-competitive atmosphere. Instead of complaining, as we had done many times in the past, my friend (the one who worked for INCO) and I simply called up a dozen people who we identified as our 'competition' and invited them to a meeting at my studio. The result of the meeting was the creation of an informal professional association which meets from time to time in various studios and homes: it turns out that there is a lot of stuff like-minded competitors can share over some non-threatening beer and chips. For example: what clients are going the rounds ripping off unsuspecting suppliers of photography with untruthful promises of future work?

My experience tells me that competition

is not so fierce that well-served clients will abandon those suppliers whom they respect on the basis of price alone. That means that we can all relax and enjoy each others company and share some technical information without a lot of anxiety. In fact the process strengthens, rather than weakens, any particular individual's position in the business world. I think that the 'critical mass' for such an enterprise is nine or ten people—not a terribly inconvenient number of calls to make.

P.D. Courses, Seminars, Lectures, and Conventions

I have stated many times that boredom and intellectual stagnation go hand in hand. Resist this condition! Professional photography is just too sophisticated these days to support the dull and the apathetic. Nevertheless, self-motivation techniques do not work in a vacuum—there is a requirement for some outside stimulation, some outside source of inspiration.

Many of us—and I am a prime example—are predisposed against formal learning situations because of bad experiences in schools. Watch for, and struggle against self-limiting conditioning of this kind, since many opportunities for growth exist in various kinds of classrooms.

Here is a tip: make certain that you are on several different photo-industry mailing lists. Many large distributors and manufacturers publish monthly newsletters—get the addresses of these organizations from your photo-retailer and subscribe. Things are moving quickly these days: because the photo-press can not keep up the industry has responded by offering a plethora of educational programs for professionals. You will find that there are an astonishing number of trade shows, speakers, and short courses going on all the time. Many of these events are free, or nearly so. More intense and artistically sophisticated two or three week workshops are advertised in the big photography magazines—lead by world-class photographers, tuition might be hundreds of dollars

but remember, travel and other expenses related to professional development are tax deductible.

Lately I have become one of those people that give lectures, run seminars and organize professional development programs. My conversations with the people who attend these events lead me to believe that success in business is directly linked to a continued effort to expand one's intellectual and technical horizons. A substantial supplemental benefit is camaraderie and mutual support—you will find that many who attend lectures and conventions are from out of state, and not your direct competitors anyway. Just taking a measure of the generosity and ingenuity that exists in the professional world is inspiring in itself.

Formal Continuing Education

Where I live school teachers are paid according to a sliding scale on which experience and formal education are determining factors for salary increases. This means that many teachers, inspired by the promise of higher incomes, attend summer school or night school in order to finish degrees. I know many of these people, and I can say that although they sometimes sign up for these course kicking and screaming they benefit in more ways than the financial. It is possible to ignore the deadbeats and the internal politics and still know that universities and technical colleges are full of people dedicated to helping others achieve professional excellence. My teacher friends who make the effort to expand themselves—whatever the initial motivation—are clearly more interesting personally, and more effective professionally.

Photographers will not have the same direct financial incentive to follow the path of post-secondary education, but for all practical purposes the incentives are the same. Education inevitably pays on all levels. It is not necessary to pursue only those courses specific to one's own business or profession in order to accrue some benefit: for example, a course which explores the psychology of political propaganda could be as enlightening to a commercial advertising photographer as to an anthropologist or sociologist.

Client Education

In an earlier chapter I talked about practical responses to clients of various temperaments and abilities. Having looked at the personal advantages of continuing education, I would now like to suggest some strategies for raising the consciousness of the people for whom you work.

Client education is an exercise which combines elements of community service with self-preservation. A successful community is built around the mutual respect of its members—this is just as true for a community of business people as it is for other communities. I therefore propose that any effort to educate clients not be specialized propaganda but rather a clear-headed sharing of specialized knowledge.

Recently I was asked to join a panel discussion sponsored by the Graphic Designers Association of Canada. Myself and a colleague were asked to address problems arising between commercial photographers and graphic designer clients. Questions from the participants dealt with the accuracy of layouts, the accuracy of the quoting process, how to establish a realistic budget, and how to handle a less than perfectly executed assignment. Events like this are great for blowing away stereotypes and improving business relationships—a client education initiative skillfully tucked into a professional development agenda organized by a group of clients!

A newsletter is a useful device. How many people would you like to maintain professional contact with? Fifty? A hundred? With modest word-processing facilities and the mail one can expect a simple public relations missive to cover a lot of territory, both literally and figuratively. Another truth about human nature says that everyone is interested in everyone else's business. There is no harm in offering some personal notes and observations about successfully completed projects—after all, there is no industry quite as public as the advertising industry. Tell your story in simple, interesting language—be discrete about your clients' business affairs, but keep the tone entertaining.

A traditional tool for client education is becoming something of a dinosaur—the business lunch. With couriers, fax, and answer machines interposed between us, some of may clients don't see me in person for months at time. Its strange but true—in a age where everyone is in a hurry time flies by at an alarming rate. The occasional social contact is important: do lunch one in a while! Work to maintain a mutual image of client and supplier as actual human beings with personalities and insights and particular idiosyncrasies. It really is no fun any other way.

Since I have started giving seminars on photographic topics I have enjoyed the luxury of being able to invite clients to the various events. This is a nice thing not only in terms of exposing them to my teaching persona, but also by bringing diverse people together whose common interest is good photography. For example, at a recent event in Toronto where I instructed architects and interior designers I invited people from a professional color lab, a sales manager from Nikon, and several accomplished students of photography and architecture. The room actually buzzed as these people discovered and explored mutual interests. This sort of cross-fertilization can happen anywhere—why not invite one of your commercial clients and your favorite retouch artist out for lunch at the same time?

Recommended Reading

Although we are all visual people in the photo business, and although we are constantly inundated with words, music, and moving pictures from TV, movies, and radio, it is still necessary to spend time reading. There is so much good information and insight stored on the printed page that to waste it simply because we are distracted by other more glittery media is a crime.

I recommend subscriptions to a variety of up-to-date periodicals, among them titles that are not necessarily directly related to still photography. I like *American Cinematographer*, for example. *Communication Arts* (*CA*) is the international bible for art directors, graphic artists, and graphic designers—world class photography is accurately reproduced and presented in context with many superior examples of the other types of advertising art.

Books, old and new, are a rich source of inspiration. Ansel Adam's series on the zone system, particularly *The Negative, The Print*, and *Available Light Photography* demonstrate a marvelous juxtaposition of the profoundly practical with the profoundly passionate. Langford's *Professional Photography* and Andreas Feininger's books are also favorites from the past. Modern technical and critical books about photography are available from a number of sources—university books store are very reliable suppliers as are the photo book clubs which advertise in photography magazines. I suggest that you contact your local technical college or university an obtain their reading lists for students of photography.

For those who appreciate very compact and practical technical books I recommend the many excellent pamphlets and books published by Kodak. A list of what Kodak offers may be obtained at any large photo store or by contacting your local Kodak technical representative—look up Kodak in the white pages of your phone book, or ask your suppliers for a number to call.

21.

Stress Management

Introduction

Any occupation which demands high performance under pressure of time is stressful. With one eye on the clock and the other on the competition, photographers must control tricky technical variables, assuage the worries of demanding clients, and make a decent living. Such potentially soul-consuming preoccupations have forced many artistically gifted people out of the market place. Nevertheless, lots of others do succeed in minimizing the destructive aspects of stress and carry on profitable and fulfilling commercial careers. Like all life skills, stress management can be learned. Those who enjoy the benefits of relaxed genes may acquire the necessary experience more easily than the rest of us, but we all benefit by consciously cultivating a few simple survival techniques.

Maintaining Physical Health

The first and most obvious strategy is to pursue a state of physical well-being. Inside the studio or on location, the photographer's typical working day involves lifting and carrying equipment as well as stretching, bend-ing, and fairly constant bustling around. The ability to remain truly motionless in odd postures is a basic requirement—impossible without a sturdy, supple body.

It is not necessary to look like Arnold Schwarzenegger, but to maintain stamina it is obligatory to do some sort of aerobic exercise for twenty to thirty minutes every other day. This could be prudently supplemented with some weight training and/or vigorous Yoga for strength. A moderate diet, sufficient rest, and an avoidance of nicotine, caffeine and other unwholesome substances makes life easier in the long run, as well.

The life style of a busy photographer offers up a lot of temptations and physical pitfalls—social drinking with clients, long workdays fueled by junk-food, all-night marathons to meet impossible deadlines. A relaxed self-discipline in relation to these matters will allow occasional excesses within an overall context of self-control.

Short Term and Long Term Pressures

Maintaining equilibrium in a frantic business milieu requires an ability to identify the different types of stress inducing forces. Generally speaking, there are two varieties:

152

short term and long term. Each of these requires a different response.

The suggestions outlined above constitute a strategy for dealing with the long term physical stress that which might otherwise result in heart disease, chronic fatigue, etc. Extending the same logic into the mental/emotional arena is a little more complicated, but not impossible. It is only necessary to catalog a few of the controllable aspects of life in the photo business and then make some plans which eliminate the need for minute by minute review. Happily, this process is actually embedded in the ordinary precepts of good management: Such practices as responsible budgeting and carefully planned capital expenditures, sensible marketing and advertising, honest and regular consultation with the bank, and controlled use of credit (your own, or your clients') all contribute to long-term peace of mind and a state of creative inner harmony.

Since we can only live in one moment at a time all stress is fundamentally a short term concern. Having alleviated the long-term factors which contribute to real-time stressful experience, the next step is to discipline the mind to remember not to worry: the technique is simply to concentrate on the task at hand. There is a saying in the Zen Buddhist tradition: "When walking, walk—when eating, eat—when sleeping, sleep." This should be extended to "when taking a picture, take a picture". That is to say, do only the task at hand at any given moment, but do it completely. Many tasks will arise, but do only one at a time—completely. Keep mental noise, extraneous thoughts, to a minimum. Here is a simple but effective tip: make detailed lists of what you have to do during the day. The list can be put together and prioritized at the end of the previous working day, or first thing in the morning. New responsibilities can be added to the list as they arise: every item should be 'bite-sized'—a task that you can manage while not thinking about something else. Be hard-headed about what may be accomplished per day. It is a discipline to take on only that which can be properly handled with the time and resources available. What you are able to do will inevitably expand with experience, but that expansion is slowed or reversed if you insist on existing in a perpetually over-extended state.

At the Edge of Your Abilities

Your portfolio should demonstrate your photographic skills and accomplishments to potential clients. When you show your book you are saying: "Look here, I can do this for you . . . at a cost you can afford". It is true that much of the work which comes your way will involve a creative recycling of techniques already mastered using skills already learned. Yet if you do well, the natural course of events will lead you to new challenges and the development of new abilities. It sounds great, even wholesome—the American Way of Business. The downside is having to decide whether to take on jobs you may not be capable of handling.

The dilemma is not a straightforward one, since the pressures to accept all work offered is tough to resist. Many clients, particularly in smallish markets, will look to you to solve all visual problems with skill and speed. It is very possible that a refusal will diminish your image in the clients eyes, as well as you own—and of course, you will always need the money. What to do?

The first step is to take some to time to think. I don't mean sweaty, shallow breathing, racing heartbeat thinking, but rather 'I'll call you back tomorrow, this afternoon, in an hour' even-tempered contemplative type thinking. If your first instinct says that the job is beyond you, try to figure out why. Is it a lack of financial depth, lack of equipment, lack of experience, or lack of confidence that engendered your negative response? Which of these conditions are under your control, which of these will yield to extraordinary effort? Will expert advise make the decision easier? Are you willing to experiment, to research, to take a risk? Will your bank support the effort? Can rented equipment be flown in from a big city supplier? Can you manage self-generated fears sufficiently well to allow the concentration required to complete the job? There are answers to all these questions. And honesty is the best policy, believe me.

Dealing with Failure and Success

Unavoidably and repeatedly, you will face the decision of whether or not to extend yourself. A successful coping strategy must accommodate either success or failure should you accept the job, as well as the possibility of client rejection or personal self-doubt should you refuse the job. The key here is to develop a sense of attentive detachment. That is to say, any action is appropriate, so long as one is prepared to accept the consequences of that action with equanimity. There is not a lot of open discussion about failure in most business relationships. In fact, the unspoken agenda for business is the bred-in-the-bone expectation of never-ending success. Goal setting and positive visualization is a growth inducing process but unsubstantiated expectation is not. Be realistic, pragmatic, and honest. Distinguish between those variables over which you have a degree of influence and those which are beyond your control. Keep track of the fruits of your labors and remember to be amazed at how well most sober-minded endeavors turn out.

Worry, Burnout, and Boredom

The negative mantra, "What if? What if? What if?", will diminish the enjoyment of the most spectacular achievements. Similarly, any activity, no matter how exotic, may be reduced to something unpleasant by endless repetition. Worry itself is both a cause and a result of burnout and boredom.

The antidote to the erosion of joy is a decent life outside and beyond photography. This could mean family, professional education, hobbies, travel, or the simple ability to walk out of a frustrating situation for a period, however brief, of rest and relaxation. The key is to recognize the symptoms of distress and attribute them to the appropriate causes. In other words, learn not to blame the messenger, but instead act on the message.

Recognizing Honesty and Dishonesty in Business

There two approaches to business. One approach defines success as the defeat of the other guy, while the second recognizes that true success allows all parties in an interaction to benefit. Those in the former category tend to be aggressive and manipulative, and in the extreme, dishonest. Unsavory practices in business are just slightly denatured dishonesty—inside the law but outside the unwritten ethical code of behavior.

I have come to believe that one reaps what one sows, that one attracts negativity if one projects negativity. It is impossible to predict exactly how events will evolve, how one will be personally affected during the constant ebb and flow of human affairs. However it is possible to maintain an intention to do good and to experience life positively. If the intention is good, the results will be satisfactory most of the time.

Index

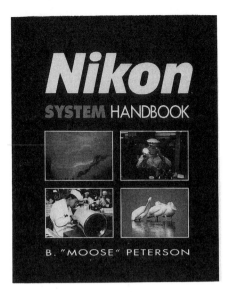

NIKON SYSTEM HANDBOOK.
By B. Moose Peterson.

Complete Nikon guide to current and older models. Lens production and comprehensive discussion of all Nikkor slr lenses produced. Illustrated guide to complete Nikon system, incl. accessories. Includes price guide to all bodies and lenses. **Only $19.95**

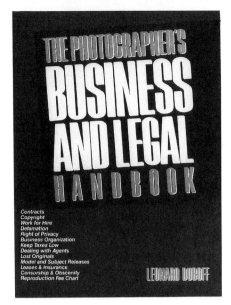

THE PHOTOGRAPHER'S BUSINESS AND LEGAL HANDBOOK. By Leonard Duboff, lawyer.

How do you protect yourself legally as a photographer? What you don't know can hurt you. This new authoritative book deals with copyright, your rights, tax tips, legal forms, contracts, reproduction fee prices, etc. **Only $18.95**

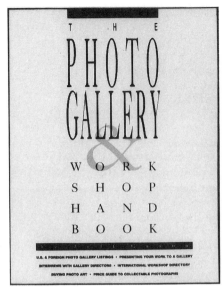

THE PHOTO GALLERY AND WORKSHOP HANDBOOK. By Jeff Cason.

U.S. & International gallery guide and workshop directory. Detailed listings, interviews w/ gallery and workshop directors, photo investing, price guides of collectible photo art, auctions, and how to present your photographs to galleries. **Only $19.95**

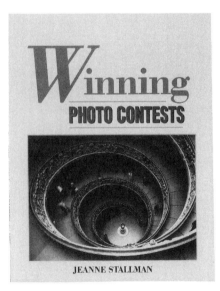

WINNING PHOTO CONTESTS.
By Jeanne Stallman.

Your guide to entering and cashing in on contests of all kinds. Included are:
• Prize-winning photos from various contests.
• Detailed contest listings with information on entry requirements and awards.
• Interviews with judges and prize winners.
• Advice on graphic impact, timing, composition, and color.
Expert advice is offered to the reader on:
• Finding the right contest for your photos.
• How to make your entry stand out.
• Model releases.
• Editing and presentation of photos.
• Contests to avoid.
Only $14.95

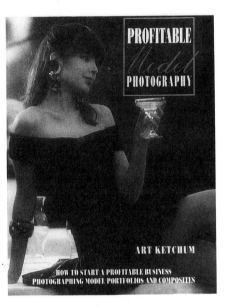

PROFITABLE MODEL PHOTOGRAPHY.
By Art Ketchum.

All you need to know to get started and manage a successful model photography studio! Build a profitable business photographing model portfolios and composites. Included in this photo-packed volume:
• Advice on preparing your portfolio.
• Advice on lab services and keeping processing costs down.
• Information on backgrounds, locations, and props.
• Lighting advice including flash and fill-flash.
• Discovering the secrets of posing and directing models.
• Advertising, promotion, and pricing your work.
• And more!
Only $18.95

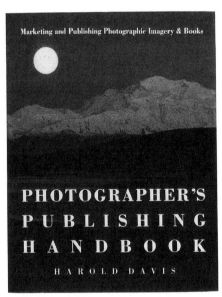

PHOTOGRAPHER'S PUBLISHING HANDBOOK.
By Harold Davis.

Comprehensive reference on all aspects of publishing photographic imagery, including photo books and paper products. How to:
• Create publishable imagery.
• Publish self-promotion pieces.
• Market stock photos to publishers.
• Self-publish.
• Create a reputation as a photographer.
Only $19.95